D0810915

Angela Davis

Angela Davis

• • •

The Making of a Revolutionary

J. A. PARKER

ARLINGTON HOUSE   *New Rochelle, N.Y.*

1771

Copyright © 1973 by J. A. Parker.

Library of Congress Catalog Card Number 72-77642
ISBN 0-87000-175-2
MANUFACTURED IN THE UNITED STATES OF AMERICA

DEDICATED TO MY WIFE *Dorothy*
WHO IS NOT A REVOLUTIONARY
AND OUR DAUGHTER *Wanda*
WHO SHOWS NO SIGNS OF BECOMING A REVOLUTIONARY.

ACKNOWLEDGMENTS

I gratefully acknowledge the major writing and research assistance of Allan C. Brownfeld. Appreciation is also due especially to Dr. Walter Darnell Jacobs for his research assistance and kind encouragement.

Angela Davis

1

THE CONTROVERSY THAT RAGES WITHIN THE BLACK COMMUNITY TO-day appears to many—particularly to interested white observers, both those who seek a society with equal citizenship for all and those who do not—to be something new. Previously, many seem to believe, black Americans were docile and unconcerned with their fate and their future. Somehow, with the dawning of a new era, there have appeared the Whitney Youngs, the Martin Luther Kings, and the Malcolm X's, as well as the Stokely Carmichaels, the Bobby Seales, and, as this study will show in some detail, the Angela Davises.

It is unfortunate that too few Americans of both races understand the passionate debates and discussions that have reverberated through black America since even before the Civil War. At a time when most black Americans were slaves, debate raged among the few who were not about what their role might be in American society in the long run. From the end of the Civil War until the time of the great civil rights awakening of our own day, there were diverse movements within the black community. There were, in fact, antecedents to the movements we witness today. The black nationalism of today is only an echo of the black nationalism of another time. So, too, is the call for integration and racial equality and harmony, as well as the strident calls for a radical restructuring of society. Although the forms these ideologies and movements have taken in our own time are unique, for history never repeats itself precisely, still they cannot be adequately understood without some knowledge of what has come before.

It is common in today's American society to say that history is "irrelevant," but in saying so too many are guilty of what the Quaker theologian Elton Trueblood called the "sin of contemporaneity"—the sin of believing that the only things that are important are those which are happening today and that the past has nothing to teach us. Whether the past has anything to teach will have to be left to the judgment of each individual. Still, no judgment can be made without some investigation.

Political activity on the part of black Americans has a long history, and it has never been a monolithic structure. Black leaders—and their white supporters—have differed sharply over both the goals that political groups should pursue and the methods that should be used in such a pursuit.

At least two diametrically opposed approaches have been termed by author Daniel Webster Wynn as (1) that of the Negro protest actionist and (2) that of the Negro revolutionist.

The revolutionary seeks to solve racial problems through a fundamental transformation of the social system, while the protest actionist accepts and works within the framework of the social system. He has no desire to transform the system but, instead, to integrate into it. He has no class definiton of his political opponents but the racial concept "white people." He has much the same conception of the values of the American social, economic, and political system as that of whites, and his goal is unrestricted inclusion in the system as it is.

In his study *The NAACP Versus Negro Revolutionary Protest,* Wynn divides black political protests into six distinct movements: Protest, symbolized by the leadership of Frederick Douglass; protest collaboration, as represented by Booker T. Washington; protest action, as represented by the NAACP; protest nationalism, as represented by Marcus Garvey; protest non-violent goodwill action, as represented in the March on Washington Movement under the leadership of the Rev. Martin Luther King, Jr.; and protest revolutionary antagonism, as represented prior to the 1960s by Paul Robeson and W. E. B. Du Bois.

Only by considering the evolution of black political activity and involvement can we understand the role of the organizations and philosophies that exist today, and only in this way can we place the important case of Angela Davis in a proper perspective.

Perhaps the first prominent spokesman for black Americans in the political arena was Frederick Douglass. Born into slavery in 1817, Douglass escaped bondage in 1838 and fled to New Bedford, Massachusetts. Because of existing laws and customs, Douglass had to learn to read and write in secrecy while still enslaved. Following his escape, Douglass worked with the Massachusetts Anti-Slavery Society as a lecturer. His formal freedom was purchased with money he raised during this time.

Frederick Douglass had a vision at this early date of an American society in which black men and white men would live as free and equal citizens. Long before the Civil War, Douglass rejected the notion that slaves should return to Africa. In a letter to Harriet Beecher Stowe written March 8, 1853, Douglass expressed this view: "The truth is, dear madam, we are here, and here we are likely to remain. Individuals emigrate— nations never. We have grown up with this republic, and I see nothing in her character or even in the character of the American people, as yet, which compels the belief that we must leave the United States."

During the Civil War and before the end of slavery, Frederick Douglass set forth his views for the future in an important article, "The Present and Future of the Colored Race in America." Appearing in his own magazine, *Douglass' Monthly,* in 1863, he stated, "I shall advocate for the Negro, his most full and complete adoption into the great national family of America. I shall demand for him the most perfect civil and political equality, and that he shall enjoy all the rights, privileges and immunities enjoyed by any other members of the body politic."

In his article, Douglass expresses as much concern for the future of the nation itself as he does for the future of those who were about to be freed from the bondage of slavery: "It [equality] is demanded not less by the terrible exigencies of the nation, than by the negro himself for the negro and the nation, are to rise or fall, be killed or cured, saved or lost together. Save the

[13]

negro and you save the nation, and to save both you must have one great law of Liberty, Equality, Fraternity for all Americans without respect to color."

The question bothering so many Americans of both races today is the very question that disturbed Frederick Douglass in 1863. At that time he asked that question and answered it frankly: "Can the white and colored people of this country be blended into a common nationality, and enjoy together, in the same country, under the same flag, the inestimable blessings of life, liberty and the pursuit of happiness, as neighborly citizens of a common country? I answer most unhesitatingly, I believe they can."

During the early period of freedom the leading figure in black America was Booker T. Washington. Born a slave April 5, 1856, in Franklin County, Virginia, Washington and his family moved to Malden, West Virginia, following the Civil War. There he attended school on an irregular basis and worked in salt furnaces and coal mines. Through determination and hard work he completed his education at Hampton Normal and Agricultural Institute and in 1881 he was selected to head the Tuskegee Normal and Industrial Institute in Alabama, a school modeled after the Hampton Institute. Philosophically, he felt that the interest of the Negro could best be realized through education, thrift, and practical skill in industry and agriculture rather than by emphasizing equality and demanding civil rights.

In *The Negro Problem,* written in 1903, he sets forth his ideas concerning the need for industrial education for the Negro: ". . . as a slave the Negro worked, and . . . as a freeman he must learn to work. There is still doubt in many quarters as to the ability of the Negro unguided, unsupported, to hew his own path and put into visible, tangible, indisputable form, products and signs of civilization. This doubt cannot be much affected by abstract arguments, no matter how delicately and convincingly woven together. Patiently, quietly, doggedly, persistently, through summer and winter, sunshine and shadow, by self-sacrifice, by foresight, by honesty and industry, we must reenforce argument with results. One farm bought, one house built, one home sweetly and intelligently kept, one man who is the largest taxpayer or has the largest bank account, one school or church maintained, one factory running successfully, one truck garden profitably cultivated, one patient cured by a Negro doctor, one sermon well preached, one office well filled, one life cleanly lived—these will tell more in our favor than all the abstract eloquence that can be summoned to plead our cause. Our pathway must be up through the soil, up through the swamps, up through forests, up through streams, the rocks, up through commerce, education and religion!"

This view is not very much different from the one expressed by Frederick Douglass prior to the Civil War. At that time Douglass urged the creation of a school that would assist free Negroes in the North to develop mechanical skills. By proving their ability, Douglass argued, prejudice would be lessened and arguments about racial inferiority would be ineffective. In 1853 he wrote: "I have, during the last dozen years, denied before the Americans that we are an inferior race; but this has been done by arguments based upon admitted principles rather than by the presentation of facts. Now, firmly believing, as I do, that there are skill, invention, power, industry and real mechanical genius among the colored people, which will bear favorable testimony for them, and which only need the means to develop them, I am decidedly in favor of the establishment of such a college [industrial] as I have mentioned. . . . There is no question in the mind of any unprejudiced person that the Negro is capable of making a good mechanic. Indeed, even those who cherish the bitterest feelings toward us have admitted that the apprehension that Negroes might be employed in their stead dictated the policy of excluding them from trades altogether."

At the Atlanta Exposition in 1900 Booker T. Washington made what was widely considered to be one of the most eloquent speeches ever heard in America. Clark Howell, the editor of the *Atlanta Constitution,* telegraphed to a New York paper the following: "I do not exaggerate when I say that Professor Booker T. Washington's address yesterday was one of the most notable speeches, both as to character and as to the warmth of its reception, ever delivered to a Southern audience. The address was a revelation. The whole speech is a platform upon which blacks and whites can stand with full justice to each

[15]

other." The *Boston Transcript* said editorially: "The speech of Booker T. Washington at the Atlanta Exposition, this week, seems to have dwarfed all the other proceedings and the Exposition itself. The sensation that it has caused in the press has never been equalled."

In the speech Washington cautions those of his own race not to expect too much too soon, and without hard work, and urges whites not to criticize Negroes for lack of achievement if they at the same time deprive them of the opportunity to achieve.

Addressing himself to the attitudes of black Americans at that time Washington said: "Our greatest danger is that in the great leap from slavery to freedom we may overlook the fact that the masses of us are to live by the production of our hands, and fail to keep in mind that we shall prosper in proportion as we learn to dignify and glorify common labour and put brains and skill into the common occupations of life; shall prosper in proportion as we learn to draw the line between the superficial and the substantial, the ornamental gewgaws of life and the useful. No race can prosper till it learns that there is as much dignity in tilling a field as in writing a poem. It is at the bottom of life we must begin, and not at the top. Nor should we permit our grievances to overshadow our opportunities. . . . In all things that are purely social we can be as separate as the fingers, yet one as the hand in all things essential to mutual progress. There is no defence or security for any of us except in the highest intelligence and development of all."

Washington was critical of those who thought that a better condition might be achieved not by training and hard work but by the application of force and power against the dominant white majority. He cautioned those who sought what he considered to be short cuts to real equality and dignity: "The wisest among my race understand that the agitation of questions of social equality is the extremest folly, and that progress in the enjoyment of all the privileges that will come to us must be the result of severe and constant struggle rather than artificial forcing. No race that has anything to contribute to the markets of the world is long in any degree ostracized. It is important and right that all privileges of the law be ours, but it is vastly more important that we be prepared for the exercises of these privi-

[16]

leges. The opportunity to earn a dollar in a factory just now is worth infinitely more than the opportunity to spend a dollar in an opera-house."

It was not the view of Booker T. Washington, however, that work in the fields and the factories would make the Negro self-sufficient and that he should be satisfied with this status in American society. His ideal was far broader than this, and his address in Atlanta was a blend of what he considered to be the practical needs of the moment together with the philosophical goals of the future. He makes this point when he declares, ". . . far above and beyond material benefits will be that higher good, that, let us pray God, will come, in a blotting out of sectional differences and racial animosities and suspicions, in a determination to administer absolute justice, in a willing obedience, among all classes to the mandates of law. This, then, coupled with our material prosperity, will bring into our beloved South, a new heaven and a new earth."

Suspicion of the rich and powerful was not an element in Washington's philosophy. He stated, "My experience in getting money for Tuskegee has taught me to have no patience with those people who are always condemning the rich because they are rich, and because they do not give more to the objects of charity . . . more and more rich people are coming to regard men and women who apply to them for help for worthy objects not as beggars, but as agents for doing their work."

The approach of Booker T. Washington, even during this early period, was bitterly opposed by that group of black leaders who believed in protest but not in collaboration. After many clashes with Washington, the black protest leaders finally determined to constrain him and carry on the movement for civil rights. This was known as the Niagara Movement, which later merged with the National Association for the Advancement of Colored People.

Gunner Myrdal, in his epic on the race question, *An American Dilemma,* feels that Washington's approach was more effective in the promotion of the cause of the Negro than is suspected by many. According to Myrdal, it is a political axiom that Negroes can never, in any period, hope to attain more in

[17]

the short-term power bargain than the most benevolent white groups are prepared to give them.

Myrdal wrote: "This much Washington attained. With shrewd insight Washington took exactly as much off the Negro protest, and it had to be a big reduction, as was needed in order to get the maximum cooperation from the only two white groups in America who in this era of ideological reaction cared anything at all about the Negroes: the Northern humanitarians and philanthropists, and the Southern upper class school of 'parallel civilization.' Both of these liberal groups demanded appeasement above all. And so the Southern conservatives were actually allowed to set the conditions upon which Washington and the Southern and Northern liberals could come to terms. For his time and for the region where he worked and where then nine tenths of all Negroes lived, his policy of abstaining from talk of rights and of 'casting down your buckets where you are' was entirely realistic. Even today it is still—in local affairs where the short-range view must dominate—the only workable Negro policy in the South."

Booker T. Washington believed that the only way to build a house, a life, or a civilization was to begin at the bottom and work up. He considered political activity on the part of freedmen unwise, like trying to start from the top. He accepted segregation and tried as best he could to silence agitation for citizenship rights. Something else, he insisted, came first. Wealth and property, trades and skills, were the immediate first objectives. In the end the farmer on his own land, the skilled carpenter or brick mason living in his own home, and the Negro businessman in his own shop would see barriers fall and attitudes change.

The attitude of Booker T. Washington, however, was not long to be the dominant approach of the Negro leadership. In 1905 Dr. W. E. B. Du Bois called a meeting of Negro leaders at Niagara Falls to organize a movement in defense of the rights of Negroes. On February 12, 1909 a meeting was held in New York to form a new organization to win full equality for the Negro. The call for this meeting came from Oswald Garrison Villard, grandson of the abolitionist William Lloyd Garrison, and was signed by prominent whites and Negroes. The objec-

[18]

tives were: (1) Abolition of all forced segregation; (2) equal educational opportunities; (3) enfranchisement of the Negro; (4) enforcement of the Fourteenth and Fifteenth Amendments. Du Bois was made director of publicity and editor of a new magazine, *The Crisis.*

Du Bois has at times been considered the father of modern black militancy. As one of the founders of the Niagara Movement and the NAACP, Du Bois, the recipient of a Ph.D. degree from Harvard University, recognized the need for organized protest. He has to his credit a number of outstanding books and articles, including *The Souls of Black Folk, Suppression of the Black African Trade,* and *Black Reconstruction.* Only during the latter years of his long life did he turn to political radicalism. One of his primary early interests was to inspire a vanguard of college-educated blacks to become leaders for their people.

In his essay, "The Talented Tenth," Du Bois addresses all Americans, but particularly white Americans, who, he argues, have as much to gain or lose as do black Americans from the final resolution of the racial crisis. He writes: "Men of America, the problem is plain before you. Here is a race transplanted through the criminal foolishness of your fathers. Whether you like it or not the millions are here, and here they will remain. If you do not lift them up, they will pull you down. Education and work are the levers to uplift a people. Work alone will not do it unless inspired by the right ideals and guided by intelligence. Education must not simply teach work—it must teach life. The Talented Tenth of the Negro race must be made leaders of thought and missionaries of culture among their people. No others can do this work and Negro colleges must train men for it. The Negro race, like all other races, is going to be saved by its exceptional men."

Later, Du Bois makes it clear that political equality is of the essence, thereby differentiating his own position from that of Booker T. Washington, who was willing to place that question in the background. Writing in *The Crisis* for April, 1915, Du Bois states: "The American Negro demands equality—political equality, industrial equality and social equality; and he is never going to rest satisfied with anything less. He demands this in no spirit of braggadocio and with no obsequious envy of others, but as an absolute measure of self-defense and the only one that will assure to the darker races their ultimate survival on earth."

In this same article, Du Bois discusses what it is that he means by the term "equality," challenging implicitly what many mean by this term at the present time. He wrote: "Human equality does not even entail, as is sometimes said, absolute equality of opportunity; for certainly the natural inequalities of inherent genius and varying gift make this a dubious phrase. But there is a more and more clearly recognized minimum of opportunity and maximum of freedom to be, to move, and to think, which the modern world denies to no being which it recognizes as a real man."

Du Bois does not even challenge the concept of schools attended by black children with black teachers and administrators. His concern is far deeper than a consideration of what he considered superificialities. In *The Crisis* of January, 1934, he wrote: ". . . there is no objection to schools attended by colored pupils and taught by colored teachers. On the contrary, colored pupils can by our contention be as fine human beings as any other sort of children, and we certainly know that there are no teachers better than trained colored teachers. But if the existence of such a school is made reason and cause for giving it worse housing, poorer facilities, poorer equipment and poorer teachers, then we do object, and the objection is not against the color of the pupils' or teachers' skins, but against the discrimination."

In 1918 a new kind of Negro movement was started, although it did have roots in the post-Civil War era. Known as the Garvey Movement, it was based on the thesis that the Negro would never receive justice in a white man's country and that the only solution was to establish an independent country. Marcus Garvey, a West Indian, felt that the first step in the founding of a Negro nation was the development of commercial pursuits among Negroes. This was to be accomplished by the setting up of restaurants and grocery stores in America and by creating social and cultural as well as economic bonds between the Negroes of America and of Africa.

[20]

Many of the programs being inaugurated by black separatists today are suggestive of those which Garvey initiated. For example, he created the Universal Negro Improvement Association and the African Communities League, and he founded the "Black Star Line," a steamship company. Throughout his life he was vitally concerned about the "unity and liberation" of black people throughout the world. To him, the racist exploitation of Africa was as intolerable as that in America.

Garvey's views are somewhat more complex than they would appear at first glance. It was his view that the black race would not earn the respect of other races until they were doing for themselves what other races were doing for themselves. In his view, this involved not imitating the white race, but developing a unique style and culture different and distinct from that by which black Americans were surrounded.

In his "Appeal to the Conscience of the Black Race to See Itself," Garvey wrote: "Progress of and among any people will advance them in the respect and appreciation of the rest of their fellows. It is such a progress that the Negro must attach to himself if he is to rise above the prejudice of the world. The reliance of our race upon the progress and achievements of others for a consideration in sympathy, justice and rights is like a dependence upon a broken stick, resting upon which will eventually consign you to the ground."

Discussing the aims and purposes of the organization he had founded, Garvey declared: "The Universal Negro Improvement Association teaches our race self-help and self-reliance, not only in one essential, but in all those things that contribute to human happiness and well-being. The disposition of the many to depend upon the other races for a kindly and sympathetic consideration of their needs, without making the effort to do for themselves, has been the race's standing disgrace by which we have been judged and through which we have created the strongest prejudice against ourselves."

The concept of a return to Africa was, consequently, more than a mere political judgment that black Americans could never live full lives in the predominantly white American society. It was an effort, however utopian, to develop a self-respect and sense of achievement and worth which would permit the black man to stand with his head high every place in the world.

"The Negro," Garvey said, "needs a nation and a country of his own, where he can best show evidence of his own ability in the art of human progress. Scattered as an unmixed and un-recognized part of alien nations and civilizations is but to dem-onstrate his imbecility, and point him out as an unworthy dere-lict, fit neither for the society of Greek, Jew, nor Gentile. No Negro, let him be American, European, West Indian or African, shall be truly respected until the race as a whole has eman-cipated itself, through self-achievement and progress, from universal prejudice. The Negro will have to build his own gov-ernment, industry, art, science, literature and culture before the world will stop to consider him."

Marcus Garvey had little respect for those Negroes who wanted to imitate the dominant white culture, and little also for those who begged for charity and welfare at the hands of the dominant group. In the long run, he believed, no one helps those who will not help themselves. To those of his own race who followed either the path of imitation or the path of urging charity, Garvey had these words:

"There is no progress in aping white people and telling us that they represent the best in the race, for in that respect any dressed monkey would represent the best of its species, irre-spective of the creative matter of the monkey instinct. . . . It is the slave spirit of dependence that causes our 'so-called leading men' (apes) to seek the shelter, leadership, protection and pa-tronage of the 'master' in their organization and so-called ad-vancement work. It is the spirit of feeling secured as good ser-vants of the master, rather than as independents, why our modern Uncle Toms take pride in laboring under alien leader-ship and becoming surprised at the audacity of the Universal Negro Improvement Association in proclaiming for racial lib-erty and independence.

"The best of the great white race doesn't fawn before and beg black, brown or yellow man; they go out, create for self and thus demonstrate the fitness of the race to survive; and so the white race of America and the world will be informed that the best in the Negro race is not the class of beggars who send out to other races piteous appeals annually for donations to maintain their coterie, but the groups within us that are honestly striving to do for themselves with the voluntary help and appreciation of that class of other races that is reasonable, just and liberal enough to give each and every one a fair chance in the promotion of those ideals that tend to greater human progress and human love."

In 1921 the Empire of Africa was finally announced and Garvey was inaugurated as President General of the Universal Negro Improvement Association and Provisional President of Africa. The movement reached its peak in 1920–21. To implement his program, Garvey sold stock and was convicted on the charge of using the mails to defraud and was sent to the Federal penitentiary in Atlanta. In 1927 he was deported as an undesirable alien.

An attempt was made to organize the Negro protest into a political movement allied to radical white labor after 1917. Left-wing publications in which interracial solidarity was preached were started by young Negro socialists such as A. Philip Randolph and Chandler Owen. On the extreme left Negroes were appealed to by the Communists. This group appealed to them as an oppressed people under imperialist domination. They promised "self-determination" for the Negro in the Black Belt which was to be realized by setting up an independent black republic. The new republic would comprise those areas in the South where Negroes were in a majority.

To the right there was a Negro intellectual chauvinism, and glorification of the artistic and intellectual achievements of Negroes. This was done by Du Bois, as editor of *The Crisis,* Charles Johnson, editor of *Opportunity,* and Alaine Locke, editor of *The New Negro.*

A movement to discover a cultural tradition for American Negroes grew up in the 1920s and 1930s. This attempt to provide Negroes with a respectable past led to numerous slave biographies, the most important of which was the *Narrative of the Life and Times of Frederick Douglass.* Born a slave, Douglass had been freed and spent much of his time during the Civil War raising Negro troops for the Northern Army, had met several times with Abraham Lincoln, and was considered a great orator of the period.

Moving closer to the present we find the beginning of what has been termed "protest nonviolent goodwill action." During World War II a mass protest movement was started among Negroes and was under the leadership of A. Philip Randolph of the Brotherhood of Sleeping Car Porters, and was known as the March on Washington Movement. It grew out of the failure of the government to include Negroes in the defense program. Conferences were arranged between the President and members of the committee and resulted in Executive Order 8802 on June 25, 1941. The policy of nondiscrimination in the government was reaffirmed and contractors handling government orders were prohibited from discriminating. This was an example of a limited aim and technique used by bringing pressure through threats to march on Washington.

The Negro movement which can be termed that of protest revolutionary antagonism had two major leaders in this earlier period—W. E. B. Du Bois and Paul Robeson. In 1949, Du Bois stated: "Gentlemen, make no mistake. Russia and communism are not your enemies. Your enemy, ruthless and implacable, is the soulless and utterly selfish corporate wealth, organized for profit and willing to kill your sons in order to retain its present absolute power. . . . Socialism, whether accomplished by communism or reformed capitalism or both, is the natural and inevitable end of the modern world, and grows out of the industrial revolution as a fruit out of the seed."

Explaining why many young Negroes have turned to leftist and Communist movements, Richard Wright, himself an ex-Communist, wrote the following in his book *White Man, Listen:* "Many a black boy in America has seized upon the rungs of the Red ladder to climb out of his Black Belt. And well he may, if there are no other ways out of it. Hence, ideology here becomes a means towards social intimacy. Yes, I know that such a notion is somewhat shocking. But it is true. Many an African in Paris and London, and many a Negro in New York and Chicago, crossed the class and racial line for the first time by accepting the ideology of Marxism, whether he really believed it or not. The role of ideology here served as a function; it enables the

[24]

Negro or Asian to meet revolutionary fragments of the hostile race on a plane of equality. No doubt the oppressed, educated young man said to himself: 'I don't believe in this stuff, but it works.' "

In the important volume *The God That Failed,* a number of former Communists such as Ignazio Silone, Arthur Koestler, and André Gide present the story of how and why they first entered the Communist Party—and how and why they left it. One of the contributors to this book was Richard Wright. His first experience was a visit to a Communist-dominated writers' club in Chicago. He presented this report:

"I felt that Communists could not possibly have a sincere interest in Negroes. I was cynical and I would rather have heard a white man say that he hated Negroes, which I could have readily believed, than to have heard him say that he respected Negroes, which would have made me doubt him. I sat in a corner and listened while they discussed their magazine, *Left Front.* Were they treating me courteously because I was a Negro? I must let cold reason guide me with these people, I told myself. I was asked to contribute something to the magazine, and I said vaguely that I would consider it. After the meeting I met an Irish girl who worked for an advertising agency, a girl who did social work, a school-teacher, and the wife of a prominent university professor. I had once worked as a servant for people like these and I was skeptical. I tried to fathom their motives, but I could detect no condescension in them."

Richard Wright decided to become a Communist. He reasoned: ". . . here, at last, in the realm of revolutionary expression, Negro experience could find a home." One of the developments in the Soviet Union which impressed Wright and other young Negro intellectuals was the idea of backward peoples being led to unity on a national scale. Wright remembers that "I had read with awe how the Communists had sent phonetic experts into the vast regions of Russia to listen to the stammering dialects of peoples oppressed for centuries by the czars. I had made the first total emotional commitment of my life when I read how the phonetic experts had given these tongueless people a language, newspapers, institutions. I had read how these forgotten folk had been encouraged to keep their old cul-

[25]

tures, to see in their ancient customs meanings and satisfactions as deep as those contained in supposedly superior ways of living. And I had exclaimed to myself how different this was from the way in which Negroes were sneered at in America."

It was some time before Richard Wright discovered that minority groups in the Soviet Union fared much worse than did Negroes in the United States. The stated goal of providing "autonomy" to such groups as the Ukrainians, Jews, Armenians and Georgians was simply a smoke screen for those in the West who advocated such a benevolent approach. The policy of Russification, the destruction of such "alien" forces as the Jewish religion and the Ukrainian language, went forward with more brutality, loss of life, and destruction of culture than anything imagined or experienced by black Americans in the post-Civil War era.

Richard Wright learned all of these things, but he learned a good deal about the internal operation of the Communist Party as well. He remembers, "I found myself arguing alone against the majority opinion, and then I made still another amazing discovery, I saw that even those who agreed with me would not support me. . . . I learned that when a man was informed of the wish of the Party he submitted, even though he knew with all the strength of his brain that the wish was not a wise one, was one that would ultimately hurt the Party's interests."

Wright recalls that "It was not courage that made me oppose the Party. I simply did not know any better. It was inconceivable to me, though bred in the lap of Southern hate, that a man could not have his say. I had spent a third of my life traveling from the place of my birth to the North just to talk freely, to escape the pressure of fear. And now I was facing fear again."

In 1935 Wright attended a National Writer's Congress in New York, sponsored by the John Reed Club, a Communist-front organization of which he was a member in Chicago. Even among these enlightened advocates of the coming revolution which would free all men of their prejudices, he found difficulty on the same human level upon which he had encountered difficulty so many times in the past. He waited while one white Communist called another white Communist to his side and discussed what could be done to get him, a black Chicago Com-

[26]

munist, housed. He writes: "During the trip I had not thought of myself as a Negro; I had been mulling over the problems of the young left-wing writers I knew. Now, as I stood watching one white comrade talk frantically to another about the color of my skin, I felt disgusted. . . . I cursed under my breath. Several people standing nearby observed the white Communist trying to find a black Communist a place to sleep. I burned with shame. A few minutes later the white Communist returned, frantic-eyed, sweating. 'Did you find anything?' I asked. 'No, not yet,' he said, panting. 'Just a moment. I'm going to call somebody I know. Say, give me a nickel for the phone.' 'Forget it,' I said. My legs felt like water. 'I'll find a place. But I'd like to put my suitcase somewhere until after the meeting tonight.' "

The personal anguish which this young, talented black writer felt as a part of the revolutionary left was followed by a broader understanding of why it is that communism hates intellectuals, and must hate all free and open thought if it is to survive. Richard Wright came to this assessment and understanding far more quickly than did many of his white colleagues who spent many years doing the bidding of the Communist Party, only to their ultimate regret and degradation. He came to this conclusion: "In trying to grasp why Communists hated intellectuals, my mind was led back again to the accounts I had read of the Russian Revolution. There had existed in Old Russia millions of poor, ignorant people who were exploited by a few educated, arrogant noblemen, and it became natural for the Russian Communists to associate betrayal with intellectualism. But there existed in the Western world an element that baffled and frightened the Communist Party: the prevalence of self-achieved literacy. Even a Negro, entrapped by ignorance and exploitation —as I had been—could, if he had the will and the love for it, learn to read and understand the world in which he lived. And it was these people that the Communists could not understand."

While Richard Wright toyed with communism, and Marcus Garvey urged a return to Africa, and other black voices expressed other views, the burden of the mainstream effort to achieve equality under the law and integration into the American society was conducted under the auspices of the National Association for the Advancement of Colored People.

The theme of the NAACP has been that the attack upon Negro citizenship rights is an attack upon white Americans and democracy as well. The organization conducted its activities in the traditional pattern of lobbying activity, legal procedures, education, and persuasion. Officers have been of both races, although there has never been a mass following and the organization has had a high percentage of upper class members.

Walter White, long a leading NAACP spokesman, said the following at the forty-third convention of the organization in Oklahoma City in 1952: "We know that we may not win full equality tomorrow. But we are going to continue fighting for it with every democratic weapon at our command and we will never let up in that fight. Let us never forget that it is better to die on our feet than live on our knees."

It is generally agreed that the NAACP accomplished the following: (1) It successfully fought the election or appointment to public office of many persons who were prejudiced toward Negroes. (2) It reached the alert strata of the Negro community through the Negro press. (3) It won notable victories in efforts to end Jim Crow education, to put an end to lynchings, to abolish segregation in the armed forces, and to improve opportunities in employment and housing. (4) It was often successful in influencing politicians by threatening, in its lobbying, to influence the Negro vote against them. (5) The lawyers of the association participated in hundreds of cases and were successful in saving Negroes from unfair treatment in courts. It succeeded in having "grandfather clauses" of Southern state constitutions declared unconstitutional, and it attacked unequal salaries of Negro teachers as well as urging an antilynching law.

The NAACP has employed an observer in each branch of Congress and has been influential in preventing the passage of discriminatory bills. It was successful, for example, in fighting against discriminatory provisions in the Wages and Hours Act and against discrimination in WPA projects and in the TVA.

Protest revolutionary antagonists charge that the NAACP evades the central issue, which is economic. Many young Negroes share with some other Americans a feeling that haphazard laws directed at symptoms and not at causes and without much consideration for social facts are bound to fail because social change cannot be achieved by legislation alone. But, that line of argument has been developed to its ultimate degree by the semirevolutionary groups later to arise in the 1960s and early 1970s. The role of the older revolutionary groups provides at least some perspective from which to observe present-day manifestations of what is a very similar feeling and viewpoint.

Concerning the NAACP, Ralph Bunche said: "The NAACP does not have a mass basis. It has never assumed the proportions of a crusade, nor has it ever, in any single instance, attracted the masses of people to its banner. It is not impressed upon the mass consciousness, and it is a bald truth that the average Negro in the street has never heard of the Association nor of any of its leaders. It has shown a pitiful lack of knowledge of mass technique and of how to pitch an appeal so as to reach the ears of the masses."

The revolutionary movement was set in order when, at the close of the 1930s, Max Yergan and Paul Robeson set up a Council on African Affairs in New York. In the latter part of the 1940s the Council was put on the Attorney General's "subversive" list. In 1948, after being dismissed by the NAACP as director of special research, W. E. B. Du Bois became vice chairman of the Council on African Affairs. In 1949 in a speech Paul Robeson said that he hoped Negroes would never fight Russia, because it was the sole nation on earth that had made race prejudice a crime. He felt that the winning of peace was necessary for the winning of complete civil rights for Negroes. In August, 1950, Paul Robeson urged 900 members of the American Negro Labor Congress and League of Struggle For Negro Rights to sign the Stockholm Peace Pledge. In 1948, the Progressive Party placed Du Bois, Earl B. Dickerson, Larkin Marshall and Charles Howard in leadership positions, with Robeson as co-chairman. In spite of this the Party failed to get a majority of the Negro vote, and their candidate for President received only 14 percent of the total Negro vote in five election districts in Harlem.

Dr. Du Bois summed up the attitude of Negro protest revolutionary antagonism toward America: "It would not be true for me to say that I 'love my country' for it has enslaved, impoverished, murdered and insulted my people. I do not believe that loyalty to the United States involves hatred for other peoples, nor will I compromise to support my country 'right or wrong.' I will defend this country when it is right. I will condemn it when it is wrong. While I am and expect to be a loyal citizen of the United States, I also respect and admire the U.S.S.R. I regard that land as today the most hopeful nation on earth, not because of what it has accomplished. The greatest single fact about Russia which holds my faith in its future is its system of popular education. There is in the world no system equal to it. If American Negroes had one half the chance of the Russians to learn to read, write, and count, there would be no Negro question today. Social control of production and distribution of wealth is coming as sure as the rolling of the stars. The whole concept of property is changing, and must change."

Comparing the successes of the two approaches to practical problems of the American Negro, we would find that in such major areas as constitutional rights, the franchise, lynching, fair employment practice legislation, education, public accommodations, and discrimination in the armed forces, it is the NAACP that has made the major gains, while the revolutionary approach has made virtually no gains. The revolutionary approach all through the nineteen twenties, thirties, forties, and fifties met with only minimal support within the Negro community and had even less of an impact within the larger American society.

It may fairly be said, in fact, that the great successes over the years of the NAACP and its approach of working within the legal system and through the democratic process is the reason why we have been facing in the sixties and early seventies a Negro protest movement which, in many respects, may be seen as part of the revolutionary movement which Negroes (and white civil rights supporters) rejected in the forties and are tending to accept today.

In his book *The Negro Revolt*, Louis Lomax points out that the NAACP is the victim of its own history. It was created by upper-class Negroes and still reflects this view, although rank and file membership has shifted from the elite to a broader representation of the black community. Lomax feels that while the NAACP has fought many battles for the common man the feeling is widespread that its main involvement is with the "talented tenth," the exceptional Negroes who prove the Negro's right to equality. This remains true despite the fact that the very make-up of the NAACP has changed, and 80 percent of its members are now Negroes. He points out several major reasons for the decline in faith in the traditional Negro leadership:

(1) Negro leadership organizations are dominated by white liberals and middle-class whites. The result has been an attack on segregation that reflected "class" rather than "mass."

(2) Even after it became apparent that legalism and "class" concerns could not accomplish the swift change demanded by both the temper of our times and the mood of the Negro people, these organizations persisted in their basic philosophical approach to the problems of segregation. They interpreted any desire to debate the question as an attack upon the organizations and individuals who head them.

(3) These organizations failed to make room for the younger, educated Negroes who were coming to power in the Negro communities. The irony of this is that many, if not most, of the younger educated Negroes are educated and inspired because of the work of the very organizations which now refuse to make room for them.

The Negro revolt which began in the late 1950s, he feels, is more than a revolt against the white world. It is also a revolt of the Negro masses against their own leadership and goals. The "modern" phase of the Negro revolt on civil rights movements is dated from December 1, 1955, when the Montgomery bus boycott brought the Rev. Martin Luther King, Jr., to the forefront of national attention. The question faced by Negroes was: Shall we wend our way through the courts in order to get civil rights or shall we set off mass demonstrations and by dint of strength, numbers and moral right crush segregation and discrimination on the spot now? The NAACP, it seems, took one position, and many Negroes seem to have taken another.

Speaking at Spelman College in 1961, Roy Wilkins stated:

[31]

"The principal task before any community is the abolition of the segregated school. The inadequate and unequal education our children are receiving under this system is literally placing them in leg irons to run the race of life."

Lomax states that the sentiment expressed by Wilkins in this speech is the key to all of the trouble concerning the NAACP, its philosophy, and its action proₐₐₘ. Although school segregation is certainly important, he believes, placing this as the central point of the civil rights movement did not involve enough people. It provided no immediate relief for those who had already finished school or for those who had no intention of attending school. It is a slow process and the very nature of this battle sidelines the best Negro brains in the various local communities.

On February 1, 1960, in Greensboro, North Carolina, four freshmen from all-black Agricultural and Technical College sat down at an all-white lunch-counter in Woolworth's. This, following Montgomery in 1955, marked the second major battle in the Negro revolt against both segregation and the entrenched Negro leaders. This sit-in activity was sponsored by the Congress of Racial Equality. Started in 1942, CORE felt that legalism was not enough. Its technique involved nonviolent direct mass action; through persistent use of this tactic, CORE shaped it into an art at the very time when the NAACP was locked in bitter debate over whether or not it should embark on a policy of mass action. Sit-ins raged throughout the spring of 1960 and convinced even more people that direct mass action was the shorter, more effective route to the goal of desegregation.

Lomax notes that "This new gospel of the American Negro is rooted in the theology of desegregation; its missionaries are several thousand Negro students who—like Paul, Silas and Peter of the early Christian era—are braving great dangers and employing new techniques to spread the faith. It is not an easy faith, for it names the conservative Negro leadership class as sinners along with segregation. Yet this gospel is being preached by clergymen and laymen alike wherever Negroes gather."

On May 4, 1961, a freedom ride was sponsored by CORE.

[32]

These rides involved over 1,000 persons, and cost more than $300,000. In the opinion of many they did the job and all but eliminated segregation in interstate terminals. These rides mark the emergence of CORE, whose leaders were not drawn from the conservative elements that supported the NAACP but tended to be people of action, the kind who believed in picket lines and marches.

Jackie Robinson, an NAACP board member, had this to say about the role of his organization: "We are not meeting the needs of the masses. We don't know the people; the people don't know us. I have been asked by many people to form another civil rights organization, one that would be closer to the masses. I'm all for a new organization if we can do it without interfering with what the NAACP is doing. Maybe a new organization is the answer. We must do something; we can't go on as we are now."

At least one NAACP national official at this time felt that the NAACP could not embrace sit-ins and freedom rides without violating the fundamental philosophy of the organization. This is what Dr. John Marsell, executive assistant to Roy Wilkins, said about the techniques of Martin Luther King and CORE: "We can hardly advocate or condone a policy of mass civil disobedience, except under such extreme conditions that would warrant the complete abandonment of the entire philosophy of operations which has sustained us for fifty years."

The Negro leadership of the period prior to the mid-1960s wanted the job done in the nice, clean quiet of the courtroom, but the opposition rejected this approach. Central to this opposition was the Negro masses' lack of faith in the "white power structure." They did not believe that this power structure intended to keep bargains made at the race-relations conference table; thus they demanded legalism to reduce these verbal agreements to court decrees. Early school segregation cases in New York and in Newark and Englewood, New Jersey, were handled by young Negro lawyer Paul Zuber, and not by the NAACP.

In the early 1960s many black leaders cautioned that if this crisis was not resolved and if the white power structure refused to deal with responsible Negroes and bring about change, then,

[33]

in the words of Baptist minister Dr. Gardner C. Taylor, "The leadership of Negroes, particularly in our large cities, will fall into the hands of extremists whose preachments of violence endanger everything America stands for."

Any consideration of the extremist trends within the Negro protest movement must consider the Black Muslims. Their withdrawal from America is almost complete. They speak of themselves as a "nation," indicating that they are not of the American body politic; they do not vote nor do they participate in political affairs. They have their own stores, supermarkets, barbershops, department stores and fish markets. Their "good news" for the black man is that he is on the verge of recapturing his position as ruler of the universe. Totally separate from the white men, they have their own home-grown American Negro religion. God and black are one, and all Negroes are divine.

According to Lomax, "Although they are bitter ideological enemies, there is only a thin line between Muhammed and Martin Luther King. King, of course, will have none of Muhammed's blanket indictment of the white man; nor will King abide black supremacy notions. But both King and Muhammed are saying that the purpose of a religion is to explain life for the people who adopt or create it and that the function of the gospel is to speak to the frustration of a people. Muhammed's gospel as a whole will not be accepted by the Negro. But—and this is the important thing—no gospel that fails to answer Muhammed's criticism of Christianity will be accepted either."

The Black Muslims represent an extreme reaction to the difficulty of being a Negro in America today. Instead of working to improve conditions within the framework of American society, as do other Negro leadership organizations, the Black Muslims react by turning their backs on that society entirely. Their one positive aspect is that they work to make Negroes proud of being Negro. More and more black militants are becoming increasingly antiwhite, and the presence of many white people within the civil rights movement is often credited as a reason for its not becoming totally antiwhite.

Another approach to the difficulty of the American Negro has also been heard, and it is that of the National Urban League.

[34]

This group states quite frankly that if the American Negro is to fulfill his role in the American society he must become more responsible than he now is. The view is that for a long time Negroes could justly blame the white man for their weaknesses and shortcomings, but that this day is about over. They say that the Negro crime rate is too high and that Negro welfare chiselers are an abomination. Lomax states that the quiet joke among Negroes is that the Urban League has opened up more job opportunities for Negroes in "white" industry than it can find Negroes to fill. There is a disturbing view held by many Negroes in high places that 300 years of first slavery and then discrimination have destroyed the inner fiber of the American Negro masses; that, perhaps, they are not spiritually capable of becoming first-class citizens.

Whitney Young of the Urban League stated that "The Negro family as a unit must be strengthened. All too often current society has battered and broken the Negro family and then placed the blame on that family for what happened to it."

It was his view that the family broke down from lack of a consistent breadwinner, and from ignorance of, or apathy toward, community institutions designed to help families in moments of crisis. Young suggested that the Negro masses be certified as an underdeveloped people, and that they be given special, accelerated treatment in order for them to assume full responsibility in American society. The current Negro generation must be moved forward en masse and at a swifter pace than the current white generation. Young's thesis was, and the Urban League's thesis has remained, that white business and industry must now take Negroes under their wings and train them, just as, for example, Britain did Africans in Nigeria.

In the face of the many and diverse groups which have appeared on the political scene in recent years within the Negro community, many have asked this question: Does the Negro really want to be an American and integrate into the society, does he want to tear it down and remake it—or does he want to escape from it?

Richard Wright has written, "The Negro American is the only American in America who says: 'I want to be an American.' More or less all other Americans are born Americans and

[35]

take their Americanism for granted. Hence, the American Negro's effort to be an American is a self-conscious thing. America is something outside of him and he wishes to become part of that America. But, since color easily marks him off from being an ordinary American, and since he lives amidst social conditions pregnant with racism, he becomes a kind of negative American. The psychological situation resulting from this stance is a peculiar one. The Negro in America is so constantly striving to become an American that he has no time to become or try to become anything else. When he becomes a publisher, he is a 'Negro publisher'; when he becomes a physician, he is a Negro physician, when he becomes an athlete, he is a Negro athlete. This is the answer to the question that so many people have asked about American Negroes: Why do not American Negroes rebel? Aside from the fact that they are a minority and their rebellion would be futile, they haven't got time to rebel. Why are Negroes so loyal to America? They are passionately loyal because they are not psychologically free enough to be traitors. They are trapped in and by their loyalties. But that loyalty has kept them in a negative position."

Dr. Kenneth Clark, Negro psychologist, notes that "There is no point in talk, regardless of· how poetic it may be, about whether the Negro wants to integrate with America. He has no choice. He is involved, inextricably so, with America and he knows it. And the sensible Negro is the man who takes pride in this involvement and accepts it as a mandate to work for the change that is written in the way of things."

Though these sentiments are still true for the majority of Negroes, there appears to be an ever growing minority for whom it is not true. During the early 1960s the civil rights movement became more and more of a revolutionary movement, and less and less one of reform. In the midst of the rioting in Harlem in 1964 William Epton, head of the Harlem Defense Council, stated that "The state must be smashed . . . we're going to have to kill cops and judges." A detective in attendance at a secret Harlem meeting made this report: "There was talk of bloodshed, violence, missiles being thrown and warnings that all white sympathizers were to stay away."

William Stringfellow, a white lawyer who participated in an

[36]

interracial Protestant ministry activity in Harlem, wrote that "The Negro revolution is . . . an authentic revolution, in which the whole prevailing social order of the nation is being over-turned in the face of three hundred years of slavery, segrega-tion, discrimination, and de facto racism throughout the coun-try. . . . Every important institution in the public life of the nation—education, employment, unions, churches, entertain-ment, housing, politics, commerce—is immediately affected by this revolution, and this revolution will not spend its course until every institution surrenders to its objectives. The only real question is the means by which the inevitable integration of American public life will take place—peaceably or violently."

At the time when violence was first being urged as a valid policy tactic by extremist leaders, Professor Oscar Handlin pointed out the very fact of the destructiveness of such efforts. He stated: "When the Rev. Milton A. Galamison, chairman of the New York City Committee for Integrated Schools, publicly states that he would rather see the city school system destroyed than permit it to perpetuate de facto segregation, he expresses a nihilism that can only damage the whole society. That is the Northern Negro equivalent of the white attitude in Prince Ed-ward County, Virginia."

Speaking in Cairo, Egypt, Malcolm X noted that "There are more Negroes in America than police, and the time has come for our people to fight." In New York City on July 29, 1964, Jesse Gray, the leader of the Harlem Rent Strike, called for "100 skilled black revolutionaries who are ready to die" to correct what he called "the police brutality situation in Harlem." He stated: "This city can be changed only by 50,000 well organized Negroes . . . and they can determine what will happen in New York."

In a telegram to Jesse Gray, civil rights leader Martin Luther King, allegedly a supporter of nonviolent means, wrote the fol-lowing: "You have my absolute support in your righteous and courageous effort to expose the outrageous conditions that Negroes confront as a result of substandard housing condi-tions." Gray was named a Communist in sworn testimony before a committee of the House of Representatives in 1960.

By the mid-1960s the civil rights movement had accepted the

philosophy of civil disobedience almost totally. In his book *Why We Can't Wait,* Martin Luther King stated clearly that "there are just laws and there are unjust laws. . . . I submit that an individual who breaks a law that conscience tells him is unjust and willingly accepts the penalty . . . is in reality expressing the highest respect for the law."

Among many others, James Baldwin has suggested that Negroes have little to preserve in the American civilization. It has, he has repeatedly stated, enslaved and degraded them. There are, however, some Negro leaders who have not accepted this negative approach. Some have realized that not only is this approach negative, but that Negroes cannot use their race as a crutch in modern America very much longer. The Rev. Dr. John J. Hicks, pastor of St. Marks Methodist Church in Harlem, stated, "If we are going to be judged without discrimination, then we will be judged also without pity." The pastor, who was the first Negro president of the St. Louis Board of Education, said that the opportunities for success were great but that they "go hand in hand with enemies—within and without." The enemies without, he said, are those who are "callous to humanity." The enemies within, he added, are doubt and fear.

Still, comments such as those by Dr. Hicks have been few. Younger and more militant Negroes have heaped increasing scorn upon those who express such conciliatory views. As the 1960s progressed, many more moderate Negro leaders, in order to maintain their own positions of leadership within the Negro community, have been forced to take extreme positions which they know to be unwise.

In 1963 the civil rights groups conducted a March on Washington which, although peaceful, had in the background threats that if the Civil Rights Bill desired by the participating groups was not passed by the Congress, then violence would ensue. The bill was passed and, for the moment, violence was averted. How close, however, can leaders come to preaching the doctrine of violence, even as a threat, without having members of their groups pursue such a course actively? The answer seems to be that once violence has been threatened, the odds favor its occurrence. Once it is stated that law need not be obeyed unless it is "good law," then the beginning of an end to

[38]

rule by law has been initiated. ("People say it's against the law," Adam Clayton Powell has said, "What law? And who made them? There is only one great and unbreakable law, and that is the law of God.")

With the advent of the war in Vietnam the nation witnessed a steady progression toward a more extreme outlook on the part of Negro protest groups. On the one hand we witnessed armed bands being formed among Negroes, as in North Carolina, and on the other we saw the beginning of a coalition between the civil rights movement and the antiwar movement.

At the beginning of the antiwar movement, columnists Rowland Evans and Robert Novak wrote that the Assembly of Unrepresented Peoples to Declare Peace, a mass rally in Washington whose stated purpose was to get antiwar protesters arrested at the door of the White House and at the Capitol, was being run from the headquarters of the Student Nonviolent Coordinating Committee. Robert Moses, who headed SNCC's summer project in Mississippi in 1964, helped to plan the assembly together with Russell Nixon, general manager of the Communist newspaper the *National Guardian*. Martin Luther King, in a speech in Farmville, Virginia, called for an end to United States involvement in Vietnam, and the Mississippi Freedom Democratic Party urged Negroes of draft age in Mississippi to refuse to report if called to military service. CORE passed a similar resolution at its convention, calling for an end to the American role in Vietnam, but then surprisingly reversed itself.

In a book hailing the Student Nonviolent Coordinating Committee, Professor Howard Zinn of Boston University, a leading New Left theoretician, points up the "more exciting possibilities" of the civil rights movement. In *SNCC: The New Abolitionists,* he expresses his dislike for private property and demands the imposition of severe limitations on practically every enterprise. He calls for a "reorganization of national wealth which should be on the basis of justice rather than either luck or ability." Negroes having finally entered the social and economic room from which they were previously barred, now find, Zinn states, "that most of the furniture is occupied and the only place to sit is on the floor."

Urging violence against whites, a column by Mrs. S. Sparks

[39]

in *Challenge* asks: "Must we continue to eat ourselves alive with hatred and kill one another because we dare not kill the man who is our enemy and oppressor? Will our anger never spill over and, like molten lava, bury our enemy where he lies?" Discussing more moderate Negroes she stated, "Conditions are being created where any blacks who betray, in any way, the cause of complete freedom will have to go. Just over the horizon is the time when a black man will be unable to stand before the white oppressor and accuse his black brother of any crime without being in fear of his own life."

After Black Muslim leader Malcolm X was murdered, Bayard Rustin, leader of the 1963 March on Washington, predicted that "Malcolm X-ism is here to stay unless the nation is ready to revolutionize its spirit and its institutions. Violence is inevitable, fighting in the streets is inevitable"—unless the nation eliminates ghetto slums, segregated schools, and other symptoms of injustice.

Concerning the much publicized March on Selma, Rabbi Richard Rubinstein, who accompanied a group of University of Pittsburgh students, said that SNCC had "wanted dead bodies, our bodies." He accused SNCC leaders of being "activists and revolutionaries" who wanted to cause trouble rather than further civil rights. Addressing a rally called by the NAACP in Pittsburgh he said, "We were assured by SNCC in Montgomery that police permission had been granted for demonstrations there. That was a lie. As we moved down the streets in the demonstrations, SNCC leaders went into a high school and asked young children to leave their classes and join the demonstration. That was both immoral and illegal." He said that the performance was repeated in a grammar school, and that in the demonstration SNCC leaders under James Forman "broke from police lines, against all orders, and even told one of our students to come across the line—that police had given permission for it."

Even at this time, some Negro leaders challenged the new course of the civil rights movement. Roy Wilkins of the NAACP expressed his opinion about the growing coalition of civil rights groups with peace groups: "When you mix the question of Vietnam into the questions of Mississippi and Alabama and vote all the things that the American Negroes in this country want, you sort of confuse the issue. The American Negro can be a greater aid to foreign policy and other problems as he grows stronger in this country. His first thought ought to be to strengthen his position as an American. If he's a third-rate citizen his opinions on South Vietnam will have no effect."

James Farmer of CORE expressed this view: "CORE should not be a peace movement. It would divert too much of our energies. Yet on specific issues the two should be coordinated. As an individual I object to our Vietnam policies. As individuals we should and would be involved in both."

The fact is that as the 1960s progressed, and despite all disclaimers, the nature of the civil rights movement in America changed significantly. For far too many it was no longer a movement seeking to integrate black Americans into a society which, for too long, had put barriers in his path. It was no longer simply an effort to make sure that black Americans could vote, or sit in the front of the bus, or serve in an integrated army or navy. These things had been accomplished, even if some of the details remained to be perfected. It was, in addition, far more than a movement seeking jobs, and the training necessary to prepare men and women to fill them. The black protest movement had, by the mid-1960s, reached its own crisis of identity, for so many of its original goals had become realities.

It is always true historically that violent revolution comes not when people suffer in the depths of depression, but when they begin finally to see the light of a brighter day. The French Revolution came at a time when the monarchy was weak—not strong. The Russian Revolution occurred after the czar had embarked upon a policy of liberalization, not during the period of tyranny and brutal pogroms. Similarly, the most extreme and violent rhetoric and action on the part of the Negro protest movement has come not during those times when hope did not exist and despair was all pervasive. It has come in the late 1960s and early 1970s, years when racial barriers have been falling dramatically, when there are more black representatives in Congress than ever before, when several large cities have black mayors, when there is a black Supreme Court Justice and a black United States Senator.

[41]

It is at a time such as this that black militants proclaim that they no longer seek integration, that "black is beautiful," and that black nationalism rather than a common American nationality is the real answer to the American race problem. It is at a time such as this that organized groups of militant blacks call for revolution, arguing that only when the American economic, social, and political structure is destroyed can real equality and racial harmony exist.

There are, of course, a number of reasons for the rise of black militancy at this time, and the case of Angela Davis cannot adequately be understood without understanding at the same time the roots of the black protest movement which nourished and antedated the scene we witness today. The case of Angela Davis, moreover, is important because it crystallizes the transition of the black protest movement and its interrelationship beginning in approximately 1965 with the predominantly white and middle class New Left.

Still, few take the trouble to see any connection between Malcolm X, Roy Wilkins, Whitney Young and other current and contemporary spokesmen and those who came before them—Frederick Douglass, Booker T. Washington, W. E. B. Du Bois, and Marcus Garvey. The fact is, of course, that no people's history exists in a vacuum. It is impossible to understand present-day England without understanding the imperial past and the subsequent decline and need for reassessment and reorientation. It is impossible to understand the inclinations and desires of the American people without being aware of our tradition as a frontier society and our current transformation from a rural to an urban society.

It is particularly difficult to understand the attitudes and goals of black Americans because they must be considered in the context not only of what it is like to be a black American in the mid-twentieth century, but what it is like to be an American at all at this time. All of the forces of technology, the mass media, urbanization, drugs, crime, and the much discussed "identity crisis" affect all Americans, but they do so in different ways. Black Americans have, in the past decade, had to cope not only with the problems that are unique to their own minority, but to the broader problems faced by the society as a whole. It

[42]

is no wonder that it has been a difficult task to come to grips with many of these strange and ever-changing phenomena.

Just as in the early days following the Civil War there were divergent views—and just as there were the conflicting views of integration, black nationalism, and return to Africa, as well as the notion that only through a revolution within America could a common and color-blind American nationality emerge at the turn of the century and beyond—so today many divergent views and opinions exist within the black community.

For a variety of reasons, some of which will be explored, the mass media has seen fit to expose white Americans primarily to the inflammatory and radical rhetoric of what, by any estimate, represents only a small part of the thinking of black Americans. Black Americans are, after all, individuals. There are as many views and approaches as there are individuals, even though these find expression in several general themes.

The times in which we live are difficult to understand and to adjust to for the most comfortable, affluent and well educated members of our society. The same is true for its black members, except that for them the problem is even more complex and more difficult. Thus, it is little wonder that a case such as that of Angela Davis should arise at this time—combining within it many of the elements of the political life, thought, and passion of this time.

2

IN MANY RESPECTS 1966 MARKED THE POINT OF SERIOUS DIVISION within what had previously been the civil rights movement. At a week-long meeting at a campsite near Nashville, Tennessee, May 8–15, 1966, the Student Nonviolent Coordinating Committee elected new officers. The new chairman was Stokely Carmichael, who had worked in Mississippi and other parts of the South and in early 1965 began organizing in Lowndes County, Alabama. With other SNCC workers he helped organize the Lowndes County Freedom Organization, known as the Black Panther Party. Carmichael clearly discounted integration as a valid goal of the black protest movement.

He said that "It [integration] is not the solution to segregation because telling black people to integrate is telling them that they cannot get together and solve their own problems, that they need white people to solve the problems for them. It is telling them that they are inherently inferior. And it is telling them that white people are better. . . . Our goal has been fighting against white supremacy, not fighting for integration."

Carmichael stated that under his leadership SNCC would begin a campaign to resist the military draft, and he stated that SNCC's opposition to the war in Vietnam stemmed from " opposition to the whole foreign policy of this country, which we see as a policy which exploits nonwhite people across the world. And since we are nonwhite, when we take part in that system, we are exploiting our fellow nonwhites. Therefore, we cannot be a part of it. So we have to oppose it. We are also opposed to the draft. We think that no man has the right to tell any man where he should spend two years of his life, what he should be doing, and whom he should be killing."

Students for a Democratic Society, the leading New Left organization at that time, issued a strong statement supporting SNCC in its organizational emphasis on "black power" and its condemnation of the Vietnam war. Addressing itself to SNCC's liberal critics, the national council of SDS declared the following on June 18, 1966: "We know that not all SNCC's critics resemble George Wallace. That is precisely why we try to lay bare the liberal assumptions that lead to attacks on SNCC. We are struck with the fact that among the critics are liberals vociferous in their praise of an America in which minorities organize themselves and preserve their cultural integrity. They are now denouncing SNCC's 'black conciousness' as racism in reverse. We doubt these critics would find themselves so upset if SNCC sought to accept the major premises of American life: it is because SNCC is revolutionary, because it is trying to bring about a fundamental rearrangement of power in America that they shrink in horror."

In January, 1967, Stokely Carmichael flew to Puerto Rico where he made an alliance with Castroite groups working for Puerto Rican independence. He met with Juan Maris Bras, a follower of Fidel Castro who has had training in Cuba, and in a protocol of cooperation signed January 26 at the San Juan International Airport, Carmichael and Bras proclaimed their organizations as "in the vanguard of a common struggle against U.S. imperialism."

Floyd McKissick, national director of the Congress of Racial Equality, also changed the approach of that organization from one that advocated integration and civil rights legislation to one advocating "black power." He saw this significance in the events of 1966: "I've said that 1966 marked the year when the Negro became the black man. Secondly, 1966 was the moment of truth for the struggle of the black people in this country. It transferred the struggle from a moral one to one for power—recognizing that power can bring about far more changes than

[45]

an appeal to man's morality. It was also the year that we had to educate the black man as to what his fight was. . . ."

There was, of course, no unanimity within the civil rights movement concerning the new course being pursued by organizations such as SNCC and CORE. These organizations and the other advocates of "black power" were sharply criticized at the fifty-seventh annual convention of the NAACP, held in Los Angeles in July, 1966. Roy Wilkins, the association's executive secretary, denounced black power as black racism and said that it could lead only "to a black death." He also denounced the SNCC and CORE modification of the doctrine of nonviolence as one that could lead to white counterforce, lynchings, and widespread police actions of repression against the Negro people. Wilkins condemned SNCC, CORE, and the Mississippi Freedom Democratic Party for their refusal to join "in a strong nationwide effort to pass the Civil Rights Act."

Writing in *The Journal of Negro History* in January, 1968, psychologist Kenneth Clark compares the emerging black racism with the white racism of the past: "A critical danger . . . between the determinants of retrogression in the first post-Reconstruction period and the present is that whereas the promises of racial progress were reversed in the nineteenth century by the fanaticism, irrationality, and cruel strength of white segregationists—the impending racial retrogression of today might come about largely through self-hatred leading to the fanaticism, dogmatism, rigidity, and self-destructive cruelty of black separatists."

"Black power," declared Dr. Clark, "is a bitter retreat from the possibility of the attainment of the goals of any serious racial integration in America. . . . It is an attempt to make a verbal virtue of involuntary racial segregation. . . . It is the sour grapes phenomenon on the American racial scene. . . . 'Black power' is the contemporary form of the Booker T. Washington accommodation to white America's resistance to making democracy real for Negro Americans. While Booker T. made his adjustment to and acceptance of white racism under the guise of conservatism, many if not all of the 'black power' advocates are seeking to sell the same shoddy moral product disguised in the gaudy package of racial militance."

[46]

Dr. Clark is critical of those who disagree with the extremists but, nevertheless, permit them to occupy the center of the stage. He states, "White segregationists were able to inflict and perpetuate racial injustices upon Negroes because rational, sophisticated, and moderate whites were silent in the face of barbarities. They permitted themselves to be intimidated and bullied by white extremists until they were morally and almost functionally indistinguishable from their worst and most ignorant elements. A similar threat and dilemma face the rational, thoughtful Negro today. If he permits himself to be cowed into silence by unrealistic Negro racists, he will be an active partner in fastening the yoke of impossible racial separatism more tightly around the neck of America."

In his important book, *A Prophetic Minority,* Jack Newfield discusses the transformation of SNCC by noting that it "began as a religious band of middle class rather square reformers, seeking only 'our rights.'" The lunch counter, he points out, was their entrance to the American dream and their guiding spirit was not even Ghandi so much as the Bill of Rights, the Thirteenth, Fourteenth, and Fifteenth Amendments, and the Bible. They were, simply, "black, liberal integrationists grappling with segregation."

But at the SNCC meeting in Nashville in May, 1966, when the leadership was finally changed and the militant Stokely Carmichael came to power, "One field secretary seriously suggested that SNCC arrange for 100 Negroes to study nuclear physics at UCLA and then be sent to an African country to help to construct an atomic bomb to 'blow up America.' Another proposed that only the black press and the African press be invited to all future SNCC press conferences."

It was this kind of metamorphosis that transformed SNCC and CORE from civil rights organizations into revolutionary forces calling not for the entrance of Negroes into society but for the revolutionary reconstruction of the society. It was this change that provided them with a common basis for union with other New Left organizations, which also sought the revolutionary transformation of society, one in which integration, as they saw it, would become a possibility. Until then, every-

[47]

thing about the status quo had to be challenged, whether it was the selective service system or the war.

Perhaps the major fusion of the civil rights movement with the New Left was found, however, in the person of the late Martin Luther King.

The assassination of Dr. King in Memphis was, of course, an unspeakable tragedy, an affront to civilized man. For this reason, all too many observers have refrained from frankly discussing his role in the radicalization of the civil rights movement. Still, any discussion of the developing relations between the New Left and the civil rights movement is impossible without noting the role played by Dr. King in these developments in the closing years of his career. Martin Luther King, when he first emerged as leader of the civil rights movement, made a number of positive contributions for which he has rightly been honored. During this early period, among other things, he insisted on nonviolence and he avoided open association with extremists. Before his death, however, he had moved into an increasingly open alliance with the extremists and he had become increasingly reckless in his criticism of American foreign policy.

Speaking in New York on April 4, 1967, King called on "all who find the American course in Vietnam a dishonorable and unjust one" to apply as conscientious objectors to military service. He described the U. S. Government as the "greatest purveyor of violence in the world today."

Dr. King's position was supported by Leonid Ilyich Brezhnev, General Secretary of the Communist Party of the Soviet Union, at a meeting of Communist and workers' parties held in Moscow in June, 1969. Brezhnev said: "The antagonism between imperialism, which intensifies social oppression and rejects democracy, and the masses, who are fighting for their vital rights and striving for freedom and democracy, is growing sharper. In some countries popular discontent is so great that sometimes as little as a spark is enough to set off a powerful social explosion. Such explosions are becoming ever more frequent, also, in the United States, where the acute social contradictions, the struggle against the war in Vietnam and the fight for Negro civil rights, are tangled in a tight knot. It is a long time since imperialism has been confronted with such violent forms of social protest and with general democratic actions of the present scale and pitch. Ever more frequently broad masses of peasants, intellectuals, white-collar workers, students, and urban middle class strata actively join with the working class in this struggle."

Commenting on Dr. King's speech, Floyd McKissick, CORE leader, said that "Dr. King has come around and I'm glad to have him with us." A challenge came from Whitney Young, executive director of the Urban League. He said that since Negroes "have as their first priority the immediate problem of survival in this country . . . the limited resources and personnel available to civil rights agencies for work in their behalf should not be diverted into other channels."

On April 24, 1967, in Cambridge, Massachusetts, Martin Luther King, in his capacity as chairman of the Southern Christian Leadership Conference, announced a "Vietnam summer drive" against the war and against U.S. foreign policy. He said that the drive would include antidraft activities, sponsorship of peace candidates in local and state elections, and referendums in municipal elections asking for an end to the war. "We throughout the nation who oppose the war must reach others who are concerned," Dr. King said. "It is time to move from demonstrations and university teach-ins to a nationwide community teach-out."

Dr. King was joined at a news conference by pediatrician Dr. Benjamin Spock and Robert Scheer, editor of the radical *Ramparts* magazine. A pamphlet distributed at the conference stated the long-range aim of the organizing effort was the creation of a vocal, strong antiwar block by 1968. "We aim at more than changing a vote or two in Congress," the pamphlet said. "We seek to defeat Lyndon Johnson and his war."

A statement issued by Freedom House strongly criticized Martin Luther King for lending his "mantle of respectability" to an anti-Vietnam war coalition that included well-known Communist allies and luminaries of the American left. The paper said that Dr. King had "emerged as the public spear-carrier of a civil disobedience program that is demagogic and irresponsible in its attacks on our government." Joining in this

[49]

statement was Roy Wilkins, executive secretary of the NAACP and a member of the board of directors of Freedom House.

The antidraft aspect of the New Left has also been adopted by many within the civil rights movement. On May 1, 1967, Cleveland L. Sellers, Jr., one of the three major officers of the Student Nonviolent Coordinating Committee, refused to be inducted into the Army. He called the Vietnamese war a "racist conflict" and joined with Stokely Carmichael, then student committee chairman, in accusing the United States of drafting large numbers of Negroes as part of a plan to commit "calculated genocide." At the same time, Carmichael announced that fifteen other student committee workers had refused induction within the previous three months as part of the organization's campaign against the war in Vietnam.

In an interview, the Reverend James Bevel, assistant to Martin Luther King and head of an antiwar march in New York and San Francisco, was asked how he would "implement" antidraft sympathies. "You don't need a whole lot of complicated plans," Bevel said. "When Mr. Johnson comes around to get you, you just say: 'I won't go.'" He expressed the view that "Mr. Johnson is not going to stop, but we won't stop either. We're going to organize students by the thousands to go to jail by the thousands. . . . We're going to have a radical summer. We're going to say to young people, you must get out of the school and into the streets. . . . Close down New York City. . . . Tell Mr. Johnson plain that he is going to have to stop killing the folks in Vietnam."

An antidraft organization was established at predominantly Negro Morehouse College in Atlanta, Georgia. Seventy-eight students signed a petition declaring, "We cannot conscientiously permit ourselves to be used as objects in war." Henry Bass, a spokesman for the Atlanta Committee to End the War in Vietnam, said, ". . . the Morehouse guys are pledged to seek legal classification as CO's; that is, they are pledged not merely to opt out by going to Canada, staying in graduate school, fathering children, etc., but actually to combat the draft."

At the antiwar meeting in New York on April 15, 1967, Dr. Martin Luther King found himself doing what he once said he would not do. He appeared on the same platform with black power advocates Stokely Carmichael and Floyd McKissick. Writing in the *New York Times,* Gene Roberts pointed out that ". . . in attacking the war, Dr. King automatically aligned himself with the black power wing of the civil rights movement, which had long preached against the war, and cut himself adrift from the moderate wing of the movement."

The double standard implicit in Dr. King's condemnation of the role of the United States in Vietnam was discussed editorially by the *New York Times.* That paper stated, "Dr. King can only antagonize opinion in this country instead of winning recruits to the peace movement by recklessly comparing American military methods to those of the Nazis testing 'new medicine and new tortures in the concentration camps of Europe.' The facts are harsh, but they do not justify such slander. Furthermore, it is possible to disagree with many aspects of U.S. policy in Vietnam without white-washing Hanoi."

Jackie Robinson, at that time Governor Rockefeller's special assistant on community affairs, said, "Dr. King has always been my favorite civil rights leader, but I don't agree with him on this issue." Whitney Young, executive director of the National Urban League, said, "the urgent domestic programs of civil rights and the issue of the war in Vietnam should remain separate. The limited resources and personnel available to civil rights agencies for work in their behalf should not be diverted into other channels."

In criticizing the war in Vietnam, Dr. King overlooked not only the circumstances of Vietcong assassinations and the stated aims of North Vietnam's dictatorial regime to expand Communist control by force, but also an important set of figures that would indicate that his view was shared by only a small minority of the Negro population. The Negro rate of first-term enlistments in the armed forces was three times that for whites, and the rate for career personnel re-enlistment was 10 percent higher. Although Dr. King stated that "twice as many Negroes as whites are in combat," his figures were inaccurate. Actual figures as of March, 1967, showed that 10 percent of all U. S. servicemen in Vietnam were Negro while 10.5 percent of Americans are Negro.

Not only did the New Left element within the civil rights

movement vocally express its opposition to the war in Vietnam, but it did not hesitate to threaten violence in the event that some of its domestic and foreign policy demands were not adhered to.

In April, 1967, Dr. King warned that at least ten cities across the nation could "explode in racial violence this summer." Speaking in New York, Roy Wilkins said he thought that Dr. King was sincere in making the prediction, "But I think it's dangerous . . . less disciplined persons" might interpret such warnings as encouragement to riot.

The leader of a group of West Side Negro ministers in Chicago declared that Dr. Martin Luther King should "get the hell out of here" because his civil rights marching in Chicago the previous summer "created hate." The Rev. Henry Mitchell said, "If he wants to march on the West Side, let him march with rakes, brooms, and grass seed." He noted that the ministers represented the sentiments of 50,000 Chicago Negroes who wanted "peace, love, and harmony," did not approve of civil rights marches, and "just wanted to live in their communities and upgrade them."

Scores of Howard University students chanted "Burn, baby, burn" as an effigy of Selective Service Director Lewis B. Hershey was set afire during a campus rally on April 19, 1967. The burning followed hangings of effigies of Hershey, University President James M. Nabrit, Jr., and Dean Frank Snowden of Howard's College of Liberal Arts. After the hangings and a round of speeches denouncing Nabrit and Snowden as "Uncle Toms," someone in the crowd of more than 400 students yelled, "Burn that white muffinhead." Other students quickly took up the cry, shouting "Burn him" and "Napalm him."

Before the "hangings," more of the crowd jammed into a hallway in a campus building where a number of students were facing disciplinary charges for forcing General Hershey to cancel a speech at Howard on March 21. Outside the building Ronald O. Ross, co-chairman of the Project Awareness student committee that had invited Hershey to speak, said: "I'm sorry I invited him. I don't want him to speak. He's a white man." Referring to university charges that the students "disrupted the . . . orderly operation of the school," Ross continued: "With this rope we're going to disrupt it some more. We don't intend to be responsible. We intend to be black. . . . He [Nabrit] is reading Homer and shooting this university to pot. I say we don't have time for Homer. First let's get rid of every Uncle Tom around here."

A cache of arms, ranging from a slingshot to a sawed-off rifle, was uncovered by police in a raid on a Harlem theater noted for its production of plays with antiwhite themes. A police inspector said the raiding party also found a rifle practice range in the basement of the Black Arts Repertory Theater. Officers arrested six men, including one who was armed and tried to block detectives at the door. Police said they found a sign inside the theater which read: "All weapons cleaned and sharpened by 6 P.M. All weapons will be inspected by Khan, the leader." The theater is the same one founded by bitterly antiwhite poet-playwright LeRoi Jones with partial support from antipoverty funds.

Le Roi Jones (Imamu Amiri Baraka) has not hesitated to make his philosophy quite explicit. In his essay "The Legacy of Malcolm X, and the Coming of the Black Nation," written in 1966, he states, ". . . any talk of nationalism also must take this concept of land and its primary importance into consideration because, finally, any nationalism which is not intent on restoring or securing autonomous space for a people, i.e., a nation, is at the very least short-sighted."

Jones quotes Elijah Muhammed, founder of the Black Muslims, who said, "We want our people in America, whose parents or grandparents were descendants from slaves, to be allowed to establish a separate state or territory of their own—either on this continent or elsewhere. We believe that our former slavemasters are obligated to provide such land and that the area must be fertile and minerally rich."

Calling for a total separation of black and white, Jones expresses the view that "The black man's paths are alien to the white man. Black Culture is alien to the white man. . . . the solution of the Black Man's problems will come only through Black National Consciousness. We also know that the focus of change will be racial. If we feel differently, we have different ideas. Race is feeling. Where the body and the organs come in.

[53]

Culture is the preservation of these feelings in superrational to rational form. . . . In order for the black man in the West to absolutely know himself, it is necessary for him to see himself first as culturally separate from the white man."

Le Roi Jones sees major international ramifications in the efforts of black Americans to separate themselves from the American society and, if possible, help to destroy it. He writes: "Only a united Black Consciousness can save Black People from annihilation at the white man's hands. And no other nation on earth is safe, unless the Black Man in America is safe. Not even the Chinese can be absolutely certain of their continued sovereignty as long as the white man is alive. And there is only one people on the planet who can slay the white man. The people who know him best. His ex-slaves."

Here we have it quite clearly. For Le Roi Jones "black power," "black consciousness," and "black pride" all add up to one thing: destruction of the white man and of the American society. In his essay "State/Meant," he writes, "The Black Artist's role in America is to aid in the destruction of America as he knows it."

In May, 1967, a band of young Negroes armed with loaded rifles, pistols, and shotguns entered the State Capitol of California and barged into the assembly during a debate. Twenty-six men, aged seventeen to twenty-five, were booked on suspicion of a variety of charges, including brandishing a gun in a threatening manner and possession of two sawed-off shotguns. Fifteen weapons were confiscated. Members of the group said they represented the Black Panther Party of the Oakland area and had come to protest a bill restricting the carrying of loaded weapons within city limits. One of the group shouted that the bill was introduced for the "racist Oakland police force."

The Black Panthers make it clear that their goal is not to integrate into American society but, instead, to destroy that society totally. One of the founders of the Black Panthers and one of its long-time leaders is Huey P. Newton. Newton was born in a small Louisiana town on February 17, 1942; when he was three the family moved to Oakland, California. While in high school he was jailed for the first time for assault. Upon completing high school he attended Merrit College, where he

[54]

became instrumental in founding the Black Panther Party in October, 1966. Writing in the Black Panther newspaper, Newton declares that "The Black People of America are the only people who can free the world, loosen the yoke of colonialism and destroy the war machine. As long as the wheels of the imperialistic war machine are turning there is no country that can defeat this monster of the West. But black people can make a malfunction of this machine from within. America cannot stand to fight every Black country in the world and fight a civil war at the same time."

Newton's advice to black Americans is simple, and clearly destructive: "The people must oppose everything the oppressor supports and support everything that he opposes. . . . The racist dog oppressors have no rights which oppressed black people are bound to respect. As long as the racist dogs pollute the earth with the evil of their actions, they do not deserve any respect at all, and the rules of their game, written in the people's blood, are beneath contempt."

Huey Newton and the Black Panthers are, of course, open advocates of violence. They make no attempt to hide this fact. Newton writes: "When a mechanic wants to fix a broken-down car engine, he must have the necessary tools to do the job. When the people move for liberation, they must have the basic tool of liberation: the gun. Only with the power of the gun can the Black masses halt the terror and brutality perpetuated against them by the armed racist power structure; and in one sense only by the power of the gun can the whole world be transformed into the earthly paradise dreamed of by the people from time immemorial."

Who are the heroes of the Black Panthers? Huey Newton is also quite frank in responding to this question: "One successful practitioner of the art and science of national liberation and self-defense, Brother Mao Tse-tung, put it this way: 'We are advocates of the abolition of war, we do not want war; but war can only be abolished through war, and in order to get rid of the gun it is necessary to take up the gun'. . . . We were forced to build America and, if forced to, we will tear it down. The immediate result of this destruction will be suffering and blood-

[55]

shed. But the end result will be the perpetual peace for all mankind."

The Panther approach to man and society is really quite simple. Man is good, the Panthers argue, but the institutions of the American society are corrupt. Therefore, once man can destroy these corrupt institutions he will create a benevolent and humane society with which to replace it. Violence, accordingly, becomes a cleansing process to the Panthers and those who advocate this philosophy. Integration as a goal is, of course, corrupt—for only those who are themselves degraded would want to participate in this degraded American society. Given these assumptions, however naive, the rest of the Panther philosophy follows with simple logic.

Another prominent Black Panther spokesman is Eldridge Cleaver. Cleaver, also a convicted rapist, wrote an article entitled "Revolution in the White Mother Country and National Liberation in the Black Colony" in the July-August, 1968, issue of the *North American Review*. In this article he calls for a coalition between militant black groups such as the Panthers and Communist and other radical white organizations: "We start with the basic definition: that black people in America are a colonized people in every sense of the term and that white America is an organized imperialist force holding black people in colonial bondage. From this definition our task becomes clearer: what we need is a revolution in the white mother country and national liberation for the black colony. To achieve these ends we believe that political and military machinery that does not exist now and has never existed must be created."

What would be the nature of this new political and military machinery? Cleaver continues: "We believe that cooperation between revolutionary forces in the mother country and their counterpart in the black colony is absolutely and unequivocally desirable and necessary. We believe that it is suicidal and nonsensical for such political allies to remain aloof and isolated from each other any longer."

Making it clear that the kind of "revolution" being urged by the Panthers and other black militants is one that accepts the basic terminology of communism, H. Rap Brown, another Panther leader, wrote the following in his volume, *Die Nigger Die,* published in 1969: "You have to destroy the system. You can destroy the power structure and leave the system intact. But if you get the system, you get the power structure. That's the job which confronts us . . . we cannot end racism, capitalism, colonialism and imperialism until the reins of state power are in the hands of those people who understand that the wealth, the total wealth of any country and the world, belongs equally to all people. Societies and countries based on the profit motive will never insure a new humanism or eliminate poverty and racism . . . the power necessary to end racism, colonialism, capitalism and imperialism will only come through long, protracted, bloody, brutal and violent wars with our oppressors."

Whether Rap Brown realizes that communism has not produced a "classless" society but has developed, instead, the "New Class" of bureaucrats about whom Milovan Djilas, the Yugoslav Marxist, has written so eloquently, we cannot be sure. Whether Rap Brown realizes that what we call poverty in the United States would seem affluent by the standards of China or Eastern Europe, societies he urges us to emulate, it is not possible to know. But whether his "communism" is as a result of ignorance or real dedication, the fact remains that the philosophy which he and the Panthers enunciate is clearly one which ties them to the radical left.

Rap Brown declares that black Americans not only have the power to "liberate" their own country, but to do the same for the entire world. In this same volume, *Die Nigger Die,* he states that "We hold the key to liberation around the world. The freedom of people around the world depends upon what we do. This is true, because this country is the chief oppressor around the world. If we view this country as an octopus, then we see that her tentacles stretch around the globe. Like in Vietnam, Africa, Latin America—if these countries cut off a tentacle, it can be replaced. But we got his eye; we live in the belly of the monster. So it's up to us to destroy its brain. When we do this not only will Africa be free but all people oppressed by 'the man.' It is because of America's racism and greed that Black people and people of color around the world are oppressed. . . . The question of violence has been cleared up. This country was born of violence. Violence is as American as cherry pie. . . . Violence is a necessary part of revolutionary struggle. Nonviolence as it is advocated by Negroes is merely a preparation for genocide. . . . Power indeed must come from the barrel of a gun."

Beginning in 1965 many factors combined to make the limited coalition of some members of the civil rights movement and the New Left a serious concern, for both the traditional civil rights movement and the nation at large.

On the one hand, Negroes are told to separate themselves from other Americans, to have their own foreign policy, their own reaction to the Selective Service System, their own spokesmen concerning the war in Vietnam. On the other hand, of course, they are told to work for integration, for the war on poverty, for an end to discrimination and for increased economic opportunities. The black power element has been challenging the very concept of integration into the democratic American society by calling for a social, political, and economic revolution.

While leaders of traditional civil rights organizations have been saying that America is essentially a decent society in which for too long they have been deprived of their equal rights, the black power advocates of the New Left are saying that America is corrupt to its very core, and that a revolution is required. It is for this reason that the objection to the war in Vietnam has been a compelling one in the eyes of the Negro New Left. The war in Vietnam appears to be a defense of such things, while the Communist revolutionaries to them represent a contrary and perhaps more hopeful system. The contradictions, the inhumanity, the total denial of human freedom which characterize communism are totally overlooked, while America is frequently compared with Nazi Germany.

The militancy of the extremist black power organizations and the white New Left coalition is, therefore, not a militancy directed to those goals which for so long guided such organizations as the NAACP, the Urban League, and Dr. King's Southern Christian Leadership Conference. The latter groups called for equality under the law, integration, and a society which treated citizens as individuals, not as members of a particular race. The new organizations preach revolution, racial consciousness, and hostility to all establishments, both good and

[58]

bad. They are, in a sense, against things as they are, regardless of whether the things be beneficial or detrimental.

It is for this reason, too, that violence becomes a tactic which in the eyes of the Negro New Left is wholly permissible. It is, after all, the established order of doing things to call for rational discourse and debate, and a democratic and peaceful settlement of disputes. If the New Left–black power coalition disputes the establishment in all areas, it also disputes the establishment with regard to the use of violence.

Despite the efforts of the militants, Negro participation in antiwar protests has been slight. Many see a parallel with past efforts of the Communist Party to enlist Negro support for a separate Negro Republic in the South by identifying themselves with civil rights activities. But for the limited response to the black power appeal, it would appear that the current New Left attempt to use the Negro as a catalyst for revolution will fail as dismally as have past efforts to exploit the American Negro for revolutionary purposes. Meanwhile, the split that has been growing in the civil rights movement since the association of some of its members with the New Left, antiwar movement, has seen conflicting organizations and viewpoints arise.

Ex-convict Eldridge Cleaver, for some time the Black Panthers' "Minister of Information" and presidential nominee of the Peace and Freedom Party, explained his revolutionary goals to a group of San Francisco lawyers: "America is up against the wall. This whole apparatus, this capitalistic system and its institutions and police . . . all need to be assigned to the garbage can of history and I don't give a ——— who doesn't like it. If we can't have it, nobody's gonna have it. We'd rather provoke a situation . . . that will disrupt cities and the economy so that the enemies of America could come in and pick the gold teeth of these Babylonian pigs. . . . The right to revolution can't be taken from the people. . . . We can go nowhere unless we have the right to defend ourselves against the pig cops. . . ."

Cleaver attacked white society, stating that "You're all chasing dollars, but there are other people who are chasing dollars to buy guns, to kill judges and police and corporation lawyers. . . . We need lawyers today who have a lawbook in one hand and a gun in the other . . . so that if he goes to court and that ——

[59]

— doesn't come out right, he can pull out his gun and start shooting."

The trial of Huey Newton, the Black Panther leader, in Oakland, California, for the murder of a white policeman led to mass demonstrations both inside and outside the courtroom. The far-left newspaper *The National Guardian* placed the trial in this perspective: "With the world focusing on the voluntary manslaughter verdict of the Huey Newton trial, there is a tendency to forget the real importance of the case. This has been the first major political trial of the New Left run in a totally political fashion. Inside and outside the courtroom, major attempts to educate and radicalize the community were combined with an all-out effort to question and begin to restructure the judicial system." In many instances, the trial of Huey Newton in Oakland is an important forerunner to the case of Angela Davis.

Newton, who served as minister for defense of the Black Panther Party and candidate for U.S. Congress on the Peace and Freedom Party ticket, is a close associate of Eldridge Cleaver and of Stokely Carmichael, who resigned from SNCC and transferred his organizational support to the Black Panthers. Cleaver expressed the Black Panther philosophy this way: "If I could get two machine guns . . . I wouldn't care if you applauded me or threw glasses at me. . . . I hope you'll take your guns and shoot judges and police. . . . Kill some white people or make them act in a prescribed manner."

Explaining what he meant by the term "black power" when it first came into common usage, Stokely Carmichael wrote an article entitled "Toward Black Liberation" in *The Massachusetts Review* in 1966. In this article he states, "Traditionally, for each new ethnic group, the route to social and political integration into America's pluralistic society has been through the organization of their own institutions with which to represent the communal needs within the larger society. This is simply stating what the advocates of black power are saying. The strident outcry, particularly from the liberal community, that has been evoked by this proposal can only be understood by examining the historic relationship between Negro and White power in this country."

[60]

But, for Carmichael, "black power" is far more than a means by which equality is to be reached in an open and pluralistic society. He continues: "According to the advocates of integration, social justice will be accomplished by 'integrating the Negro into the mainstream institutions of the society from which he has been traditionally excluded.' It is very significant that each time I have heard this formulation it has been in terms of 'the Negro,' the individual Negro, rather than in terms of the community. . . . Thus the goal of the movement for integration was simply to loosen up the restrictions barring the entry of Negroes into the white community. Goals around which the struggle took place, such as public accommodation, open housing, job opportunity on the executive level . . . are quite simply middle-class goals, articulated by a tiny group of Negroes who had middle-class aspirations. . . . Now, black people must look beyond these goals, to the issue of collective power."

Thus, for Carmichael, the goal of a free and open society in which all men are judged as individuals and in which the law itself is colorblind, had become only a "middle-class" aspiration. The new goal was obvious: Revolution!

Prior to leaving SNCC, Carmichael traveled around the world, meeting with Communist leaders in various countries. Castro's newspaper *Granma* quoted Carmichael as saying, "Brothers, we see our fight connected with the patriotic struggle of the peoples of Africa, Asia, and Latin America against foreign oppression, especially U.S. oppression." *Granma* published an interview with Carmichael in which he said that "Fidel Castro is a source of inspiration" and that Cuban communism had a special importance "because it is the nearest system." Carmichael stated: "We are moving toward urban guerrilla warfare within the United States." He linked the purposes of his guerrilla warfare to Communist objectives: "When the United States has 50 Vietnams inside and 50 outside, this will mean the death of imperialism."

Carmichael is, of course, not the only Negro spokesman who has maintained close ties with Castro. A long-distance call between H. Rap Brown, former SNCC leader, and a Castro functionary in Havana was broadcast throughout Latin America on

August 13, 1967. Brown told Havana: "Our rebellion is against the power and structure of white America." He bragged that black power is now proficient in the terrorist urban tactics of the Vietcong, and said of the summer of 1967: "Each city in America which has a large Negro population can predict with confidence that it will have a rebellion. . . . We live in the stomach of a monster and we can destroy him from within."

Separatism and the advocacy of violence seem to be major characteristics of the new, militant breed of "black power" organizations. In Washington, D.C., the Black United Front was formed, under the leadership of Stokely Carmichael, in January, 1968. This was established as a coalition of both militant and moderate organizations, including the Washington Urban League. Whites were not admitted as members, and white members of the press were not welcomed. Among those in leadership positions in this organization were the Rev. Walter Fauntroy, then Vice Chairman of the District of Columbia City Council and now the D.C. nonvoting delegate to the U.S. House of Representatives, and the Rev. Channing Phillips, Democratic National Committeeman from Washington, D.C.

In July, 1968, this organization issued a statement describing the slaying of a white District of Columbia policeman as a "justifiable homicide." The statement said, in part: "The methods of self-defense used by the family charged with the alleged slaying of the honky cop is justifiable homicide in the same sense that police are allowed to kill black people and call it justifiable homicide."

Several hours later, Mayor Walter Washington, himself a Negro, asserted that "The Black United Front resolution with respect to the slaying of Officer Stephen A. Williams . . . is inflammatory, irresponsible, and unfortunate. . . . If this community is to thrive and prosper, it must do so within the framework of law. As citizens we must continue to work together—black and white, policeman and civilian, so that law and order, with justice, will be the code for all."

The D.C. Federation of Civic Associations voted to oppose the Black United Front resolution. Through its executive committee, the Federation also endorsed Mayor Walter Washington's condemnation of the Front statement and voted to send a condolence card and $50 to the family of Private Stephen A. Williams, the slain officer, and an additional $50 and a card to Private Frederick L. Matteson, who recovered from the July 2 shooting. The D.C. Federation of Civic Associations is a predominantly Negro organization.

There is virtually conclusive evidence that the violence that has occurred in urban areas has been the direct result of action by extremist organizations. The violence in Cleveland in July, 1968, for example, was described this way by that city's black mayor, Carl B. Stokes: "The [violence] was not at all related to any kind of honest reaction to an environment, not at all. This was a planned, deliberate, and previously contrived plot to damage."

Stokes noted: "You must not confuse some of the many disturbances around our country that have reflected the reaction of people to an unresponsive city administration or to a continually frustrating environment. The acts of the people the other night were just deliberately contrived lawlessness and determination to commit violence among this small group."

Experts state that the key figure in the conspiracy was Fred "Ahmed" Evans, a local black power leader who has been linked to the pro-Peking Revolutionary Action Movement. In May, 1967, Detective Sergeant John Ungvary, head of the Cleveland Police Department's Subversive Squad, said that terrorists under Evans' direction were plotting a "black revolution" to coincide with "a war between Red China and the United States." Evans, who was arrested during the riots, was charged with shooting to kill. "If my carbine hadn't jammed I would have killed you three," police quoted him as saying. "I had you in my sights when my rifle jammed." Evans told police that he and seventeen others had organized the sniper attacks that resulted in the deaths of three policemen. Told that three of his snipers had been slain, Evans said, "They died for a worthy cause." Phil Hutchings, militant head of SNCC, told newsmen that the Cleveland outbreaks were "the first stage of revolutionary armed violence."

The same story can be told about the background of the rioting which took place in Newark, New Jersey. In that city, the crystallizing force arrived during the summer of 1964. Students

[63]

for a Democratic Society sent a group of organizers there, headed by Tom Hayden. By 1967, just three weeks before the Newark riot, SDS national secretary Gregory Calvert boasted to a *New York Times* reporter: "We are working to build a guerrilla force in an urban environment. We are actively organizing sedition."

By the summer of 1965, according to a document presented to Congressional hearings on the Newark riot, Hayden was able to claim "We had taken control [electoral] of the major offices in the community action part of the war on poverty here."

In two short years, assaults on policemen in Newark's streets doubled—from 92 in 1964 to 187 in 1966. The antipolice campaign also immobilized the police department in a crucial and ultimately deadly way. Police Commissioner Dominick A. Spina later told the New Jersey Governor's commission in explanation of his department's total lack of preparation for civil disorders that he had purposely refused to institute riot training. The reason? He feared the antipolice propagandists would have a field day.

A sound truck, rented with Federal antipoverty funds, toured the city daily, agitating the abrasive issues and urging Negroes to attend City Hall hearings. Commissioner Spina wired President Lyndon Johnson and his O.E.O. Director Sargent Shriver, protesting the use of Federally paid antipoverty workers "for the purpose of fomenting and agitating against" the Newark city government. "The acceleration of this kind of practice by the antipoverty agency will undoubtedly lead to riots and anarchy in our city."

Who rioted in Newark? Three out of every four of those arrested in the riot had jobs. As Governor Hughes' investigative commission later concluded, with 11.5 percent of Newark's Negroes jobless and 27 percent of those who were arrested jobless, unemployment was obviously a riot disposing factor, but jobs, though important, were not the whole answer. Otherwise, asked the commission, how explain the fact that 73 percent of those arrested had jobs? The Newark police department had prior arrest records on 867—74 percent—of its adult arrestees; 55.6 percent of the juveniles had prior offense records. Checking 1,089 fingerprint sets sent to Washington, the FBI found that

708, or 65 percent, had prior records on file, either from the Newark police or other departments that file arrest records.

It is clear that riots in our large urban areas were fomented by advocates of violence and revolution. Stokely Carmichael quoted Ernesto "Che" Guevara's statement, "Hatred is an element of the struggle, transforming man into an effective, violent, selective and cold killing maching." At the 1968 SDS convention at Michigan State University, Dave Gilbert of the Philadelphia SDS colony proclaimed: "The ability to manipulate people through violence and mass media has never been greater, and the potential for liberation for us as radicals has never been more exciting than now."

Unfortunately, much of the public discussion about the urban violence we have faced refuses to confront the real facts of the situation. An example is the report issued by the Kerner Commission. At the time of the Commission's findings, then Attorney General Nicholas Katzenbach expressed the view that responsibility for riots rested not with individuals, but with disease, despair, joblessness, rat-infested housing, and long-impacted cynicism. According to that report, riots were caused by everyone but those who had in fact perpetrated them. The blame was spread over a wide range. Government was to blame, for its programs had not effectively reached the people. Judges and police were to blame, for they were often too harsh and disrespectful. The press was to blame, for they exhibited a lack of understanding. The real cause, according to the Commission, was white racism.

The approach taken by the Commission was characterized this way by columnist Joseph Kraft. He said that such an approach is based on the notion—the Marxian notion—that economic deprivation is the root of social unrest: "It thus prescribes elaborate programs to improve economic opportunity through welfare payments, public housing, educational subsidies. The result of that approach has been what might be called 'reservationism'—the herding of Negroes into core cities— guarded by the police, and on a monthly hand-out of whiskey and blankets in the form of Federal programs." Kraft noted that the Commission had taken into account the noneconomic causes of the riots and that the Commission itself showed that rioters did not emerge from a background of hopeless poverty. Still, its recommendations are all based on this fallacious economic theory, a theory which has been shown to be completely invalid.

Professor Irving Rueben, head of the University of Michigan Center for Urban Studies, made a survey of those who had been arrested for rioting in Detroit. He stated that solutions based primarily on improving schools, housing, and employment for urban Negroes are not responsive to the deeper needs behind the violence. They are comfortable solutions, things our society knows how to do best. But they are not what the riots are all about. In the main riot areas of Detroit, according to the University of Michigan survey, the median annual income of Negro households is $6,200. This is only slightly lower than the figure for all Negro households in Detroit—$6,400. And it is not far below the median white household income: $6,800.

Educational attainment in Negro household heads (45 percent were high-school graduates or better) was higher in the riot area than throughout the city. Seventy percent of the Negro households in the riot area had automobiles available, and the Negroes living in the riot area were substantially better off in every respect than those who lived inside the deep core of the city. They were also somewhat better off than the whites who lived in the riot neighborhoods. Of those arrested, Detroit Police Department records show that only 10 percent of the Negroes were juveniles; 18 percent were between seventeen and nineteen years old, 24 percent between twenty and twenty-four years old, 17 percent between twenty-five and twenty-nine, and 31 percent over thirty. The Urban Law Center survey of 1,200 nonjuvenile male arrestees shows that 83 percent were employed—40 percent of them by the three major automobile companies, and an equal percentage by other large employers. No income data was gathered, but annual wages of $6,000 and more can be assumed. The conclusion of Professor Rueben is that if we deal only with housing, education, and jobs, we are sowing the seeds of even greater trouble.

The records of crime statistics show that there was much less crime in America during the Depression in 1933. Total reported crimes against the person stood about 150 per 100,000 population. This figure dropped steadily throughout the continuing years of the Depression and the enforced scarcity of World War II. As the war came to an end and prosperity returned, the line turned sharply upward and has continued to climb ever since. By 1965 the figures stood at more than 180. Judge David Pine states that during the dark days of the Depression in the early 1930s, there existed all over the land abject poverty, distress and misery. But he recalls no vast upsurge in crime. From 1931 to 1935, while the nation's population grew by better than 3 million persons, the number of robberies and auto thefts decreased by 35.2 percent; burglaries decreased 8.9 percent; and aggravated assault and larceny remained relatively constant. In 1938, Attorney General Homer Cummings announced that the preceding year had seen nearly 1,500,000 crimes committed —a number he felt, quite properly, to be enormous. The population of the United States was then estimated at 130,320,000. In 1964, no less than 2,729,659 major crimes were committed—an increase of 1.2 million. The population was then approximately 191,372,000. Crime in the United States between Depression year 1938 and boom year 1964 had increased by 80 percent. Population had increased by only 47 percent.

Professor Ernest van den Haag concludes that the countries with the lowest living standards usually have very low homicide and suicide rates. Great Britain and Sweden have more advanced welfare states than our own. The result: crime is increasing at an even more rapid pace than ours. In Sweden, known offenses against the penal code have risen from 172,000 in 1950 to 373,000 in 1965. The crime rate per 100,000 population has gone up 97 percent in fifteen years. It seems clear that the costly welfare and educational reforms in Sweden have not forestalled the significant increase in such social ills as crime, alcoholism, and drug addiction. Swedish crime has doubled since 1950, with a particular upsurge notable among young people. Officials attribute the rise in crime and antisocial behavior among young people to a deterioration of family life. It appears, they say, that the welfare state has not strengthened either family ties or moral standards. Job programs, educational improvements, and housing proposals all have merit. It remains clear, however, that the Riot Commission did not in

[67]

any sense know that these were connected with the rise in crime and in urban violence. All of the evidence points to the fact that such violence is not motivated by economics. Violence stems, at least in part, from people who have lacked a sense of values and for whom life has lost all meaning and purpose.

What the Riot Commission did not stress, and what is perhaps the key to the situation we face, is that professional agitators have made it their task to hook up every possible pool of discontent to the revolutionary strategy of disruption. Lenin himself was the author of this grand strategy of disruption. He wrote: "We must use every trace of discontent. We must collect every grain of protest." If spontaneous social conditions raise the level of frustration and free-floating aggression, the likelihood of violence increases and the agitator's job becomes easier. "A newspaper is a collective organizer," proclaimed Lenin, as well as the only way professional revolutionaries had to create "an organization ready at any time to support every protest and every outbreak and use it to build up and consolidate the fighting forces suitable for the decisive struggle."

Lenin, of course, wrote long before the impact of the mass media. It is clear that men such as Rap Brown, Stokely Carmichael, and Eldridge Cleaver would not have reached the positions of importance and influence they have, had it not been for television. All too often the black community has been given the responsibility for elevating men such as these to leadership positions. The fact is that Negroes have never voted for any of them, and none of them have ever risen to positions of responsibility in any national Negro organizations. More to the point is the fact that such black militants serve the purposes of the white liberal intellectual establishment, and it is this establishment that has proclaimed them to be the "leaders" their own community never saw fit to name them.

Recent riots in our urban areas have been blamed on poverty and discrimination, on incitement by extremists and on planned subversion by outsiders. Some of these are, of course, partially to blame. Yet, if outside influences have, in fact, shared the blame for riots in Newark, Detroit, Los Angeles, Harlem, Cincinnati and other cities, some evidence suggests that television has indirectly fulfilled such a role. Toledo's

[68]

Mayor John W. Potter cited television coverage of other riots as a major cause of his city's troubles: "The Detroit situation had much to do with starting it. It was young people who felt they wanted to get into the act. They saw on television how Detroit police just monitored without stopping looting." In Newark, Donald Malafronte, administrative aide to the city's mayor, said that a key reason for the riots was the press and television coverage which had given too much attention to the militant demands of black nationalist groups, demands which, he said, the city government "did not give weight to."

Television's impact on rioting was not new in the "long, hot summer" of 1967. Mayor Richard Daley of Chicago charged earlier that "In disturbances resulting from protest marches, the television cameras didn't seek the violence, the violence sought the camera."

An NBC television newsman has told how, in Cambridge, Maryland, at the time of its original racial unrest, the civil rights demonstrators conferred with the assembled broadcast cameramen and moved their demonstrations back from 8 P.M. to 6 P.M., so the cameramen would have time to get their film flown to New York for the 11 P.M. news roundups. Yet, the public was given the impression that they were seeing largely "spontaneous crowds of protestors."

Does television coverage of violence, in fact, cause some people to react in a violent way? Commenting upon the contagiousness of televised appeals to violence, Dr. Alfred A. Messer, an Atlanta psychiatrist who specializes in family treatment, stated: "Who can forget the scene on television . . . in which a Negro speaker in Detroit was haranguing a group of young Negro adolescents that they must get an education, do better in life than their parents, live decently, etc. In the midst of this harangue, the speaker turned directly to the television cameras and exploded, 'And if they don't let you, we'll burn America down!' . . . Seeing this scene on television, the individual might have one of two reactions. A person in sympathy with the rioters could be stirred to similar violence. On the other hand, a person fearful that the rioters would injure him might be influenced to obtain guns or other means of protecting himself."

New York's Mayor John Lindsay referred to the rioting as a

"fever" and said that "fever can spread . . . there are aspects of contagion here." Television may be one of the prime carriers of the disease.

This has been reminiscent of the famed Orson Welles broadcast on Halloween weekend, 1938. At that time a small company of radio actors broadcast in semi-news style a dramatized version of H. G. Wells' fictional account of a Martian invasion of earth. Though clear announcements that the production was purely fictional punctuated the program, many listeners by some mental process simply tuned qualification out. Thousands literally believed that a mysterious interplanetary cylinder had landed in New Jersey, disgorging giant machines that soon were wading across the Hudson River and blasting Manhattan with invincible death rays. Widespread panic ensued. People rushed from their homes in tears and prayed in the streets. Several died of heart attacks. Hardier souls grabbed shotguns and prepared to fight for their lives, or fled to the woods and hills.

If radio can convince people the Martians are coming and send them into the streets with shotguns, it is hardly surprising that television broadcasts of inflammatory speeches of Stokely Carmichael and Rap Brown can convince people that they are being exploited by a "brutal colonial welfare system" and "mad-dog president" and "white power structure" and send them into the streets with firebombs to "shoot these honkie cops" and "burn America down."

The fact that such extremist leaders do desire violence should, by this time, be beyond question. On August 29, 1966, for example, SNCC held a fund-raising meeting in Harlem that featured Stokely Carmichael as the speaker. He attacked the United States as an aggressor in Vietnam and then discussed the 1966 riots in Cleveland. He said that in "Cleveland they're building stores with no windows. All brick. I don't know what they think they'll accomplish. It just means we have to move from Molotov cocktails to dynamite." He added, "They say we're stupid and don't do anybody any good and we deserve to be called that, because if we had any sense we'd have bombed those ghettoes long ago."

It is spokesmen such as these who have occupied much of our

prime viewing time in recent days. Whitney Young criticized the stress placed on extremists by television and the press and said, "The press lacks sophistication. They ought to be covering where Negroes move in and whites don't move out. At CORE's convention in Baltimore there was a tiny number of delegates but almost twice as many reporters. At the Urban League there were 1,500 delegates and less than 30 reporters."

There is, of course, nothing new about psychological epidemics. They have occurred throughout history. But the combination of electronic communication and mass urbanization has loosed some new dynamics totally unprecedented in scale in the history of civilization. The news of the Declaration of Independence required a month to travel from Philadelphia to Georgia. In 1960, however, 70 million people watched the Kennedy-Nixon debates. In addition, television's reach is far greater than that of the printed media, for it influences those who either cannot or do not read.

The world of television news differs greatly from the world of the printed word. Henry Fairlie, Washington correspondent for the *London Express,* notes that "not only is the core of television the public and the spectacular, but there is an important sense in which television has a vested interest in disaster. From the point of view of a good story, both newspapers and television prefer covering a major strike to covering negotiations which prevent a strike. But what can television do with negotiations? . . . Violence—movement—is the stuff of television, something it cannot help emphasizing." Yet, "as television cameramen and reporters move into the street literally looking for trouble they add an external provocation. The crowds begin to play up to them. Television, merely by its presence, helps to create incidents."

Ed Haddad, President of the Radio and Television News Association of Southern California, wrote in the *Columbia Journalism Review* detailing how television newsmen in Los Angeles had actually incited crowds on Sunset Strip by calling out, "C'mon, let's have some action—you're on TV now—C'mon roll an auto. . . ."

Writing in the *Washington Star,* Crosby Noyes pointed out, "All of these extremist leaders are utterly dependent on the publicity they receive from the press and television. The more outrageous their public behavior . . . the surer they are of making headlines, followed up . . . by indignant editorials and invitations to appear on television panel shows."

Newark, New Jersey, mayoralty aide Donald Malfronte said that in the Newark riots, television cameras "picked on every black face who proclaimed himself a leader. Casuals who had never raised a voice in community affairs all of a sudden were spokesmen on television."

Events were similar in Plainfield, New Jersey. Here, Mayor George F. Hetfield said, "they gave the impression that the whole town was going up in flames. Soon we had busloads of people coming in from Philadelphia and Newark who were professional manipulators."

In many respects we have entered a new technological age in which, as Marshall McLuhan has instructed us, electronic media are replacing the printed word. James Burnham goes so far as to see television serving as a free tool for revolutionary aims. Writing in 1967, he noted: "This summer's riot sequence shows spectacularly how television has become the revolution's collective organizer—provided for free by the 'imperialist enemy.' There is no longer any need for an elaborate, disciplined, far-flung apparatus. Instead, intelligence, communication, guidance, example and directive are given through the TV net. Following the pioneering breakthrough made by . . . Martin Luther King in the Selma March, the young Black Power revolutionists are rapidly learning how to exploit TV's revolutionary potential as organizer and agitator."

There is something very wrong with news coverage which makes the average American aware of a Rap Brown and not of a Whitney Young. It creates two mistaken impressions. One is that men such as Brown are truly Negro leaders and that responsible spokesmen do not exist. The other is the one fostered among Negroes that the white community views such extremists as being true representatives. Hearst and Pulitzer may have created the Spanish-American War out of their headline-hunting competition. We cannot afford such a sacrifice to similar headline-hunting crusades by modern television. The stakes are much too high.

[72]

In an important book published in 1971, *The News Twisters,* Edith Efron of *TV Guide* provides conclusive proof that the major television networks have stereotyped the black American. Miss Efron shows that the stereotype "was that of a 'thug-revolutionary,' a violent criminal on whom network men lavished sympathy and used to threaten whites." She also provides evidence that "blacks of intellectual and moral distinction and great achievement were largely kept off the air . . . and that network news was indifferent to black victims of black crime, a classic expression of racism."

Beyond this, *The News Twisters* shows that "network reporters equated the concept of law and order with 'racism,' thus reinforcing the racist view that all blacks are lawless. . . . The networks falsified the views of the black community, portraying it monolithically as racist, pro-separatism, and pro-violence."

It is clear that a certain segment of the "civil rights" movement has turned to separatism and to violence. With the help of the mass media, it has joined forces with the New Left in opposing the very structure of American society, and in calling for defeat abroad and revolution at home.

Those who truly seek civil rights, who truly seek an American society in which Negroes and whites share a common citizenship, are disturbed with this trend among younger, more militant Negro spokesmen. This concern was expressed by former Secretary of Health, Education, and Welfare John Gardner: "Negro extremists who advocate violence assert that nonviolence did not work. It is untrue. The greatest gains for the American Negro came in response to the nonviolent campaigns of Martin Luther King, Jr., and (before it turned violent) SNCC. It is the fashion now to belittle those gains, but they were great and undeniable. They were registered in historic civil rights legislation and even more emphatically in social practice. . . . The violent tactics of the past two years have brought nothing but deepened hostility between the two races and a slowing down of progress in the necessary drive toward social justice. Nor do those who condone violence ever speak of the legacy of bitterness and division that will be left by increasingly harsh outbursts of destructive interaction. What good will

[73]

it do to dramatize the problem if, in the process, hatreds burn themselves so deep that the wounds permanently cripple our society. . . . To date the moderates—both Negro and white—have been all too silent."

The joining of forces between the New Left and certain elements of the civil rights movement is a dangerous symbol of the extremism toward which we are moving. Part of the reason for its success, as both Secretary Gardner and psychologist Kenneth Clark have said, is that the moderates have not stemmed the tide. In many cases, and with the assistance of the mass media, they have encouraged it, fearing to lose their own leadership role. If this continues, and it has been continuing, society will face an ever more serious problem. Violence begets violence, and the gains of the past will be in danger. This would, of course, be harmful to all Americans.

The kind of desperate rebellion we are witnessing on the part of black militants is by no means a new phenomenon in the world. The French Revolution, and the Reign of Terror that followed it, had many elements that are similar to the situation we have seen emerging within the black extremist movement.

In his classic volume, *The Rebel,* Albert Camus provides this analysis: "Every rebellion implies some kind of unity. The rebellion of 1789 demands the unity of the whole country. Saint-Just dreams of an ideal city . . . and if factions arise to interrupt this dream, passion will exaggerate its logic. . . . Saint-Just said that 'A patriot is he who supports the Republic in general; whoever opposes it in detail is a traitor.' When neither reason nor the free expression of individual opinion succeeds in systematically establishing unity, it must be decided to suppress all alien elements. . . . Marat wrote day and night in the most monotonous vocabulary imaginable, of the necessity of killing in order to create. He wrote again, by candlelight deep down in his cellar, during the September nights when his henchmen were installing spectators' benches in prison courtyards—men on the right, women on the left, to display to them, as a gracious example of philanthropy, the spectacle of the aristocrats having their heads cut off."

Camus continues: ". . . rebellion, when it gets out of hand, swings from the annihilation of others to the destruction of the

[74]

self. . . . Saint-Just agreed to go to his death for love of principle and despite all the realities of the situation, since the opinion of the Assembly could only really be swayed by the eloquence and fanaticism of a faction. . . . Rousseau, who was not wanting in common sense, understood very well that the society envisioned by the Social Contract was suitable only for gods. His successors took him at his word and tried to establish the divinity of man. . . . From the moment that eternal principles are put in doubt simultaneously with formal virtue, and when every value is discredited, reason will start to act without reference to anything but its own successes. It would like to rule, denying everything that has been and affirming all that is to come. . . . The Jacobin Revolution, which tried to institute the religion of virtue in order to establish unity upon it, will be followed by the cynical revolutions, which can be either of the right or of the left and which will try to achieve the unity of the world so as to found, at last, the religion of man. . . ."

Many of these thoughts concerning the French Revolution and the Reign of Terror are applicable to the calls for a violent revolution which supposedly would produce an earthly utopia, calls which we hear so often from advocates of a "cleansing" kind of violence today. Unfortunately, too few of us today have sufficient knowledge of history to make the comparisons and to expose ideas which are presented to us as "new" and "revolutionary" as really being the shopworn failures of the past.

It is from this background that we face the real turn toward violence, revolution, and black racism which we have seen emerging in the 1970s. This extremism turns not only against the white society and the "white establishment," but also against all Negroes who disagree with the goal of destruction and revolution, who continue to believe that racism is an evil whether practiced by black men or white men, and who believe that the real progress of the past decade is an indication that Americans can live together in peace and harmony in a nation whose concept of nationality is not tied to a common race, religion, or ethnic background—a concept of nationality which has been called by some historians "the only new thing in history."

The responsibility for the emergence of this black extremism is difficult to assess. The mass media bears a certain large measure of responsibility, as do those institutions of society which have paid attention only to black spokesmen who attacked American society and not to those who sought to improve it and correct its flaws and shortcomings. A share of the responsibility also belongs to those professional revolutionaries—of both races—who have sought to use the natural dissatisfaction within the Negro community for their own devious purposes.

All of these forces combine at this time to give us the complex case of Angela Davis, the bright young honor student, taught at the nation's best universities, a product not of the slums or deprivation but of the black middle class, who stood accused of murder and whose philosophy is one of destroying American society.

The preceding review provides only briefly some insight into the background leading to today's black militance. No man lives in a vacuum, and all of us are a part of the times in which we have been nurtured and grown to adulthood. In this sense, Angela Davis is more than a solitary individual, although she is surely that. She is also a symbol and is seen as such by those who revere her and those who revile her. Only by understanding both the person and the symbol can we hope to make sense of the situation at hand.

3

IN AN EXCLUSIVE INTERVIEW IN THE BLACK MUSLIM NEWSPAPER *Muhammed Speaks,* Angela Davis stated that "The Communist Party recognizes that Black people not only constitute the most oppressed collection of people in the United States but also that we are the product of the most militant tradition of resistance within the confines of the country. Therefore we as Black people are the natural leaders of a revolution which must ultimately overthrow the American ruling class, thus freeing the masses of the American people. . . ."

Miss Davis added: "We realize in our struggle that racism in this country is all pervasive. This we learned in the experiences we encountered during the civil rights era in which many well-meaning whites unconsciously perpetuated racism by taking the patronizing posture that they must help us Black people, which meant to assist us in the futile task of integrating ourselves into a dying culture."

Integration, according to Miss Davis, is a false goal. The only proper and valid one is revolution, completely destroying the American social, political and economic fabric and replacing it with one designed by the Communist Party. This was the clearly stated philosophy of a young woman who now occupied the center of the stage of American radicalism, who had even found herself upon the FBI's "Ten Most Wanted" list. It was a long distance from her comfortable childhood, education in good schools, and position as a college professor of philosophy. The journey taken by Angela Davis in her short life had brought her to an unexpected juncture—arrest and jail on the charge of murder. What the future might hold, no one could tell. The past, however, was much like an open book, and the progression from bright and promising student to dedicated and perhaps violent revolutionary was surprisingly swift.

The thumbnail biography of Angela Davis presented by *Ebony* magazine read like this:

Name: Angela Yvonne Davis.

Date of Birth: January 26, 1944.

Hometown: Birmingham, Alabama.

Present address: Jail section, Marin County Civic Center, San Rafael, California; awaiting trial on kidnap, murder and conspiracy charges; accused of providing guns used during August 7, 1970, attempt of Jonathan Jackson, 17, to free several black prisoners during a trial in Marin County Court House.

Childhood Interests: Sunday school, church youth discussion groups; played piano, clarinet and saxophone; Girl Scouts of America (won many badges and certificates, participated in Girl Scouts 1959 national roundup in Colorado); marched, picketed etc. to protest racial segregation in Birmingham.

Education: Attended elementary school and Parker High School in Birmingham; graduate (with honors), Elisabeth Irwin High School, New York City; graduate (French literature major, magna cum laude, Phi Beta Kappa), Brandeis University, Waltham, Massachusetts; student of French literature and philosophy, the Sorbonne, Paris, France; graduate student of philosophy, the Johann Wolfgang von Goethe University, Frankfurt, Germany; graduate student (for master's degree in philosophy), the University of California at San Diego; doctoral student (for Ph.D. in philosophy), the University of California at San Diego. Currently completing dissertation for Ph.D. degree.

Profession: Previously employed as acting assistant professor of philosophy, the University of California at Los Angeles.

Politics: Communist.

Political Affiliation: Member, Che Lumumba Club, an all-black collective of the Communist Party of Southern California.

Relatives: Father, B. Frank Davis, former schoolteacher, presently a service station operator in Birmingham; mother, Mrs. Sallye.E. Davis, public schoolteacher in Birmingham; sister, Mrs. Fania Davis Jordan, graduate of Swarthmore College, graduate student at University of California at San Diego, national co-coordinator of National United Committee to Free Angela Davis, Berkeley, California; brother, Benjamin Davis, graduate of Defiance (Ohio) College, professional football player with Cleveland Browns, Cleveland, Ohio; brother, Reginald Davis, a student at Defiance College.

This, then, is Angela Davis. But is anyone's life, even that of one so young, so easily described and disposed of? Is not a man or woman's life far more than the vital statistics, the names and dates and places, the degrees and jobs and awards? It has been said that a good novel could be written about the life of almost any man, and if this statement bears any degree of truth, which it seems to, then the life of Angela Davis would provide a field much more fertile than the average. Here, after all, was a young lady who psychologically accepted the mantle of the oppressed and downtrodden while, in her life, taking advantage of opportunities that come only to those in a more fortunate position. But, fortunate or unfortunate, life is even more complex, for man is not only the sum total of his experiences and the effect upon him of people who have passed through his existence, but also the manner in which he has seen and observed these phenomena.

Many of these, of course, involve things one can never really know about another. It is for this reason that men can never truly be understood, and that their motives, in the long run, remain their own. Yet, to the extent that their lives touch those

[79]

of the community at large, that community has both the right and the responsibility to attempt to understand.

Angela Davis is the daughter of a schoolteacher and a reasonably prosperous service-station owner. Her mother has an M.A. degree from New York University, and while still very young Angela had opportunities afforded few other black children in Birmingham, Alabama.

At the age of two she began piano lessons, and her parents rewarded her with a Wurlitzer console piano on her sixth birthday. When she was three, her mother took her to a poetry reading by Langston Hughes and led her up to see the poet after it was over. Angela demonstrated her cultural precocity by addressing the poet: "I like your poems, Mr. Hughes," she said. "I know one too—'Mary had a little lamb. . . .' " This incident, however, was unusual and most of her teachers, both then and later, sensed that she was a shy, stand-offish girl. "At school," her mother recalls, "she'd never volunteer. But if she was called on, she'd know the answer. I'd tell her, 'Angela, you've got to speak up. If you know something, you've got to express yourself.' "

Growing up in Birmingham in the mid-1950s was difficult for a black child. The city was tightly segregated, and racial passions ran rampant, particularly among workers at the city's many steel mills. Birmingham had long been known as the "Pittsburgh of the South," and like any industrial city it had large numbers of factory workers, most of them recent arrivals from rural areas in which segregation and racial division had been even more pronounced than they had been in Birmingham. In a tense atmosphere such as this, it was not possible to shield even a fortunate black child from the often grim realities of what life was like for a Negro in that environment.

The Davis family lived, together with many other middle-class Negroes, on what came to be called "Dynamite Hill" after white nightriders began bomb attacks on the homes of the civil rights leaders living there. Angela knew some of the four black girls killed in the blast that devastated a church and Sunday school in September, 1963. Later on, Angela was to state, "My political involvement stems from my existence in the South."

When Angela was fifteen, a representative of New York's

Elisabeth Irwin High School, a progressive and innovative school, came to Birmingham looking for talented black children to recruit. Her own high school recommended her, and she readily accepted. Things were not easy for her at Elisabeth Irwin. The financial burden, however, was significantly eased by a scholarship from the American Friends Service Committee, a Quaker organization often closely affiliated with political causes. Moving into the frequently bohemian life of New York from the more restrained, provincial existence of Birmingham provided a certain degree of cultural shock. Angela had never had many of the academic subjects which were now presented to her at Elisabeth Irwin. One of these new academic demands was that of French. In response to the challenge, Angela decided to major in French.

Moving to New York and away from her family had a major influence on Angela Davis' life. While studying at Elisabeth Irwin High School, she lived at the home of white Episcopal Minister William Howard Melish. In August, 1959, Angela arrived at New York's Pennsylvania Station and was met by Melish and his wife, Mary Anne, and began her new life.

Melish, a highly controversial figure in New York because of his pro-Communist views and vocal support for the Soviet Union, had been involved in a battle with the members of his congregation who wanted to remove him as associate rector at Holy Trinity Church in Brooklyn, where his father was rector. Melish recently said, "I have never been a member of the Communist Party. I am sympathetic with the Socialist viewpoint." Whether this is true or not is difficult to say. Clearer is the fact that his far-left views had a significant impact upon the young and impressionable Angela Davis.

Mary Jane Melish recalls that Angela greeted her with a kiss on the cheek. "She was a well brought up girl—nice, quiet, pleasant," Mrs. Melish says. Angela lived with the Melish family for two years. They had a large home in Brooklyn on the edge of the Bedford-Stuyvesant black ghetto. The Elisabeth Irwin School was located in Greenwich Village, and the combined impact of life with the Melishes and school in Greenwich Village must have greatly influenced Angela's evolving ideas. The Melishes had three sons—John, then nineteen, William, sixteen, and Howard, eleven. All have since been graduated from Harvard.

The school that gave Angela Davis a scholarship was no ordinary educational institution, just as the Rev. Melish was no ordinary Episcopal clergyman. The *New York Times* guide to New York City private schools says this of Elisabeth Irwin: "The school encourages an image of socially aware students who have a desire to be active in bringing about change. They tend to be informal in dress and manner." The description does not, of course, give any indication of what it is that students are encouraged to "change" from or what it is that they are encouraged to "change" to. Academic policies at the school are arrived at by "democratic decisions" through meetings of the faculty. As part of their studies, students are required to spend several hours each week in some kind of community service work.

Though she had been an A student in high school in Birmingham, Angela had difficulty at Elisabeth Irwin. She was a very lovely, eager-beaver student when she came up, the Rev. Melish recalls. "But she had pretty rough going at Elisabeth Irwin. The standards were much tougher than she had been accustomed to in Birmingham at Parker High. . . . The school advised her to do the junior year over. It turned out that it was very wise advice. She was too young and she had these holes in her education to fill." Melish said that she was "crazy about drama and the theater. They had a good teacher and coach at Elisabeth Irwin and she was in everything."

A girl in Angela's class, however, who took part in all of the drama activities, could not recall Angela being very active in anything. Amy Saltz, director of the off-Broadway production "Touch," and an assistant director of the original production of "Hair," had trouble recalling much about Angela. She told Jack Fox of United Press International that Angela "was a total nebbish—she never said anything, she never did anything."

Miss Saltz contrasted Angela with another of their classmates, Kathy Boudin. Miss Boudin was one of the two known survivors, along with Kathy Wilkerson, of the explosion of March 6, 1970, that wrecked a Greenwich Village townhouse where young radicals were making bombs. "She [Miss Boudin] was very active politically, doing everything there was to do—

going to Cuba. She was the idol of the school. She was very active, very bright, involved in things."

One of the teachers at Elisabeth Irwin, in an interview, agreed that Angela Davis was hardly an outstanding student. "I remember something about nearly every student I have had —an essay, a report, something—but I don't remember a thing about Angela," the teacher says.

The Rev. Melish agrees that Angela, at the time, had little awareness of or interest in the civil rights movement. Her parents, he said, "had tried to shield their children from the difficulties of Birmingham. Angela was not active at this time. Angela's political interests came after she moved here."

Two years before Angela came to New York, the Rev. Melish had left the church staff and in 1959 was eastern representative of the Southern Conference Educational Fund. At least twice a year he went through the South to talk to people in the civil rights movement and to meet emerging black leaders. He invited a number of them to come up and join him in speaking tours of Northern cities, when they would stay with the Melishes in their home.

"They were all coming through our house while Angela was there," he says. "The whole atmosphere was one of activism. There probably were very few homes in the country where she would have been exposed to the movement as she was here."

During her senior year at Elisabeth Irwin, Angela applied to several colleges, all of them in the North. She was accepted at three: Mount Holyoke in South Hadley, Massachusetts, Brandeis University in Waltham, Massachusetts, and Western Reserve in Cleveland, where she had applied because of the medical school and with the thought that she might want to be a pediatrician.

"But of the three," Melish recalls, "only Brandeis offered a scholarship, a very generous one, four years at $1,500 a year." Angela chose Brandeis, and for a variety of reasons this choice was to loom large in her future life.

During the pre-Civil War days the Underground Railroad was a network through which slaves were transported from slave states to free states, manned by men and women dedicated to ending human slavery. There are certain surface similarities between the antislavery Underground Railroad of those days and the left-wing political network which seems to have chosen a bright young black girl from Alabama and provided her with the best education America's "progressive" elements could provide. A scholarship from the far-left American Friends Service Committee enabled Angela Davis to go to the far-left Elisabeth Irwin High School. Living at the home of far-left clergyman William Howard Melish enabled her to become familiar with the radical movement with which she was later to be so closely identified. The choice of Brandeis University was also important in the transformation of Angela Davis from a child of the black middle class to a leader of the radical left. Whether her attendance at Brandeis was stimulated by the Rev. Melish or was due only to the accidental incentive of a scholarship award cannot be known. Subsequent events at Brandeis, however, show beyond any doubt that Angela Davis' radicalization underwent an important alteration and advance there.

French had been Angela's most difficult subject at Elisabeth Irwin, and with a drive to overcome any obstacle which seemed to stand in her way, she chose French literature as her major subject at Brandeis and moved into Brandeis' "French House," where only that language was spoken.

Her first two years at Brandeis were marked mainly by her lack of noticeability as contrasted to the important and prominent figure she was later to become. Her academic performance, however, was outstanding, and she was later to graduate magna cum laude, one of 32 persons in a class of about 300 with that honor. Her inclinations at Brandeis were aesthetic and literary. She concentrated on French literature and wrote her honors thesis on the novelist Alain Robbe-Grillet. One of a dozen blacks in her class, Angela spent three of her four college years at Brandeis, and spent her junior year at the Sorbonne in Paris.

In her sophomore year, she met a young German exchange student, Manfred Clemenz, who was majoring in philosophy. He introduced her to the writings of Nietzsche and Marcuse, and they spent much time discussing politics. When Angela went to Paris under the junior year abroad program in 1964,

Clemenz also returned to Europe. It was clear by this time that they had fallen in love, a fact which was met with consternation both by his family in Germany and by the Davises in Birmingham.

The Rev. Melish, who had been corresponding with Angela and her family regularly, said that after the young couple went to Europe Manfred wrote to Angela's parents asking their permission to marry. "Manfred wrote Sallye [Mrs. Davis] a very formal letter asking for Angela's hand in marriage," Melish said. "Mama hit the roof. She wrote me enclosing a copy of the letter from Manfred. Her letter was very emotional. It said Angela was very unhappy at Brandeis and didn't want to go back there." Melish noted, "I told Sallye that if you refuse this and try to break it up, they'll elope. But if you leave things alone, it will take care of itself. Just sit tight."

Manfred and Angela went skiing together in the Alps, and spent much time exploring Paris. The young man's parents were as much opposed to the interracial marriage as was Mrs. Davis and the relationship eventually cooled.

In an article entitled "The radicalization of Angela Davis," *Ebony* magazine said this of Angela's year in Paris: "Birmingham was the root, but the radicalization of Angela Davis was hastened by what she heard and saw and began thinking about in Paris, France. It was there, at twenty, hearing, seeing, thinking, that she began achieving psychological distance from the kind of 'educated Negro middle class' identity for which so much had fitted her. In Paris, Angela began extending her intellectual interests beyond Rabelais, Montaigne, Balzac and other *maîtres* of French literature. She began delving into philosophical thought. Phenomenology interested her; existential truths became ever more clear. Kant and Hegel offered much, but a favorite was the political philosopher Karl Marx."

During her period in Paris Angela mingled with Algerian students and became interested in the cause of Algerian independence. *Ebony* reports, "Often during her year of study in Paris Angela saw things that reminded her of home. The police constantly harassed Algerians and seemed delighted at every opportunity to slam their truncheons across Algerian heads. Angela had known Birmingham and the South very well. . . .

[85]

She had seen and felt the rage of whites and knew that what she saw in Paris was yet another example of white people reacting against previously enslaved black people they were being forced to free. How little difference she could discern between the elegantly caparisoned Paris police in kepi and cape and the bull-necked Birmingham cops in sweaty shirts who grinned as they bludgeoned black marchers and used electric cattle prods on young girls."

After her year in Paris, Angela returned to complete her senior year at Brandeis. It was at this time that she took a course with Herbert Marcuse, the guru of the modern Marxist New Left. This experience seems to have rechanneled her intellectual interests. Marcuse, in his 70s, had been at Brandeis for eleven years after teaching at Western European universities. A German Marxist during the period of the Weimar Republic, Marcuse called for the abolition of the democratic government because of its weakness and ineptitude. Whatever followed, he argued, would be better. Hitler followed, however, forcing Marcuse to flee from his native country. At the time Angela Davis met him, Herbert Marcuse was in his final year at Brandeis, a philosopher who laid stress on subtle forms of repression within capitalist democracies and the psychic need for individual acts of refusal to break society's molds. Angela found herself strongly attracted to his views. She began the study of philosophy, and this was to change her life.

Marcuse does not discount the role he played in shaping Angela Davis' evolving ideas, but he says that it is probably exaggerated. "If it hadn't been me, it would have been someone much like me," he says.

In order to understand adequately the influence of Herbert Marcuse upon the young and impressionable Angela Davis it is essential to be aware of his complex and often confusing philosophy, as well as his method of presenting it to his students.

In his volume *Marcuse*, Alasdair MacIntyre points out that Marcuse's whole manner of thought and style of presentation "do not invite questioning, but suggest that the teacher is delivering truths to the pupil which the pupil has merely to receive." He goes on to tell his readers that Marcuse does not give any reasons for believing that what he says is true. Instead, he

[86]

illustrates his points but never offers evidence in a systematic manner.

In another book. *The Meaning of Marcuse*, Robert W. Marks writes that "Marcuse is a master of the polemics of obscurity. His meanings are seldom completely clear even to the reader who approaches him with the necessary background and with sympathetic interest." Farther on, Marks notes, "The essential conclusion, perhaps, is that Marcuse is not so much a philosopher of revolution as a pamphleteer. He is an exhorter—in the tradition of the Nietzsche of Zarathustra." Another professor recalls: "I have been told by a colleague of his at Brandeis that his student followers accepted him uncritically as a prophet, a Fuhrer of a political-intellectual ideology which his followers neither questioned nor allowed anyone else to question."

One thing quite clear about Professor Marcuse is that if he were in charge of our universities, or of society as a whole, free speech would surely be eliminated. In his *Critique Of Pure Tolerance,* Marcuse, who has been referred to as the "foremost literary symbol of the New Left" by the *New York Times*, states that people who are confused about politics really don't know how to use freedom of speech correctly; they turn it into "an instrument for absolving servitude," so that "that which is radically evil now appears as good." Having established this premise, Marcuse recommends "the withdrawal of toleration of speech and assembly from groups which promote aggressive policies, armament, chauvinism, racial and religious discrimination or which oppose the extension of public services." For him, the correct political attitude is one of "intolerance against movements from the right and toleration of movements from the left."

Professor Marcuse's philosophy, put into action by militant New Left students, has resulted in an erosion of free speech on a number of campuses. Platforms have been stormed, speakers have been prevented from expressing their point of view, classes have been suspended. Discussing these New Left efforts, Charles Susskind, a professor of electrical engineering at Berkeley who had lived through the period of Nazi ascendancy in Germany, stated, "I don't know why they think of themselves as the New Left. Their methods look to me much more

[87]

like those of the Nazi students whom I saw in the 1930s harassing deans, hounding professors and their families, making public disturbances and interfering with lectures, until only professors sympathetic with the Nazi cause remained."

Herbert Marcuse's philosophy, however, is not that easy to pinpoint. His book *Eros And Civilization*, for example is an effort to challenge the thesis of Sigmund Freud's *Civilization and Its Discontents*. Marcuse sets forth the thesis that we can avoid Freud's gloomy view of man if we only distinguish between "labor" and "work." Labor, he states, is the result of domination and brings about alienation and misery. It is "surplus repression" which traditionally was the repression of workers but in our modern American society has become the repression of everyone.

A rational system of socialism, argues Marcuse, would release man from both repression and work so that he would then be able to "play and display." The result, according to Marcuse, would be a world in which human beings would no longer be under the "tyranny of the genital." Men would no longer be used as machines for the performance of labor, they would be "resexualized." Marcuse argues that "genital supremacy" would decline and "pregenital polymorphous sexuality and narcissism" would take its place. With the end of repression and labor, "Eros" would dominate, and life would become a pleasant rather than a tortuous experience. Under Marcuse's system, the life of the mind would be seriously downgraded.

Marcuse's goal seems to be the creation of the kind of primitive life which some 19th-century Westerners believed men could live in the preindustrial South Sea islands. Freud's approach is, of course, exactly the opposite. Freud sets forth the proposition that life is valuable and that civilization is a valid goal and that it is the result of sublimation of man's primitive instincts. Marcuse calls, in effect, for the elimination of civilization as we know it, and his philosophy has as its basic premise the destruction of the institutions of Western society. It is a philosophy which is wholly negative, and Marcuse himself admits this.

In his book *One Dimensional Man*, he writes: "The critical theory of society [that is, Marcuse's theory] possesses no concepts which could bridge the gap between the present and the future: holding no promise and showing no success, it remains negative."

Herbert Marcuse has given words a meaning all his own. He argues, to cite one example, that American society is "totalitarian." He provides this explanation for the charge: "Free election of masters does not abolish the masters or the slaves ... 'totalitarian' is not only a terroristic economic-technical coordination of society, but also a non-terroristic economic-technical coordination which operated through the manipulation of needs by vested interests." When Angela Davis declares that American society is "totalitarian," something she declares with some frequency, we must understand that she is using this term in a sense far different from that which is generally accepted in rational discourse, and far different from any dictionary definition. Marcuse suggests that our society is totalitarian in precisely the same sense that Nazi Germany was and, he admits, Russia and China are (an admission no longer shared by his one-time student Angela Davis). He writes: "Those whose life is the hell of the Affluent Society are kept in line by a brutality which revives medieval and early modern practices."

American society is condemned by Professor Marcuse for what many observers have long considered to be one of its great strengths, namely the ability to respond to changing and challenging situations through the democratic process. He argues that our society is constructed in such a way as to manipulate the needs and wants of its members and then satisfy them. In *One Dimensional Man* he notes that American society is "capable of containing social change—qualitative change which would establish essentially different institutions, a new direction of the productive process, new modes of human existence."

Also overlooked by Professor Marcuse is the fact that in modern American society increased freedom from labor is being steadily achieved by an increasingly large number of workers, due primarily to automation and other new productive techniques. Part of the reason for his refusal to accept this change as an advance is that he disapproves of the manner in which workers have freely and voluntarily seen fit to use their new

[89]

leisure time. A *New York Times* report quoted Marcuse as stating that the civil rights movement has accomplished nothing so far because the Negroes were choosing middle-class values; Marcuse expressed the view that they had no real right to choose such values.

Whatever else may be said about the philosophy of Herbert Marcuse, it is clear that such philosophy does not embody the idea that one man's rights end where another man's rights begin. It does involve the view that society itself is dangerous and corrupt, and it rejects the idea that man has some role in the world other than pleasure, or that man is more than merely a material being with material wants and needs. It challenges traditional ideas of right and wrong and good and evil, and it likewise rejects the idea that man is capable of deciding for himself the important questions in his own life. Herbert Marcuse has created an elitist philosophy which places his own judgment above all things.

Discussing Marcuse's philosophy and nonscientific approach, Professor Eliseo Vivas notes: "Marcuse repudiates in advance the code of conduct that allows a man to apply for membership in the academic world. Consider: No science department in the nation would hire a man who announced in advance of his being hired that he did not have the least intention of doing his work with an open mind, who wrote that he did not intend to listen to the criticisms of his hypotheses advanced by his colleagues, because he knew they were wrong and he had contempt for them; and that he had every intention of preventing them from carrying on the experiments they had planned, because he knew in advance of their being performed that they were nonsense. . . . Such a man is not a scientist. He is not a scholar. He is unfit for an academic post."

It is clear that Professor Marcuse's approach to the problems he sees fit to consider is not that of a scholar, and as a young student Angela Davis closely observed not the approach of a scholarly mind working at an academic discipline, but of a brilliant man advancing an elitist philosophy of control over other people with himself being in the position of controller. His denouncements of American society and of all nonmaterial views of the nature of man may be correct or incorrect, but they

[90]

are presented ex cathedra, with no supporting evidence that would be considered valid in any academic discussion of the question. As we observe Angela Davis' "scholarly" method emerging, we will see that what she has done is to learn the lessons that Herbert Marcuse laboriously taught her very well. Whether this adds up to scholarship or to something else remains an open question.

Summing up the attitude of much of the academic community to the method and approach of Herbert Marcuse, Professor Vivas writes of "what Marcuse the 'philosopher' and 'social scientist' declares to be one basic tenet of his thought— tolerance toward the left, repression of the right. He knows, and knows in advance, and knows beyond argument, that he is right and those who disagree with him are wrong. Which is to say that he is neither a philosopher nor a social scientist but an intellectual energumen. A man with a closed mind may be fit for any number of things. . . . But a man with a closed mind is not fit to serve in a philosophy department or in the division of the social sciences of a university. A man like that is not fit to be an academic man. He has already settled the question of freedom by announcing that he does not believe in it."

As Angela Davis completed her senior year at Brandeis, her literature teachers urged her to spend the next year teaching at a Southern university. But, at Marcuse's urging, she rejected this advice and went on from Brandeis to study for two years at Johann Wolfgang von Goethe University in Frankfurt, Germany. She studied at the Marxist-oriented Institute of Social Research; one of her professors was Marcuse's old Marxist friend and colleague, Theodore W. Adorno, who has since died.

In Frankfurt, recalls sociology professor Oskar Negt, "she learned German in a remarkably short period and grasped Kant and Hegel in equally amazing fashion." He particularly remembers a first-rate seminar paper of hers on 'The Conception of Interest in Kant's Critique of the Powers of Pure Reason."

When Angela first arrived in Frankfurt, she lived in a residence for 1,000 foreign students studying at Goethe, which had an enrollment of about 17,000. A short time later she moved in with radical sociology students who had taken over an old abandoned building dubbed "The Factory."

A student friend, David Wittenberg, recalls that she had become increasingly concerned about racial developments in America and, as one of her teachers said, "felt that she could no longer tolerate the deterioration of the situation in the United States without becoming actively involved." Wittenberg recalls that she had a number of visitors from the United States who kept her posted on racial developments. "The amazing thing about Angela," he says, "was that she didn't treat this racial thing as a personal issue. She had an ability to keep her own feelings out of her assessment of the American racial situation. This allowed her to arrive at rational rather than emotional conclusions." One of these conclusions was that it was time for her to return home. For a variety of reasons, theoretical speculations had begun to lose their appeal for her. In 1967 she left Germany, as one of her teachers explained, to become involved in what she considered to be a worsening situation for Negroes in the United States.

Upon her return from two years in Germany, Angela resumed her studies under Professor Herbert Marcuse, this time at the University of California at San Diego, where Marcuse had moved from Brandeis. During this period she lived for almost a year with another graduate student, his wife, and their infant son.

The young man was Barry Shapiro, who was also working under Marcuse for his doctorate degree in philosophy. He had rented an old house at Cardiff-by-the-Sea, north of the campus, and he subleased a big downstairs room with an ocean view to Angela. Shapiro found her warm, easy to be around, and quick to become involved in the life of others. "I remember her teaching our baby, Aaron, how to walk and talk when he was only six or eight months old," Shapiro recalls.

Often, Angela would have the evening meal with the Shapiros, help with the dishes and then go to her room to study. "She would read until she fell asleep with the book in her lap," Shapiro said. "I was studying hard, too, but I would finally give up and go to bed. But many mornings I came downstairs to find the lights still on and her asleep in the chair. She seemed to feel that she didn't have time for things like sleep."

At this time Angela's career was still following a rather orthodox academic pattern. Her interest in practical politics, in demonstrations and picket lines, in the rhetoric of black militancy and radicalism, remained somewhat dormant. Her choice of a Ph.D. thesis topic—Kant's analysis of violence in the French Revolution—did, however, seem to signal a gradual shift in the focus of her scholarly interests, and she also began to dip into the organizing of the black community then beginning to emerge in San Diego.

"She was at all the meetings, constantly around and nibbling at the edges," recalls Tom Johnson, a journalist who was head of the San Diego NAACP at that time. "I remember she wasn't really that involved—she was always concerned but aloof. She seemed to be a detached observer at that time, always asking questions without saying very much herself. It seemed as if she was merely intellectually curious. . . . In fact, she seemed so determined to get a feel of what was happening on the street level in the community that I first thought that she was an FBI plant."

During the last months she was living with the Shapiros, she rented a small one-story wooden apartment in back of a house in south-central Los Angeles, not far from Watts, scene of the first big city black riot in 1965. She commuted regularly the 120 miles between La Jolla and Los Angeles, driving a 1959 station wagon. Shapiro said that one of the things he envied most was her "mobility," her independence that permitted her to be away for days. This was the period when, according to Helen Dudar of the *New York Post*, ". . . she made her commitment. The cool intellectual with the carriage of a duchess, the detached onlooker, became a full participant—a rangy, chain smoking black woman in a glorious Afro who ran with the Panthers and signed up with the Communists, reconciling in some mysterious way Marcuse's off-brand ideology with the more standard variety dowdily pursued by the old party."

Angela first began to involve herself with black militant groups in Los Angeles. One was an organization called US, a

[93]

black nationalist extremist cult headed by Ron Karenga; it and the Black Panthers had emerged as the two best-known militant factions among young blacks.

Ron Karenga attended the University of California at Los Angeles and was graduated cum laude. He has a master's degree and is working toward a doctorate in political science. In addition to these educational accomplishments, he has been employed as a social worker and has lectured on numerous topics such as urban problems and African history. He has also served as an instructor of Swahili. In addition, Karenga reads Spanish and French and is studying several other languages. In 1965, shortly after the Watts riot, he founded US, one of whose primary goals was to achieve unity among black people.

Karenga urges the white community not to intervene at all in the activities of the black community; he urges it to provide the black community with "foreign aid," and advocates that it spend time, money and resources in the process of "civilizing itself." Then, he hopes, some sort of "balance of power" between blacks and whites might emerge.

In an essay entitled "The Black Community and the University: A Community Organizer's Perspective," Karenga sets forth his ideas:

"There are three things I see the university as needing to do. First, nonintervention with regard to the black community; stop imposing yourself through projects that only benefit you and the white community, or the business community. Stop trying to make political decisions about what we do. Do not pass value judgments on what we do. Second, afford us foreign aid —financial and technical. As I said before, the university is one of the largest financial institutions in the country, and as a matter of reparations perhaps some kind of transaction could be made so that we could be repaid for some of the efforts that our forefathers made. Technical aid should be given in terms of universitites having the facilities and personnel to collect data that we can interpret and use to our own benefit. Third, and the most important thing, create a civilizing movement in this country among whites."

Discussing what he calls the "civilizing movement" for the white community, Karenga states: "I think that if you don't have any social content in this educational thing, then the academic institution is of no importance at all. That is why we concluded long ago that we use reason too well to be overly impressed by other people's use of it. We are more interested in living life than in discussing it. I would suggest that this civilizing movement start from the university—this on the very basis that the university has always had an avowed tradition of liberalism, humanitarianism, and a few other 'isms' that are related, but should not be mentioned, lest you be bored by the long list of complimentary adjectives, and forget what else I have said."

Although Angela Davis was attracted by US, she felt strongly that it had at least two weaknesses. Initially, it rejected association with the white community in bringing about social upheaval, and she felt that this was unrealistic. Secondly, it treated women as "servants" to the men, and this was something that Angela would not tolerate, regardless of ideology and other considerations. At this time she became closer to the Black Panthers, although there is no evidence that she ever joined the Panther Party. She did, however, become involved in their activities and was in later speeches to hail Bobby Seale, Huey Newton and other Panther leaders in jail as martyrs to the black struggle.

Bobby Seale, when asked by *Time* magazine where the black American should go in his drive for a racially equal society, responded: "Black people, brothers and sisters in this country, have to move to a level of revolutionary struggle in terms of what we understand to be the true enemy, the enemy who perpetuates tyranny and oppression, poverty and the wretched conditions that we're subjected to in the black community. This enemy, as Eldridge Cleaver always puts it, is at three levels of oppression: the big-time, tycooning, avaricious businessmen, the lying, demagogic, trick politicians, and the fascist pig cops, militia, and pig agents who work for the avaricious, demagogic ruling class. Black people's direction should be to wage a relentless revolutionary struggle against the three levels of oppression. But it can't be handled alone by blacks. We need alliances with those whose own self-interest is to seek communities free of disorders."

[95]

It seems clear that at this point in her intellectual development, Angela Davis had abandoned the academic goals which had once been her primary motivation and had placed them somewhat in the background, although by no means rejecting them totally. Her study and experience had, for a variety of reasons, led her to the conclusion that there was no way for black and white Americans to live peacefully in equality under the system of democracy and free enterprise. Only if democracy was eliminated and free enterprise replaced with total state control might an equal society emerge.

Given this conclusion, it became only natural for Angela to devote herself to revolution, to the overthrow and destruction of the existing society and social, economic, and political order. Angela's only problem, at this stage, was which organization, which ideology, which crusade, would best achieve these goals. For a short time she felt that Ron Karenga's US had the answers, then she moved over to the Panthers. Neither of these groups, however, totally satisfied her emotional and intellectual needs for the real and total answer. Something more, she felt, was needed.

The attraction the Communist Party had for Angela Davis seemed to stem from a severe rationalism rather than from a ghetto soul or emotional racial commitment. There was in Angela Davis the need to find a philosophy that explained the nature of the world's problems and provided an answer to them, a path to follow at the end of which understanding might be achieved.

The world makes little sense to the reasonable man, and never has. Why so often is it the good who suffer, and the bad who receive earthly rewards? This, of course, was the dilemma faced in the Book of Job. It is as old as creation. Man, from the religious view, is seen as being created in the image of God. No one has seen God and, as a result, it is clear that man is created in the image of an enigma, and remains an enigma himself. Those who try to explain man with one theory or another always seem to be defied by man's own inexplicable nature. Yet, the years of philosophical study at the hands of such advocates of the material nature of man as Herbert Marcuse and Theodore Adorno led Angela inevitably to search for an ideology which tied all of reality together and provided some hope for a utopian future. This the Communist Party seemed to provide, a substitute religion for those whose God was man's own mind. Though her teachers saw that, in many respects, the communism practiced in the Soviet Union or in China was no better than the democracy and capitalism to which they objected in the West, Angela Davis seemed to cast aside all of their doubts, becoming a "true believer" in the traditional communism of Marx and Lenin, not the theory alone but even its practice in the "Peoples' republics" of today.

During this period of political and philosophical transformation, Angela had emerged as a leading figure among blacks on campus, helping to set up a Black Students Council and drafting guidelines for the "Third College," an experimental school-within-a-school run by and for minorities. In many respects, however, her role was hampered by her tendency to speak in conceptual and grandiose philosophical terms, and her effectiveness was relative to the ability of other students to understand and appreciate what she was really talking about. There continued to exist the aloofness about which others had commented in the past. "She was never really hung up on that leadership thing," says Tyra Garlington, a San Diego girl friend. "It was always something personal with her—if others wanted to follow, that was their worry, not hers."

The University of California at San Diego was one of the newest and most modern of the nine universities in the California state system of higher education. This school had been planned for tremendous expansion beyond its 7,000 member student body, a program which was later curtailed because of the crisis in educational funding. The University branch in San Diego had two colleges, Revelle and Muir, and at the time Angela Davis arrived in 1967, the university was proceeding toward a third college along the same lines, under the leadership of Chancellor William McGill.

Angela, together with other black and Mexican-American militants, demanded that the Administration change the entire format so that it would be devoted almost entirely to Negro and Mexican-American students with minority instructors and a curriculum to be chosen largely by the students. This became

[97]

a major issue on campus, and McGill offered a compromise under which it would be a two-year experimental college, pending determination about whether academic standards would be lowered otherwise.

"I remember there was a meeting of the academic senate [faculty] and the militants presented a list of nonnegotiable demands," recalls Dr. Avrum Stroll, now head of the philosophy department at Revelle College. "A number of blacks moved into the hall and took over the platform and warned that we were in trouble if we didn't approve the demands."

Discussing this performance of academic blackmail and the introduction of force into the once staid deliberations of the University's faculty senate, Jack Fox of United Press International notes that "In short, Angela Davis and the militants won. There is now a 'third college' at the University of California at San Diego. It has 167 students, almost all black or Chicano, with 12 to 14 faculty members. The classes are conducted in old Marine huts. The curriculum is weighted heavily toward minority studies, sociology, political theory, anthropology. Its future is uncertain, but it bears the stamp of Angela Davis."

At this time Angela Davis seems to have abandoned the scholarly pursuits which once motivated her and she appears to have rejected all ideas of the university as an institution in which scholarship was to be pursued and through which cultural continuity was to be maintained. Instead, she adopted the philosophy of the university advocated by the New Left—one calling for the University to become a political institution, a base from which revolutionary activity aiming at the destruction of the existing social order might be launched.

More and more, New Left spokesmen have come to see the university not as the repository of wisdom and the transmitter of culture, but simply as a defender of the status quo and as the place where its various elites are trained. In an essay entitled "A Student Syndicalist Movement—University Reform Revisited," Carl Davidson, a former vice president of Students for a Democratic Society, explained why university reform is a matter of concern that transcends the campus: "We have named the system in this country corporate liberalism and if we bother to look, its penetration into the campus community is awesome. Its elite is trained in our colleges of business administration. Its defenders are trained in our law schools. Its apologists can be found in the political science departments. The colleges of social science produce its own manipulators. For propagandists, it relies on the schools of journalism. It insures its own future growth in the colleges of education. If some of us don't quite fit in, we are brainwashed in the division of counseling. And we all know only too well what goes on in the classrooms of the military science buildings. . . . It is on our assembly lines in the universities that the leaders of U. S. society are molded into what they are."

Davidson concludes by asking: "What would happen to a manipulative society if its means of creating manipulable people were done away with?"

For many in the New Left the kind of campus reform which Angela Davis urged at the University of California at San Diego has as its long-range goal not simply the creation of a politically involved college community, but the total alteration of the social, economic, and political structure of society.

The Port Huron Statement, adopted by the Students for a Democratic Society in 1962, describes the modern American university as "the cumbersome academic bureaucracy extending throughout the academic as well as extra-curricular structures, contributing to the sense of outer complexity and inner powerlessness that transforms so many students from honest searching to ratification of convention and worse, to a numbness to present and future catastrophes. The size and financing systems of the University enhance the permanent trusteeship of the administrative bureaucracy, their power leading to a shift to the value standards of business and administrative mentality within the university . . . a new left must start controversy across the land if national policies and national apathy are to be reversed. The ideal university is a community of controversy, within itself and in its effects on communities beyond. . . . To turn these possibilities into realities will involve national efforts at university reform by an alliance of students and faculty."

What must be done, the SDS statement says, is that such students and faculty members "must wrest control of the edu-

[99]

cational process from the adminstrative bureaucracy. . . . They must consciously build a base for their assault upon the loci of power."

Many in the New Left criticize the university for being "too political" today, for being too closely tied to the Pentagon, with the nation's war policies, and with government and large foundation grants. While such criticisms are, in many instances, the same ones which were made by more conservative critics of the concept of federal aid to education, the fact remains that the New Left seeks a "political" university, only with a different kind of politics. In neither instance is real education or real scholarship provided.

The New Left also makes what many consider to be the serious mistake of believing that all of society's problems may be solved within the context of the kind of university they seek to create. Professor Eli Ginzburg of Columbia University notes that "The central mistake we made in the United States was to oversell education as the solution to all problems. The last three Presidents made this mistake. There are a lot of myths about the importance of higher education. One is that you can earn more money with more education. Long-distance truck drivers earn more than teachers. Education is good for certain people. Educators have bollixed things by claiming that because some education is good for everybody, more education is better. The country is degree crazy."

Many New Left students and their faculty supporters, including Angela Davis, have adopted the view that the university is responsible for everything, and is capable of all things. They expect the university to end the war in Vietnam, to eliminate racism, and to decontaminate the cities. They want, as Professor Henry Steele Commager has said, ". . . the university to be contemporary, to deal with every issue as it arises, plunge into every controversy, offer courses in every problem, be involved in everything."

Dr. Commager contrasts the activists' attitude with the more traditional idea of the academic community, an idea which Angela Davis seems to have shared during the first portion of her education: "They are unable to understand . . . that the university is the one institution whose conspicuous duty is not

[100]

to be involved in everything, and above all not to be so involved in contemporary problems that it cannot deal with problems that are not merely contemporary. The solution of contemporary problems is the business of politics and government. The business of the university is to preserve the heritage of the past, to anticipate the problems of the future, and to train students able to solve the problems of the present."

Many are now demanding that education be made "relevant." Often it is claimed that the colleges and universities are far removed from the needs of society, that four years of undergraduate education is essentially cloistered unreality. Yet, the question of what is truly "relevant" with regard to education is not quite so simple. Neither is the question of what kind of education best prepares students to cope with such practical problems as race relations, urban renewal, war, and poverty.

Addressing the graduating class at Amherst college several years ago, Dr. Kenneth B. Clark, Negro psychologist and professor at the City University of New York, made an impassioned defense of what he termed "nonrelevant" education. He called on colleges to recognize the needs of those who did not seek immediate relevance in their studies—students whom he called "the forgotten men of the present ferment of campus confrontation." He said: "It is from these perverse, lonely, nonrelevant, educated persons that a practical society receives antidotes to a terrifying sense of inner emptiness and despair. From these impracticals come our poets, our artists, our novelists, our satirists, our humorists, who, because of their perspective of education and their restless search for insights, continue to try to educate us. They make the life of the thinking human being more endurable and the thought of a future tolerable."

What do people such as Angela Davis mean when they raise the question of relevance? Relevance to what? What they ought to mean, perhaps, is "relevant to wisdom," though many think only of "relevance to current affairs." The notion of "adjournment to modern society," however, may not be relevant to what we have traditionally called higher education. In his novel *Scott King's Modern Europe,* Evelyn Waugh's hero learns by a summer's experience of modern society that it would be infinitely wicked to teach young men to adjust to the modern

[101]

world. Professor Russell Kirk notes that "to adjust to the age of the mass state, of the concentration camp, the secret police and injustice triumphant, would be sin and shame. The higher learning is not meant to inculcate conformity to passing fad and foible, nor necessarily to present domination and powers. It is intended, rather, to reveal to us the norms, the enduring standards, for the person and the republic. Adjustment to abnormality is ruinous policy."

Modern technology alters so rapidly that, as Peter Drucker has pointed out, the college and university cannot possibly keep abreast of industrial methods. What higher education should do is discipline the intellect so that it may be applied in future productive processes as to many other matters. The truly relevant things in a college are the permanent things, in T. S. Eliot's phrase. They are the body of knowledge, not undone by the machinations of the modern world. Is such an education "relevant"? Dr. Kirk says, "If a formal education does not bear at all upon our personal and social difficulties today, of course it is a sham and worthless; in that, the students of the New Left are quite right. But no modern authors are more genuinely relevant than are Plato and Augustine today. Preoccupation with the passing pageant is merely the sort of 'relevance' which the big commercial bookclubs sell; and the college and university were not endowed for that purpose."

In considering Angela Davis' approach to the role of the university as it first expressed itself at the University of California at San Diego, we must ask the question whether she and those in the New Left who agree with her approach represent an intellectual or an anti-intellectual movement and tendency. Are such individuals and groups interested in action for its own sake, and not in ideas? In *The Partisan Review,* Professor Leslie Fiedler answers rather distinctly: "The 'mutants' in our midst are nonparticipants in the past . . . dropouts from history. The withdrawal from school, so typical of this generation and so inscrutable to ours, is best understood as a lived symbol of their rejection of the notion of cultural continuity and progress, which our graded education system represents in institutional form. It is not merely a matter of their rejecting what happens to have happened just before them, as the young do, after all, in every age; but of their attempting to disavow the past, of their seeking to avoid recapitulating it step by step—up to the point of graduation into the present."

The New Left rejects the Western tradition in part because it feels that all systems of reason have come to be held more and more suspect, as Fiedler points out: "The new irrationalists ... deny all the apostles of reason, Freud as well as Socrates; and if they seem to exempt Marx, this is because they know less about him, have heard him evoked less often by the teachers they are driven to deny. Not only do they reject the Socratic adage that the examined life is the only one worth enduring at all, but they also abjure the Freudian one: 'Where id was, ego shall be,' since for them the true rallying cry is 'Let id prevail over ego, impulse over order. . . .' "

Although spokesmen for black and student militant movements frequently urge more debate, free discussion, and open consideration of all points of view, the fact is that they prefer action—the demonstration, the sit-in, the riot. They prefer what Fiedler has called "the mindless unity of an impassioned crowd, whose immediate cause is felt rather than thought out, whose ultimate cause is itself." The philosophy of Herbert Marcuse, that tolerance should be reserved only for opinions which are "correct," is one which Angela Davis came to accept almost totally, and one which her colleagues in the New Left movement dedicated themselves to implement. Her own crusade at the University of California at San Diego was, for Angela Davis, only the beginning of such an effort at implementation.

Barry Shapiro, with whose family Angela was living at the time of the controversy at San Diego, recalls that during this period Angela came home from Los Angeles one night after a shooting in the cafeteria at UCLA between US and Panther factions in which two persons were killed. She had an M-1 rifle with her for protection, he says.

"Seeing that gun frightened the hell out of us," he says. "Two people she knew had just been killed and we asked her why she didn't just split, that nothing was worth her life. But she said that if they thought they [Shapiro didn't specify who] were going to shut her up they were wrong. She said she felt she might be shot to death but it wasn't going to stop her. She wasn't like

[103]

us. She had no problem in understanding the role of violence in a revolutionary situation."

Academically, Angela was progressing well, despite her preoccupation with political and racial problems. She completed all of the requirements for her doctorate degree in a year's time, and as the subject for her dissertation chose the topic, "the problem of violence and German idealism." Her grade point average for two years was 3.8 out of a possible 4.

Yet, because of her growing involvement in political activities, Angela never found the time to write her dissertation. During this period she joined the Communist Party. She joined the Che Lumumba Club, a Marxist-oriented organization of black people. "Che Lumumba's commitment as a group of black people using Marxist principles for social change—that's what really impressed me," Angela told a friend from Brandeis, Eileen Foley.

Later, she told the Associated Press, "I feel that the most important part of my life ought to be the struggle for equality of all peoples, the struggle for economic equality, the struggle for black liberation." She said, "I have given my life to the struggle. . . . If I have to lose my life in that struggle, well, then, that's the way it will have to be."

It seemed clear that by this time Angela Davis was no longer concerned with a truly academic or scholarly career. Her commitment was one to violent revolution as the only means of achieving the kind of equality she sought. She had joined the Communist Party and had, in effect, declared war upon American society. She proclaimed her rejection of such "bourgeois" ideas as freedom of speech and respect for the rights of others. Her commitment was far different, it was no longer the search for truth but the search for power, and such power, she had come to believe, could only come, as Mao Tse-tung had said, "out of the barrel of a gun."

Angela was still living with the Shapiros when she was approached by Dr. Donald Kalish, head of the Department of Philosophy at UCLA, about coming there as an assistant professor. She was still more interested in completing work on her Ph.D. degree, but Kalish assured her she would have sufficient spare time to complete her thesis.

[104]

The reasons for Dr. Kalish's particular interest in Angela Davis were set forth this way by *Newsweek* magazine: "The UCLA philosophy department was looking for an instructor, and she seemed to fit the bill perfectly. Not only was she black —all major universities were hungering for talented Negro teachers by then—but she was strongly schooled in the Continental European philosophical tradition of Kant, Hegel, Nietzsche and the existentialists. 'The rest of us,' noted a UCLA philosophy professor, 'are under the influence of British empiricists and analytical logical positivists. Her real value was that she filled a tremendous gap in the offerings of the department.' "

Angela had a choice of jobs at this time, as she was also offered a teaching position at Swarthmore College in Pennsylvania. Her decision to teach at UCLA was to have significant ramifications, for her as well as for the California university system and the black militant movement. When she left San Diego to assume her new job in Los Angeles, Angela Davis was hardly known off the San Diego campus. Such anonymity, however, was not to be hers for very long.

What was the philosophy that Angela Davis took with her to her teaching position at the University of California at Los Angeles? In an article in *Ebony* magazine entitled "Rhetoric vs. Reality," she set forth her views in these words:

"I am a Communist because I am convinced that the centuries-old sufferings of Black people cannot be alleviated under the present social arrangement. Capitalism is based on the ownership of the gigantic economic apparatus, on which the life of the nation depends, by a small minority of privileged men. The wealth of the nation is concentrated in the hands of fewer than 500 corporations, among them General Motors, Ford, General Electric, U.S. Steel, the Standard Oil Companies, Bank of America, Chase-Manhattan Bank. But where lies the origin of their stupendous fortunes? Their wealth has been created by millions of working people who have never received the full value of their work.

"The economic system, and thus the society, functions in accordance with the irrational drive for profit. The masses of people, through their work, are mere tools for the realization of

[105]

profits which are swallowed up by that circle of corporations. This is what exploitation is all about: When people work, they take home in wages far less than the value of what they have actually produced.

"For Black people this exploitation has always been more intense, more devastating, more deadly. We have always been compelled to take the most ignoble and lowest-paying jobs. And the capitalists have fostered racism among the masses of white people in order better to exploit us. Their exploitation of white workers is also thereby facilitated, for white workers, in their racist posture, ignore their real enemies."

Angela Davis has harsh words for those black Americans who have succeeded in the free-enterprise American society, and for those who advocate a policy of "black capitalism" to help society face its racial difficulties. She writes: "The apologists for Black Capitalism are determined to render Black people oblivious to the reality that the most significant portion of this country's wealth rests with a small group of corporations and that, absent a revolution, there it will remain. Even the most assiduous and most fortunate Black capitalists can never make substantial inroads into the top ranks of the ruling class. That Rev. Leon Sullivan was recently appointed to the Board of Directors of General Motors does not contradict this. He wields no decisive power; his appointment was clearly a further measure of pacification. As a Communist, I feel that it is incumbent upon us to reject Black Capitalism."

Angela Davis' approach to the very real problems facing black Americans seems to overlook the real facts of our recent history. During the decade from 1960 to 1970 black Americans made substantial progress in jobs, incomes, education and housing. The median income of all nonwhite families has risen by 102 percent since 1960 to $6,516. That is a much bigger percentage increase than that of white incomes, which rose by 75 percent. Now, for the first time, most adult Negroes in the twenty-five to twenty-nine age bracket are high-school graduates, the figure rising from 38 percent to 56 percent during the past decade.

Illiteracy was cut about in half at the same time. Among blacks aged fourteen and above, it dropped from 7.5 percent in

1959 to 3.6 percent in 1969. The proportion of blacks who finished four years of college was more than 40 percent higher by the end of the decade, even though the numbers remained relatively small. Of all Negroes twenty-five to thirty-four, 4.3 percent were college graduates in 1960, and 6.1 percent in 1970.

Negro attendance at college rose even faster. As recently as 1965, only 10 percent of all college-age Negroes were in college. In 1970, 16 percent were enrolled. There has also been a pronounced upgrading in the kinds of jobs that were filled by blacks during the 1960s. The sharpest rise occurred in the proportionate number of nonwhites in professional technical jobs —up 131 percent between 1960 and 1970. The number in white-collar clerical jobs about doubled in the decade. At the same time, there was a major decline in the number of the nation's nonwhites engaged as laborers, farm workers, and private household workers. In 1960, about 40 percent of all nonwhite employment had been in such jobs. By 1970, the figure was down to 22 percent.

More and more black families bought their own homes in this ten year period. While 38 percent of all dwelling units occupied by Negroes were owned by their occupants in 1960, the proportion rose to 42 percent in 1970. For whites, the home-owning ratio increased only slightly during that period—from 64 to 65 percent.

More important, the quality of the housing occupied by blacks improved considerably. A decade ago, 41 percent of their dwelling units lacked at least one plumbing facility—flush toilet, private bathtub or shower, or piped hot water. By 1970, only 17 percent were in this category.

All of this does not mean that real problems do not continue to exist. It may mean, however, that Angela Davis' ideological conception that capitalism must be destroyed and replaced by communism overlooks the fact that citizens cannot boast of a median family income of over $6,000 any place in the Communist world. Quite simply, black Americans live better economically than white people anywhere in Eastern Europe, even if it continues to be true that white Americans live even better.

American society, however, has never considered economic statistics as the proper measure of the quality of a society. The dignity of the individual, his freedom, his opportunity to achieve whatever his ability will permit him to achieve—these have always been considered more valid measures. Still, Angela Davis, having accepted the materialist concepts of her teachers, has failed to show on her own terms that black Americans would fare better under Communism.

As she began her new life as a member of the faculty at UCLA, Angela approached her academic career as well as her political commitment not as a scholar, but as a revolutionary, dedicated to an ideology that tended to overlook reality and force it to bend to its own preconceptions. It was this concept of her academic role which was to bring her to national and, later, to international attention.

4

WHEN ANGELA DAVIS LEFT SAN DIEGO TO ASSUME A POSITION AS A member of the faculty of UCLA, her life was to change very rapidly and in many different respects. In a very short period she was to find herself catapulted into national prominence, rapidly becoming a hero to some and a devil to others.

Angela had been hired as an acting assistant professor in the UCLA Philosophy Department for the term beginning in the fall of 1969 at a salary of $10,260. She was hired by the head of the Philosophy Department, Professor Donald Kalish. Kalish later said that he did not know that she was a Communist Party member at the time, but he indicated that he would have hired her regardless of this fact.

Hardly had Angela been hired before a UCLA student named William Divale, an FBI underground agent, wrote to the college newspaper stating that Angela was a member of the Communist Party. The article appeared in the *Daily Bruin* on July 1, 1969, and it set off a chain of reactions climaxed by the 1972 trial for murder.

In his letter, Divale said that the UCLA Philosophy Department had hired a member of the Communist Party. Eight days later, the *San Francisco Examiner* revealed that Angela Davis was the person to whom Divale alluded. Two days after this, the regents of the University of California instructed UCLA

Chancellor Young to determine whether Angela Davis was in fact a member of the Communist Party.

Chancellor Young wrote a letter to the young instructor: "I am constrained by regental policy to request that you inform me whether or not you are a member of the Communist Party." Angela answered: "At the outset let me say that I think the question posed is impermissible. This is true on grounds of constitutional freedom as well as academic policy. However, and without waiving my objections to the question posed, my answer is that I am now a member of the Communist Party."

The Board of Regents met on September 19, 1969. After a heated discussion, the regents supported the position taken by Governor Ronald Reagan that Angela Davis' appointment be terminated. Following this action, a storm of protest broke over the UCLA campus, the ouster was challenged in the courts, and a crowd of 2,000 students and faculty turned out for her first lecture in Philosophy 199, "Recurring Philosophical Themes in Black Literature."

Newsweek magazine described this lecture in these terms: "They had, perhaps, expected a diatribe on academic freedom. What they got was a scholarly discourse on the thought of one-time slave Frederick Douglass. The process of liberation was the theme of the course, and Assistant Professor Davis began to trace what had become one of her own main preoccupations: the psychologically liberating force of the act of refusal."

"Resistance, rejection, defiance, on every level, on every front are integral elements of the voyage toward freedom," she declared. "The path of liberation is marked by resistance at every crossroads: mental resistance, physical resistance, resistance directed to the concerted attempt to obstruct the path. I think we can learn from the experience of the slave."

Although Angela Davis had been fired by the regents, a committee of the academic senate demanded that she be permitted to teach. The regents then ruled that she could teach, but not for credit, until they heard an appeal from their original decision. In the meantime, Angela continued to receive her salary.

An Associated Press story for October 7, 1969, painted this picture of Angela's first lecture, which drew an overflow crowd to the university's Royce Hall, with about 100 turned away for lack of room:

"Miss Davis, her hair in African natural style, sprinkled her lecture with quotations from Karl Marx, existentialist Jean Paul Sartre and philosopher Herbert Marcuse. Her course is called 'Recurring Philosophical Themes in Black Literature.' Miss Davis spoke of the life and times of Frederick Douglass, a slave who became an abolitionist orator and writer, and Nat Turner, who led a black insurrection. 'The history of black literature,' she said, 'provides a much more illuminating look at the concept of freedom than philosophical discourse in Western society. The pivotal theme of this course will be freedom as it has unfolded in the literary enterprise of the black people.' "

After the regents dismissed her, Angela, then twenty-five, vowed to appeal on campus and in the courts. She told a news conference on September 20, 1969, that university regents notified her by mail that she would be dismissed as an assistant philosophy professor at UCLA the following Monday unless she filed an appeal. "The sole reason they gave," she said, "is my membership in the Communist Party. They have not questioned my qualifications, my academic training or my ability to teach."

Robert Singleton, director of UCLA's Afro-American Studies Center, said the regents' decision was based upon Angela's color, not her politics. "There are white Communists teaching at the University who have not been harassed," he said, but declined to name them. A university official later denied that known Communists teach there. The regents' action, Singleton said, "will cause the biggest holocaust they've seen for a long time." He did not elaborate.

In a meeting held October 3, the University of California regents ruled that Angela Davis, already fired, must not teach on the Los Angeles campus while she appealed her case. The governing board ruled in a secret vote of 14 to 6 that Angela would, however, continue to receive her salary during the interim period. A minority of the regents said that Angela, who was ordered fired September 19, should be allowed to teach while she follows appeals procedures approved by the regents.

[111]

"I think it's a mistake," UCLA Chancellor Charles E. Young said of the board's vote. But Young smilingly told reporters: "I am going to have to play out the scenario a bit."

Some regents, contacted after the meeting, said that they believed a compromise could be worked out whereby Angela would be permitted to lecture, but not for credit courses. Governor Ronald Reagan, an ex-officio regent, said he had no comment on the regents' action during a three-hour emergency session. The Governor had said previously that Angela should be fired because regents' rules, adopted in the 1940s, forbid Communist Party members from teaching at the University. Angela maintained that the rule was unconstitutional.

Because of pressure from a committee of the academic senate, the regents finally decided that Angela could teach as long as no credit was given for her courses during the period while her appeal was pending. Discussing the meeting of the academic senate, columnist Joseph Kraft provided the following report for his readers on October 10, 1969: "At a meeting of the academic senate last week, the professors (by votes of more than 500 to less than a score) set out two basic principles. The first was that the regents' order to fire Miss Davis as a Communist should be tested in the courts. The second, based on the widely accepted presumption that the courts would rule against the regents, was that Miss Davis' capacity to teach should be decided by the regular faculty committee on appointments."

It was columnist Kraft's view that the action of Governor Reagan and the regents had provided additional and perhaps unnecessary ammunition to campus militants: "But Governor Reagan has handed the ball to the militant activists. They have opportunities galore for making trouble. They may swarm into the Davis class in a way that itself disturbs the public peace. They can—and will—organize mass meetings here at UCLA. They can—and will—organize protest referenda at campuses all across the state."

Kraft continued: "As one militant exultantly put it: 'Without Reagan, the Davis case would have interested maybe a hundred students. Now thousands are interested. When Reagan came in, there was only one Berkeley. Now he's got a potential Berkeley on every campus in the state.' "

The issue was clear: Can the Board of Regents order the firing of a faculty member on the grounds that she is a member of the Communist Party? Beyond this, what is the business of the regents? Is it to reach into one of the state universities and override a local decision reached by the faculty and the chancellor?

"This is a real case of academic freedom, because Angela Davis is an undesirable character to much of the public," said Chancellor Young, thirty-eight, the youngest chancellor in the university's history. "The place where you find out whether the system works is in tough cases, not the easy ones everybody agrees with."

Columnist William F. Buckley, Jr., posed the problem in somewhat different terms. He noted: "The law is very clear on that matter. The regents' business is to set policy for the University of California system. Now the policy the regents have traditionally set leaves it to the faculty to decide questions of academic merit. But what the regents have traditionally done is not justification for failing to use the regents' dormant powers in times of academic emergency. That these are parlous times in the universities would not be denied by anybody, least of all Angela Davis, who glories in the general convulsions, understanding them to be a way station to revolution."

Beyond this jurisdictional question is that of whether or not membership in the Communist Party is sufficient cause for denying anyone a position on the faculty of a state institution. There are, of course, many points of view on this subject. Professor Sidney Hook of New York University, a lifelong champion of academic freedom, and himself a socialist, examined the question at length in his book *Heresy, Yes, Conspiracy, No,* in which he concluded that membership in the Communist Party was sufficient ground for disqualification of any individual from a college faculty. In 1950, the Educational Policy Commission of the National Education Association filed a report condemning the hiring of Communist teachers. The report was signed by a number of college presidents, including James Bryant Conant.

On October 21, 1969, a Superior Court judge ruled that Angela Davis could not be barred from teaching in a state university on the sole ground that she is a Communist Party member. After a hearing on a taxpayers' suit filed by faculty supporters of Angela Davis, Judge Perry Pacht held that her firing was unconstitutional. He said that if she could be ousted for being a Communist, the regents could fire teachers for being members of other organizations. At this time Thomas J. Cunningham, general counsel for the regents, said that "all appropriate steps" would be taken in an attempt to have the ruling reversed.

With the court decision settled for the time being, the legal right of Angela Davis to teach seemed to have been established. During that academic year she taught classes in black literature, Kant and idealism, Marx and materialism, and one in existentialism that drew 422 students. *Newsweek* pointed out that "Miss Davis' courses that year were the most carefully monitored in the university; faculty members sat in, her lectures were tape recorded, students were thoroughly quizzed on her performance. . . . She was, by almost all accounts, well prepared, accessible to questions in or out of class, open to points of view different from her own, and very articulate." Professor Donald Kalish, then chairman of the philosophy department, stated "There were no flaws. She rated excellent in every area."

The real question of whether or not a Communist does, in fact, have a claim upon the university with regard to "academic freedom" was rarely argued in anything but nebulous terms at the time during which the Angela Davis case received national attention and interest. Professor Sidney Hook, for example, defines "academic freedom" as the freedom to pursue the truth without "any control or authority except the control or authority of the rational methods by which truth is established." Communists are disqualified as discoverers or disseminators of truth, under this theory, not for mere membership in the Party, but because membership implies a commitment to practice educational fraud. Communist beliefs are heretical, but Party membership is conspiratorial.

[114]

Specifically, a Communist knowingly accepts three obligations: (1) to inject a Marxist-Leninist analysis into every classroom; (2) without exposing himself, to exploit his teaching position so as to give students a working-class education; and (3) to go beyond injecting Marxist-Leninist doctrines into his teaching by conducting struggles around the school in a truly Bolshevik manner.

In his volume *Academic Freedom and Academic Anarchy,* published in June, 1968, Professor Hook declares that every Party member is instructed to "angle or slant his position in the classroom, and to indoctrinate for the party line." Though Professor Hook does not think that Communists who are already faculty members should be automatically dismissed, he does favor not hiring Communists in the first place, since the presumption of intent to commit educational fraud is sufficiently strong.

Are Communists really subjected to rigid discipline today, or has this changed over the years? The fact is that during this same period in Southern California Dorothy Healy, a Communist Party functionary, was discharged from the party because she criticized the Soviet Union's most recent invasion of Czechoslovakia. The presumption is strong that Angela Davis, as a member of the Communist Party in Southern California, would be equally controlled by this nonacademic, clearly totalitarian organization.

Beyond this, there is little discussion of what the term "academic freedom" means historically. Many seem to think that it means that a faculty member can say and do whatever he wants to say or do, and that those who have employed him and pay his salary (in this instance the taxpayers of California) have no recourse if they do not approve and if they feel that the faculty member's statements and actions violate his role as teacher and scholar.

In his important volume *The Degradation of the Academic Dogma,* Professor Robert Nisbet, of the University of Pennsylvania, points out that with regard to the university both tenure and freedom "spring from the profoundly feudal character of the academic community. . . . Each is closely, even functionally related to the concept of honor . . . both concepts, tenure and

[115]

freedom, are lineally descended from the most cherished of feudal legal concepts, liberty.

"A liberty," notes Professor Nisbet, "was no more than an enclave, a corporate autonomy in society that deserved its own freedom to act in porportion to the honor of its mission, the protection it gave to its members, and the importance of its contribution to society."

Concerning academic freedom in particular, Professor Nisbet writes of "the belief in rights to a special kind of security and position and a special kind of freedom of thought. Despite the astute efforts of many academic spokesmen to persuade the public—and other parts of the larger intellectual establishment—that academic freedom is no more than a simple derivation from the Bill of Rights, it is anything but this. It is instead the declaration that the university or college is a liberty, endowed with certain rights that do not belong to a business enterprise or government bureau. When medieval lawyers referred to a 'liberty' they had in mind one or other of the corporate groups, usually chartered, that could claim autonomy in society and, within this autonomy, freedom of action by members of the 'liberty.' The medieval university was a liberty in this sense . . . we miss utterly the nature of this claim to the special kind of freedom that is contained in the concept of academic freedom if we do not see its once-questioned linkage to the other concepts of honor and tenure. . . . Tenure is— or was—the bond of protection for individuals possessed of knightly honor who gave faithfully and fully their services to the academic community."

"Recently," Professor Nisbet continues, "the idea of academic freedom has become confused. We find it often invoked to justify a professor's nonacademic activities or beliefs in the surrounding social order. It is used, in short, as a kind of extra prop for the constitutional freedoms that he shares with other citizens . . . the historic concept of academic freedom was limited to faculties and faculty members. . . . Academic freedom meant to these scholars who founded the wider guild of professors in the United States freedom for the academic man: not freedom for political man, economic man, or for those who believed the university to be primarily a privileged sanctuary for each and every dereliction, delinquency, and desolation of intellect known since Adam."

The claim of "academic freedom" made for and by Angela Davis was by no means the kind of academic freedom referred to by Professor Nisbet. It was not that Angela Davis be free to pursue scholarship and teach philosophy, but that she be free to hold a faculty position at a public university while spending the bulk of her time working for the overthrow of society, and using her faculty position not to search for truth but to propagandize for revolution. Angela had long ago accepted the New Left philosophy of the university as a staging ground for revolution rather than as a repository for wisdom and a center of teaching and scholarship. Since Angela Davis had rejected a large part of the role meant to be fulfilled by an academic person, her pronouncements with regard to academic freedom, and those of her supporters, must be viewed as being less than completely frank.

Discussing this point, columnist William Buckley writes, "It is being too widely accepted that Angela Davis has otherwise than her membership in the Communist Party an exemplary record and was clearly entitled to reappointment. It isn't so. Miss Davis doesn't even have her doctorate. The faculty committee that looked into her case . . . conceded a 'concern' with the 'proposal for giving [her] appointment an unwarranted priority in the face of other . . . more pressing faculty staffing needs.' Miss Davis is a quite rabid revolutionary whose disdain for decorum is among revolutionary paraphernalia. Decorum doesn't consist in limiting your conversation to the weather when addressing the Queen of England."

Mr. Buckley points out that decorum is the kind of thing James Rowland Angell was talking about when, as President of Yale University, he wrote that "if university men are to claim freedom of teaching and freedom of thought and speech, they must in turn justify the claim not only by a decent respect for the opinions of mankind but also by sobriety of utterance on acutely controversial issues. They must be sensitive to the dictates of good sense and good taste."

Angela Davis' words during the period of her controversy with regents of the California university system were hardly temperate. In a public speech on the regents' role in the People's Park controversy she declared: "They killed, they brutalized, they murdered human beings." Discussing what to do to correct inequities, she stated: "Are we going to write resolutions and condemn them? . . . Or are we going to openly declare war against them? And that's what we have to start talking about, a general strike, demonstrative actions which will show pig forces what we can do."

Angela told her listeners, "We should call . . . things by their name. When people start saying that we ought to subvert, that we are subversive, we should say, Hell yes, we are subversive. Hell yes, and we're going to continue to be subversive until we have subverted this whole goddamned system of oppression."

Angela Davis has not, in reality, denied that her role at UCLA was primarily political, and not academic or scholarly in any traditional sense. "I think that education is inherently political," Angela has said quite openly. The fact is that the faculty and administration that voted to keep her were also engaged in politics. Both Angela and her faculty supporters sought a confrontation with the regents and this they received.

At the completion of her first year of teaching and while her case was before the California Supreme Court, the decision had to be made about whether or not Angela Davis was to be rehired for the 1970–71 school year. Chancellor Young recommended to the regents that Angela be rehired for another year, as is done routinely with probationary teachers if their work has been satisfactory. President Hitch backed him up.

The regents retaliated in a closed-door session by voting 15 to 6 to relieve Young and Hitch "of any further authority or responsibility" in the Davis case. The regents set June 19 for a decision on whether or not to fire her again. The date was after the end of the spring academic quarter, and at a time when few students would be on the UCLA campus. Regents chairman Dewitt Higgs said that while he felt hiring authority in general should rest with Hitch and Young, "as a regent I have ultimate authority, and responsibility, under the state constitution. It's mine and nobody else's."

Angela responded defiantly, saying that she would be back on the UCLA campus the following fall regardless of what the regents did. She was backed by the powerful academic senate which voted to pay her from personal donations, if necessary, the following year.

The playing out of what Chancellor Young described as "this Greek tragedy" fit in with the program of protest that Angela Davis had outlined as her goal in a speech before a fund-raising banquet for the Communist Party newspaper *People's World,* shortly after she was hired.

"An educator," Angela said, "should criticize and unmask predominant ideas for what they are." They should "expose academic freedom as a real farce" and test the validity of "bourgeois democratic concepts" such as freedom of speech, freedom of the press, and freedom of thought. Capitalism, she said, will cancel out these freedoms when the suppressed try to use them to their own advantage. "It is up to us to push these freedoms to their very limits. We have to fight these proponents of selective democracy and expose the limits of bourgeois democracy."

For a dedicated revolutionary who herself possessed no allegiance to the concept of academic freedom, who supported the totalitarian regimes of the Soviet Union and China which had eliminated the very freedoms of speech, press and thought which she argued were imperfect in the "bourgeois democracy" of the United States, this might seem contradictory. It is, however, the traditional pattern of Communists.

Long ago, Lenin urged those who were working for the Communist revolution to associate themselves with "good" ideas. Communism, it must be remembered, has never come to power in any country because the people were supporters of the philosophy of Marxism-Leninism. Lenin himself promised the people of Russia "bread, peace, and land," not communism. Mao Tse-tung told the people of China that he was an agrarian reformer, not a Communist. Castro came to power as an advocate of Western-style democracy, not communism. Once in power, however, all of these men ignored the promises they had made, and imposed upon the people of their countries as harsh a tyranny as the world has ever seen.

The clever Communist use of language to mislead those who would oppose them if they truly understood their goals is as old

[119]

as the Russian Revolution itself. In the early 1900s, Lenin and his Bolshevik supporters could not openly call for the overthrow of the Czarist government and express other radical views in their newspaper and in their handbills. To circumvent this difficulty, Lenin devised what he called an Aesopian language by employing innocuous words which disguised their real meaning. Instead of calling for "revolution," Lenin would advocate "reform," and he would refer to the "strict Marxists" instead of to the "Bolsheviks." In this way, Lenin proved quite successful in passing along revolutionary messages to his followers without detection.

By 1935, Soviet leaders came to realize that orthodox Marxist expressions such as "terror," "class warfare," "dictatorship of the proletariat," "revolution," and "labor armies" were frightening off potential support for the Communist movement. As a result, a new linguistic movement was adopted. In his study *Language as a Communist Weapon,* Professor Stefan Possony writes, "The Seventh World Congress of the Communist International laid down the law that Communists no longer should use 'sectarian language.' This means, quite simply, that the Communist message should be couched in terms which have a positive ring in the ears of the audience. Communism must be dressed up as something like democratic liberalism or patriotic nationalism. Offensive and locally unfamiliar terms must be avoided. . . . At the Seventh Comintern Congress . . . the party —the 'world authority,' that is—specifically authorized this usage of 'nonsectarian language,' which meant that any good Communist would now be able to use language which is not to be found in the classical writing of Marx and Lenin but occurs in Jefferson, Mill—or Jane Addams."

Seen in this context, it does not seem unusual for a Communist such as Angela Davis, whose goal is the destruction of the very freedoms she appeals to in her own defense, to play upon our "bourgeois" principles of justice and fairness. America becomes a "tyranny" and the Soviet Union a "just society" only when terms have ceased to have any objective meaning. This, of course, is the kind of language which George Orwell wrote of in his book *1984:*

"Newspeak was the official language of Oceania and had

been devised to meet the ideological needs of Ingsoc, or English Socialism. The purpose of Newspeak was not only to provide a medium of expression for the worldview and mental habits proper to the devotees of Ingsoc, but to make all other modes of thought impossible. . . . Its vocabulary was so constructed as to give exact and often very subtle expression to every meaning that a Party member could properly wish to express, while excluding all other meanings and also the possibility of arriving at them by indirect methods."

Angela Davis was quite successful in convincing her faculty colleagues that the real question involved was one of academic freedom and justice. To the extent that they accepted this thesis, they may, in reality, have misunderstood what was really occurring before them. They did so, it seems, with both eagerness and enthusiasm.

During her year of teaching, professors attended Angela's classes to evaluate them for her department head. Without exception they described her as an excellent teacher. "I have never seen a set of course evaluations so favorable," says David Kaplan, acting head of the Philosophy Department. Herbert Morris, a professor of law and philosophy, was one of the faculty who checked her classes. "I found the lectures and discussions stimulating," he said. "There was absolutely nothing that could be regarded even remotely as indoctrination. Indeed, the heavy and apparent emphasis was on getting the students to think for themselves."

Students, faculty, and administration appeared clearly to support Angela and her right to continue teaching at UCLA. Angela herself was defiant, declaring "There's no question about it—I'm not leaving this state or this city or this campus." On the other side were Governor Ronald Reagan, the majority of the regents, most state officials and, if public opinion polls were accurate at that time, the majority of the people of California.

Edward W. Pauley, one of the twenty-four regents, stated, "I don't propose to be a member of a board of regents or trustees that employs Communists or lets them propound their propaganda for a party that advocates the overthrow of the government of the United States." Regent John Canaday noted that the board has had a ban on hiring Communists for university jobs for thirty years. The board had recently reaffirmed that policy. "We still believe that the same fundamental reasoning that caused regents to ban Communists from teaching in 1940—because they were not free from party discipline—is valid today," Canaday said.

Governor Reagan said that professors who defend Angela Davis "should ask themselves whether there has been a change in the Communist Party—whether a member of the Communist Party can be independent and not follow party dogma while teaching." He answered himself: "I don't think so, but the professors aren't interested in that."

Reagan also accused Young and Kalish of deliberately violating the anti-Communist rule "as a provocation to bring about a confrontation." Both Young and Kalish denied knowing of Angela Davis' Communist background before she was hired, and Young said that he had nothing to do personally with her being hired. Kalish said that he was simply searching for a black faculty member when a friend told him about Angela Davis and her impressive credentials. Kalish said that he learned she had a job offer from Swarthmore College and quickly brought her before the philosophy faculty for an interview. She made "an extremely calm, sophisticated and mature appearance," he said. The committee approved her and she signed a contract as an untenured assistant professor.

On June 19, 1970, Angela was told that she no longer could teach at UCLA. University regents voted 15 to 6 against renewing her one-year contract. The board voted against renewing her contract this time not on the grounds that she was a member of the Communist Party, but because she had made "extreme" and "inflammatory" political speeches during the year. They also said that she had not progressed satisfactorily on her Ph.D. dissertation.

While noting that both faculty members and students had rated her an excellent teacher, the fifteen regents maintained that her speeches were "so extreme, so antithetical to the protection of academic freedom and so obviously deliberately false in several respects as to be inconsistent with qualification" to

[122]

teach. She often described policemen as "pigs," the regents said.

As the regents voted in a three-hour closed session, Angela Davis was marching outside the State Building in a picket line protesting murder charges against three blacks accused of killing a Soledad Prison guard in Salinas, California. The Soledad case was later to play a major part in Angela Davis' life, leading to the charge of murder for which she was tried.

Later, wearing jeans in her office at UCLA, she graded papers. There she told a newsman that the regents had "used all kinds of excuses to do what they set out to do last fall." Asked if she would teach the following fall if the faculty succeeded in circumventing the regents and providing facilities, salary, and course credit for her classes, she said that she probably would, but wanted "to know more about the conditions."

The university faculty across the state decided earlier—in anticipation of the regents' action—to take various steps and set up committees to make arrangements. Governor Reagan told newsmen at the meeting that he would oppose all efforts to allow Angela Davis to teach, even unofficially on campus. "There are rules with regard to the use of university facilities," he said. "If they want to constitute their own teaching group and set up a little schoolhouse somewhere, that's fine."

The UCLA branch of the American Federation of Teachers held a heated and agonized debate over whether to strike in Angela's defense. A young woman professor recalls the close of the session as rather strange. "Angela arrived, as usual, at the tail end of the meeting, with her phalanx, after we had voted not to strike. She was asked whether she had anything she wanted to say, and said, yes, she certainly hoped the union was going to strike. She was very quiet and polite and her attitude suggested that, well, this was our problem." Helen Dudar, writing in the *New York Post,* notes that "The narrator was hard put to explain why the episode struck her as strange. Mostly, she supposes, it was the sensation she had that Angela Davis had presented herself at that moment, not as a participant, but in some, odd, detached way, as an object."

In many respects, the entire discussion about whether or not

Angela Davis should have been permitted to continue teaching at UCLA avoided any real consideration of the question of what academic freedom, in fact, means and whether or not a Communist can fulfill the function that has traditionally been that of a teacher and a scholar. There is the additional question of whether or not a Communist—one pledged to the destruction of the existing order and its replacement with a contrary, totalitarian order—should be permitted to teach at an institution paid for by the taxpayers. In other words, should organized society financially support and encourage those who are working for its destruction?

In testimony before the U.S. Senate Internal Security Subcommittee on March 10, 1953, Dr. Bella V. Dodd, a former leading Communist official and teacher in New York City for many years, offered a relevant appraisal from first-hand experience. Miss Dodd, in her testimony, discussed slanting instruction to fit the "party line," stating that "all Communist teachers who read the literature of the Communist Party and of the Communist movement cannot help but slant their teaching in that direction. I was a teacher of economics and political science, and it was very easy for me to slant my teaching that way. As a matter of fact, I wasn't even conscious of slanting it. That was the way I was teaching it, because I had become imbued with the whole philosophy and system of communism. Yes, communism is a total philosophy. If you believe in it, you live it, you breathe it, you teach it . . . you take it with you twenty-four hours a day, seven days a week. . . . [The students] wouldn't recognize it as communism; nobody else might recognize it as communism. But there is no doubt in my mind that the Communist teacher teaches the Communist way."

Dr. Dodd was asked whether a Communist teacher or professor was free to pursue the highest ideal of academic freedom and freedom of inquiry—the search for truth, wherever it might lead. She answered: ". . . [in Russia] they had to accept the Communist Party determination as to what was the truth. Within our country, we have any number of illustrations of both professors and writers who from time to time have been called up before the control commission because they have

[124]

either written or spoken or done that which was contrary to the Marxist-Leninist philosophy."

Thus, the testimony of Bella Dodd before the Senate committee explained the rigid control and supervision that the party holds over a Communist teacher to assure adherence to the "party line." This "party line" changes frequently and rapidly and often irrationally, and Communist Party members must change along with it. Many who were most vigorous in defending Angela Davis' right to continue teaching at UCLA were also the least informed about the history of communism in America, and the control it exercises over its adherents.

How many remember, for example, how the Communists denounced Franklin Roosevelt in the early 1930s? A typical *Daily Worker* article on the New Deal, appearing November 11, 1933, is captioned "Roosevelt and Mussolini—Blood Brothers." A Moscow resolution, adopted in 1935 just before the change of the "line" on the subject, instructed Communist parties in all capitalist countries to "fight against military expenditures . . . against militarization measures taken by capitalist governments." A few months later the same parties would be calling for bigger armaments, now considering fascism and Nazism as enemies.

At the Seventh Party Congress in Moscow, under the chairmanship of Georgi Dimitrov in the summer of 1935, the chairman stated: "Comrades, you remember the ancient tale of the capture of Troy. Troy was inaccessible to the armies attacking her, thanks to her impregnable walls. And the attacking army, after suffering many sacrifices, was unable to achieve victory until with the aid of the famous Trojan Horse it managed to penetrate to the very heart of the enemy's camp." He went on to urge that Communists make friends of everyone in their own countries and "penetrate the very heart of the enemy's camp." "We must," he said, "utilize antifascist mass organizations as the Trojan Horse. Whoever does not understand such tactics or finds them degrading is a babbler and no revolutionary."

Communist leader Earl Browder followed this advice and declared, "We are an American party composed of American citizens. We view all our problems in the light of the national interest of the United States." The Communist Party described its members as "political descendants of traditional American democracy as founded by Thomas Jefferson."

On October 4, 1937, the *Daily Worker* reported U.S. Communist leader William Z. Foster as opposed to those who urged that the United States stay out of the troubles which were beginning in Europe. He stated: "This is isolationism pure and simple; it is the absurd theory that the United States can avoid the fascist aggressors by running away from them." Then, after the pact between the Soviet Union and Nazi Germany, the American Communists shifted gears completely. In 1940 the party stated that "The war between the Allies and Germany is a struggle between rival imperialist powers, hence the workers have no interest in supporting either group in the contest."

Commenting upon these two contradictory statements, both by William Z. Foster, Eugene Lyons noted, "Either of these statements may be defended. Both statements coming from the same leader of a political party constitute prima facie evidence of political trickery."

Yet, during that period, many American liberals refused to recognize communism for what it was, or the American Communist Party for what it was, essentially the agent of a foreign government which permitted itself to be dictated to by that government. One day the party considered Nazism an evil, then it became a friendly system, and then, after Hitler attacked the Soviet Union, it became an evil again. And American Communists changed with the party line. Could a professor searching for truth and employed to present established truth and discover new truth, fulfill that mission while also remaining loyal to the ever-changing Communist Party line? This proposition, which the UCLA faculty seemed to endorse in the case of Angela Davis, is as highly suspect today as it was in the years before World War II.

At the beginning of World War II, the Rev. John Haynes Holmes, the distinguished minister of the Community Church of New York and a long-time spokesman for liberal causes, chastised his fellow liberals for their blindness. He wrote the following:

"If we liberals were right on certain single aspects of the

[126]

Russian Revolution, we were wrong, disgracefully wrong, on the question as a whole. We were wrong because, in our enthusiasm over Russia's liberation from the czar, our hope for the further liberation of the Russian people from economic as well as political serfdom and our vision of a new world springing from the womb of this Russian experiment, we permitted ourselves to condone wrongs that we knew must be wrongs. We consented to violations of principle that we knew to be fatal to the moral integrity of mankind.

"We defended, or at least apologized for, evils in the case of Russia which horrified us wherever else they appeared, and by whomsoever else they were done. We accepted covertly, if not openly, the most dangerous and ultimately disastrous idea that can lodge within the human mind, namely that the end justifies the means."

The men who hired Angela Davis and the faculty which supported her right to continue as an employe of UCLA tended to overlook the very clear and public record which Angela had been busy making up to that point. While the chairman of the Philosophy Department and the University Chancellor denied any knowledge of Angela's membership in the Communist Party, they could hardly deny knowledge of the radical role she played on the San Diego campus. Did they not know that it was Angela Davis who was a leader in the move to create a college for minority students, to be called the Lumumba-Zapata College? The names refer to Patrice Lumumba, the late assassinated leader of the Congo, and Emiliano Zapata, the Mexican revolutionary hero. Along with the establishment of the Third World College, there were many other demands.

It was Angela Davis who wrote these demands, according to Avrum Stroll, chairman of the Department of Philosophy at the University of California at San Diego. An enrollment of 70 percent blacks and Mexican-Americans in this college was one of the demands. Moreover, the architects, general contractors, subcontractors and all supervisory personnel had to come from the minority community. There would also be minority control of budget, faculty, curriculum and admission quotas. Further demands, written by Angela Davis, included that minority students "must be fully supported with funds supplied by the university to the extent that they will not have to work or take out loans."

By any estimate, these demands call for the establishment of a political not an educational institution. It is based upon racial and not educational distinctions, and its goal is racial and political rather than scholarly. The public campaign led by Angela Davis for these demands made it clear to those who were to later employ her at UCLA that her view of the university was not an academic view but, instead, was the view enunciated by her contemporaries and colleagues in the New Left. Those who showed surprise must have been play-acting. Most, however, argued that despite her activist views and role, she should have been employed at UCLA. This group is, of course, more difficult to explain and understand.

While there is much discussion about Angela's "outstanding" qualifications for the UCLA teaching position, few are aware of the information that was brought to light by the *Santa Monica Evening Outlook*—that within the UCLA Philosophy Department itself a vote was taken concerning whether or not Angela Davis should be hired. The vote was eight for, five against, and three abstentions. This was hardly an overwhelming vote of confidence. Half of the department refused to support hiring Angela Davis, underlining her lack of credentials and qualifications for the position, aside from her political views and activities.

Why are so many American college professors, such as those who composed the UCLA faculty, willing to accept a Communist political activist within the community of scholars? Is it due to some sophisticated understanding of the role of the university and of academic freedom that somehow escapes others, or is it based upon imperatives which have little to do with traditional scholarly considerations? Professor Edward Bloomberg, himself a professor at the University of California at Riverside, confronts some of these questions in his book *Student Violence,* published in 1970. Professor Bloomberg indicts his colleagues for what he considers to be a variety of sins and shortcomings and places before them the responsibility for the politicization we have recently witnessed on American college and university campuses.

[128]

He notes, ". . . from the character of the American professor it is easy to deduce his attitude toward American society. His ego is constantly pricked by the larger public. He cannot help comparing his position in the pecking order with that of his colleagues from other countries. In France and Germany few have more prestige than 'Monsieur le professeur' or 'Herr Professor.' The little people of these countries bow obsequiously to professors, and literati make politics. While in America prominent businessmen are the most respected, in Europe the professor, the journalist, the writer—the intellectuals—are considered the ultimate sources of wisdom."

Dr. Bloomberg points out that "Whereas in the USSR, that worker's paradise, a professor earns three times more than a skilled worker, in the United States their pay is approximately equal. Our market economy has placed a lower value on the professor than any statist nation. Despite the lip service he pays to egalitarianism, this irks him. It is confirmation of that inferiority he senses in himself. He is therefore predisposed to critiques of the country which treats him so badly, especially to those that come from Europe, where a learned man is treated with considerable respect."

What may be true of the faculty members at UCLA and at other campuses is not so much that they are sympathetic with communism, or with the other ideas expressed by Angela Davis and her followers. The fact may be that it is their adherence to moral relativism rather than to any particular ideology that causes them to rise in defense of *any* idea against *any* form of restraint.

Discussing this point, Dr. Bloomberg states, ". . . absolute relativism is the fashion right now. Few intellectuals would be prepared to defend anything as absolutely true or absolutely good. The result is that many feel—without knowing precisely why—that nothing can be really false or evil. Therefore nothing is absolutely forbidden. . . . If one understands the proposition 'Everything is relative' is relative, how can one believe it? A contradictory idea which becomes current usually does more mischief than a clear one, no matter how evil. Since one cannot understand a contradiction, one renounces comprehension in favor of mystic complicity with a foolish refrain. Thought

[129]

becomes 'irrelevant,' and the predisposition to violence goes unchecked."

The moral relativist, according to this view, finds himself in an awkward position: "Holding no opinion to be true, he accepts all statements as equally gratuitous. When discussing an issue, he says, 'I feel that . . .' or 'It seems to me that. . . .' He never attempts to use logic to refute another's opinion or to defend his. All man can do, according to him, is 'express' himself. He can make no claim to truth. In the name of what would he do so? He must therefore place side by side as equals authoritarianism and reason, intolerance and tolerance, good and evil, absolutism and relativism. This is a perfect formula for the elimination of all tolerance, because it has no criterion for refuting intolerance."

Thus Angela Davis, the disciple of Herbert Marcuse—who openly mocks the idea of tolerance and free speech, except for ideas which he has, in advance, ordained to be "correct"—successfully used the moral relativism and general belief in tolerance of the UCLA faculty to bolster her own case, and her alleged "right" to preach violence, revolution and intolerance at the expense of the taxpayers of California to their children. This she did, of course, only until the regents of the university finally refused to renew her contract.

One of the crusades that Angela began at this time, which had a dramatic impact upon the decision of the regents, and which led directly to the more serious charge of murder against her, was that of her championing the case of the "Soledad Brothers." Soledad is the name of a state correctional institution south of San Francisco. The inmate population is 2,570, with 30 percent Mexican-American and 20 percent black. In January, 1970, a brawl broke out in an exercise yard among black inmates. A tower guard blew a whistle, and then began shooting. Three black men were killed and one guard was wounded. Three days later, a twenty-six-year old guard, John Vincent Mills, was beaten, dragged up three flights of concrete steps and tossed to his death on the cellblock floor below. Beside him was a note: "One down, two to go."

Three convicts, George L. Jackson, twenty-nine, John Cluchette, twenty-eight, and Fletta Drumgo, twenty-five, were indicted for Mills' slaying. They became the "Soledad Brothers," and Angela Davis became one of their foremost public champions. George Jackson's younger brother, Jonathan, seventeen, became her almost constant companion and bodyguard.

In the period prior to the regents' action refusing to rehire her, Angela had been spending a good deal of time in the crusade for the Soledad Brothers. Though she pledged to fight the second firing, that of June 19, 1970, in the courts, she was spending most of her time with the younger Jackson in the San Francisco area on the Soledad Brothers case.

During this period, Angela began a correspondence with George Jackson, one of the Soledad Brothers. Angela Davis' role and her own life cannot be adequately understood without also understanding the life—and the thoughts—of George Jackson. At this time, during her year of teaching at UCLA, Angela Davis tied her life closely to that of George Jackson, and it was this which catapulted her name to the national headlines. It was at this time that she abandoned any idea of an academic life and cast her lot completely with the life of revolutionary activism.

When he was eighteen, George Jackson was sentenced from one year to life for stealing $70 from a gas station. This was the culmination of a boyhood complete with numerous run-ins with the police for a variety of reasons and was the incident that landed him in Soledad.

The Soledad Brothers quickly gained fame in the radical movement as the Black Panthers, the Communist Party, and other activist groups rose in their defense. Panther leader Huey P. Newton placed George Jackson's importance in this perspective in a talk at San Luis Obispo, California, on June 30, 1970: "George Jackson is a living legend throughout the prison system. Every inmate that I've talked to, every convict who has been around the California prisons for any length of time, knows about George and has high regard for him. Even some of the white 'racist' inmates have respect for him because they view him as a man who is totally straight. They know he is going to do exactly what he says he is going to do. They know George is a 'for-real' man. George has rejected even the possibility of getting out of prison because he refuses to violate his

[131]

own integrity or the integrity of his fellow inmates. He refuses to compromise in any way to gain personal privilege. He has stood up and let himself be counted regardless of personal cost. George is a true revolutionary."

At no time was the real innocence or guilt of George Jackson or the other Soledad Brothers really the question. They rapidly became revolutionary symbols and, as such, Angela Davis made them an intrinsic and, later, almost total part of her own life and of her own revolutionary rhetoric. This, in effect, became the dominating "cause" in her life.

Angela described in her own words the manner in which the case of the Soledad Brothers had excited her attention and concern and had turned her away from the raging controversy over her teaching position at UCLA. Writing in *Ebony* magazine, she tells this story:

"While fighting for the right of a Communist—a Black woman Communist—to teach at UCLA, I encountered a case with striking parallels to my own, only infinitely more sinister, far more deadly. The events in that case had also unfolded in one of the key institutions which form the groundwork of the society. I was battling on the relatively safe terrain of the universities—industries designed to generate proficient architects and advocates of the status quo. Black men, however, were battling on the exceedingly perilous terrain of the prisons— coercive structures designed primarily to punish and erode individuals who have been victims of the selfsame status quo upheld by the universities.

"My job was in jeopardy because I had attempted in my small way and as a member of the Communist Party to defend the rights, interests and visions of my people. But in Soledad Prison, there were three Black men, one an avowed Marxist-Leninist, all three vehement exponents of Black liberation, whose very lives were in jeopardy as a consequence of their principled political stand. Had I continued to wage my own struggle without exposing the threads which tied it to the fight which had to be conducted around political repression in the prisons, I could have been correctly accused of the utmost hypocrisy."

Angela recalls, "During this period, I was bombarded with

advice to stick to the single issue of academic freedom: restricting my utterances to a defense of the right of any qualified individual to teach, unhampered by tests of a political nature, I would surely win ample support to counter Reagan's plans to fire me. Even reactionary academicians would be compelled to concede, however reluctantly, the formal principle of academic freedom."

Angela refused to take that advice that had been given to her. Instead, she chose to abandon the fight for her UCLA teaching position and to involve herself almost totally at this time with the case of the Soledad Brothers. She notes: "Notwithstanding these words from the wise, I elected to assume, or at least to approximate, the posture which I felt most closely befitted a revolutionary. And while it is true that some professors and students withdrew their support, many were now struck by the similarity between my case and the vicious predicament in which the Soledad Brothers were enmeshed. Needless to say, Black people in general instinctively grasped the affinity and generally were prepared to fight on both fronts."

Angela does not go to very great lengths to argue that the Soledad Brothers are innocent of the murder charges leveled against them. She is noncommittal on this point when she writes, "In the wake of an unprovoked assassination of three militant Blacks in January, 1970, a guard at Soledad Prison was killed. Brothers Jackson, Drumgo, and Clutchette were selected to do penance." Their real offense, she argues, was not the murder of the prison guard, which, she seems to be saying, they may or may not have committed. The *real* offense was something different: it "has been their remarkable contributions to the creation of anti-establishment consciousness in California prisons—among Blacks, but also among Chicanos and whites."

What was on trial in reality, Angela argued, was not the question of whether or not the Soledad Brothers did, in fact, commit the murder of which they were accused. The real question was "the complex, oppressive fabric of prison life as well as the contemporary political function of the penal system." Virtually overlooked is the fact that none of the Soledad Brothers was originally imprisoned for his revolutionary rhetoric.

As Angela admits, "they were initiated into the Black Liberation struggle and achieved political maturity during the course of their lives in prison." Originally, Fleeta Drumgo and John Clutchette had been sent to prison after being found guilty of second-degree burglary, and George Jackson after being found guilty of second-degree robbery, after a string of other offenses. None of these three men had been a political thinker, either revolutionary or otherwise. They were, it seems, criminals who had been found guilty of law violations which would have made them criminals in any society, capitalist or communist, democratic or totalitarian. Yet, they served a symbolic radical purpose, and Angela Davis quickly made their case her own.

Prisons, according to Angela Davis, are viewed differently by blacks and whites. Whites accept them, while blacks do not. She presents this assessment: "Most whites take the existence of prisons for granted—the vast majority of them never anticipate ever being locked up. Until recently even blacks, most of whom can expect at some time to encounter the reality of imprisonment directly or through a member of the family, have tended to accept prisons, however demeaning and however oppressive, as unavoidable. We had to wait for our brothers and sisters behind bars to uncover not only the ruthlessness of life in the dungeons, but also the repressive political function they serve."

Overlooking the fact that the three Soledad Brothers in question were in prison for having been found guilty of committing real crimes, Angela writes of "crowds of blacks, Chicanos, Puerto Ricans snatched away from their organizing activities in ghettos and barrios and sequestered in jails and prisons." Yet the Soledad Brothers were not politically active at any time in their lives before being found guilty of criminal actions. Angela Davis, in arguing against the use of police and prison systems to persecute black and other minority group political activists, has made a case that had little to do with the Soledad Brothers. These three men were not arrested and did not find themselves in prison because of their political views, yet it was on the basis of their new-found political radicalism that their case appealed to Angela Davis.

The fact is, of course, that the Communist Party and other political radicals had been working very hard within the prison systems of the country to stir up discontent among the prisoners and to channel that discontent into a revolutionary critique of society. Angela Davis was only doing her job as a revolutionary in exploiting the situation at Soledad. The guilt or innocence of the three men involved was really beside the point.

George Jackson himself was quite frank in discussing the organizing activities of Black Panthers and others within the prisons of California. In an interview published in *The Black Panther* of August 28, 1971, he was asked this question: "In the past six months, a profound change has occurred in the prison population, in terms of the consciousness of the inmates, whereas before they had been easily divided by racism, which was instigated by the prison authorities. At that time they were beginning to see the prison authorities as their enemies and inmates of all races as their natural allies. Can you tell us how that consciousness developed, how extensive it is, and what forms it took?"

Jackson replied: "Well, to begin with, of course, the recent influx of the political teachers, the political animals, from the Black Panther Party—I think they were first instrumental in the changes from conservatism that prisoners in the prison population and people, in general, here in fascist America live in. At one time the prison population, the prisoner class could have been considered one of the most conservative classes in the country. . . . We'll give credit first to the Party, and to the system for placing political teachers at our disposal here. Secondly, the support that our movement has gotten from partisans from the street, from the outside. The average convict considers himself the doomed man right from the beginning. And that ray of hope, or sense of community created by the recent expressions of solidarity from the street, that [ray] found effect on the revolutionary consciousness inside the joint. It's always been my contention that if we could raise the hard-left military and political cadre in fascist America, that cadre would come from either the prisons or the dissident elements within the armed forces."

Jackson was next asked what forms this new consciousness took within the prisons. He replied, "Some years ago, the rise

[135]

of the Black revolutionary . . . created situations here in the joint that caused polarization between all Blacks and all Whites regardless of status. And by status I mean convict-cop, convict-pig. In other words, I'm saying that the prisoner code broke down as a result of the White convicts being threatened by the political thrust and the open antipathy demonstrated by Blacks against Whites in general. At the time I guess I was part of it, too. At the time we made no efforts to distinguish between the White convict and the White guard. Because the White convicts identified openly and clearly and without reservations with right-wing ideas, and racism. So when we'd strike, we'd strike with both barrels: one at the convict, and one at the pig. And some of it is our fault. Of course, revolution is a process. We're going through a process. And well, that's the background."

The new political consciousness, according to Jackson, "stems from the fact that . . . the political teacher, the Black Panther 'concentration camp,' as a result of the political thrust on the street, brought new ideas. You know revolutionary, scientific socialism, and anti-racism. And we attempted to make them understand that we're all equally uniformly repressed by the administration."

Discussing the future of the prisons and the relationship between the prison movement and the outside movement, Jackson stated, ". . . the building of revolutionary consciousness of the prisoner class is paramount in the over-all development of a hard-left revolutionary cadre. Of course the revolution has to be carried by the masses. But we need a cadre; we need a bodyguard; a political worker needs a bodyguard. We see ourselves as performing that function. The terms of existence here in the joint conditions the brothers for that type of work. Although I have become more political recently, from listening to Comrade Newton, and from reading the Party paper, I've gained a clearer understanding of the tie-in between political and military activities. I still see my function as military."

Not hesitating to declare his belief in the use of violence, Jackson stated, "I feel that any movement on our part, political, will have to be accompanied by a latent threat. And all the

[136]

projects for survival that Comrade Newton has started and developed, I think that they're going to have to be defended. And that defense is going to depend upon cadre, cadre violence, secret sort of stuff, that we can't go into here too extensively."

It is clear that the Black Panther Party, by its own admission a Marxist-Leninist organization, is systematically exploiting social forces and aiming to destroy the institutions of American society by force and violence. Communists, it must be remembered, use social forces; they do not create them. One social force that they are using effectively is the discontent of the prison population. Conditions in prisons are, in many instances, appalling. The Communists are using the often justifiable resentment of prisoners to assist them in advancing their program for the destruction of society. Needless to say, the majority of prisoners are not aware that they are being used in this way.

Angela Davis abandoned her academic career, and all of the things that had been most important to her until her recent turn toward political activism, in order to conduct the campaign on behalf of the Soledad Brothers. She crusaded for these prisoners not because of any expressed feeling that justice had been denied, that they were being unjustly accused, or, for that matter, for anything else that had to do with these particular individuals or this particular case. She saw that within the prisons of America existed a class of men who would be easy prey for revolutionaries—men who had valid grievances, who were discontented, and who felt that they had little to lose and much to gain by associating themselves with a movement or a philosophy. By believing in the Marxist doctrine which Angela Davis preached, murderers, rapists, and thieves came to look upon themselves as a persecuted minority of political prisoners and dissenters. They had nothing to lose, Angela seemed to be telling them, but their chains. Thus, if the proletariat, the traditional working class of Marxist theory, would not make the revolution, activists would find a substitute proletariat, and one place to begin was in the prisons. The Black Panthers, the Communist Party, and other groups with which Angela had been working since she first arrived at UCLA had long been busy striving to raise the political feelings and hostilities of prisoners in California. The Soledad case provided them with an excellent opportunity to further this work.

In addition to all of this, however, is the fact that Angela began, through correspondence, to develop a deep and personal relationship with George Jackson. Jackson had been busy educating himself during his years in prison, and Angela seemed to see in him a kindred spirit, a fellow fighter against all of the injustice, racism, and barbarity that she felt surrounded her in American society. To understand the fate that has befallen Angela Davis, it is essential to understand the evolution and tragic end of George Jackson.

5

When Angela Davis began her relationship with George Jackson she could hardly have imagined that it would all end with Jackson's being killed in an escape from San Quentin Prison, and his being eulogized as a hero and martyr, not only by black radicals but by many white liberals as well.

George Jackson achieved a measure of national attention when his collection of letters, published in a volume entitled *Soledad Brother,* appeared in October, 1970. In the introduction Jean Genêt writes, "George Jackson's style is clear, carefully pitched, simple and supple, as is his thinking. Anger alone illuminates his style and his thinking, and a kind of joy in anger. . . . What follows must be read as a manifesto, as a tract, as a call to rebellion, since it is that first of all." At the time of his death, Jackson was referred to as "A talented writer, a sensitive man, a potential leader and a political thinker of great persuasiveness" by Tom Wicker, columnist for the *New York Times.*

Was George Jackson really an intellectual, a man who had studied carefully and given serious thought and consideration to his own plight, to the plight of Negroes in America and to the future of the country? Was he a man whose political thinking was sophisticated, did he show an awareness of history, was he in touch with reality? The best way to answer such questions is to present at least a part of his thinking, the same thinking hailed by Tom Wicker, Angela Davis and a large portion of the press, and permit such thinking to, in effect, speak for itself.

Jackson believed that America was a fascist state and lamented the fact that the majority of Americans were not aware of the merits of alternative economic and political systems. "They can't see the merit in socialism and communism," he writes, "because they do not possess the qualities of rational thought, generosity, and magnanimity necessary to be part of a system. They cannot understand that 'From each according to his abilities to each according to his needs' is the only way men can live together without chaos."

Neither at this point nor at any later time in his letters did George Jackson express any awareness of the fact that the slogan "From each according to his abilities, to each according to his needs" is no place implemented in the worlds he calls "socialist" or "communist." The philosophy dominating the Communist world is something far different, which says "From each according to his ability, to each according to his work." If Jackson was aware of the "New Class" referred to so eloquently by the Yugoslav writer Milovan Djilas, he gives no indication of it.

In a letter written to his mother on September 16, 1966, Jackson does show some sign of understanding the duplicity involved in much of the Communist world. He wrote this to her on her birthday:

"Dear Mama, I wish you many happy returns in the birthday department. It sounds pretty empty I know, but that's all I have to offer now, a wish. . . . All is the same here. Each day that comes and goes is like the one before; being a good boy, going to church, reading all the saints, and getting good ratings on my job for the proper attitudes.

"Are you well, are you getting any of the pleasant things that life in these United States offers? That reminds me of a thing I read recently concerning China. One of the top political leaders came to an elementary school lecture (they take education pretty seriously). He told the children to put their heads on the desk and pray to God for ice cream. After fifteen minutes of serious and sincere effort all the children lost interest and grew restive. He then told them to pray to him and the party for ice cream, whereupon a few minutes later they raised their heads from the desks and found, guess what, ice cream. Isn't that disgusting, Mama, to distort the thinking of children like that . . . ?"

Whether this letter is really an expression of George Jackson's feelings and opinions at this stage of his life is very difficult to tell. There are indications elsewhere in his letters that he wrote material of this kind precisely so that the censor would read it and arrive at the judgment that Jackson was, in fact, trying to improve himself, thereby making him eligible for parole. Even if this is the case, however, it remains significant for it portrays Jackson still, in effect, working within the system, attempting to create an image of good behavior, attempting to obtain his release through the established methods and procedures.

Another important element in his developing political thought was that of the unity of all nonwhite peoples—what has come to be called the Third World. Regardless of their racial composition, whether Arab or Chinese or Latin American, these diverse peoples and cultures somehow represented to George Jackson, and to others in the evolving radical movement, a homogeneous grouping. There may be something of the old adage that "the enemy of my enemy is my friend" in this formulation. Whatever the case, it became an important part of his thinking, as well as a crucial element in the thinking of Angela Davis.

In a letter written on January 12, 1967, Jackson expresses this view: "I have faith in the fact that we, the majority of peoples (5 to 1) on earth, can live with and complement each other's existence if we rid the earth of the barbarous influence spread by this inhuman, unnatural minority! My faith in life holds still to the principle that we men of color will soon make a harmonious world out of this chaotic travesty of facts."

Jackson was convinced, however, that this "harmonious world" could not be brought about until the American society was totally destroyed, since it was that society which represented the strength of the "enemy." He also believed that black leaders who preached nonviolence, or working within the system, were simply following false paths.

Expressing these views, he wrote: " . . . first we must destroy the malefactor and root out all of his ideals, moralities, and institutions. It is to this end that I have long since dedicated myself, to extinguish forever the lights of a perverted science in any way that I can, by any and all means. . . . King and his kind have betrayed our bosom interests with their demagogic delirium. The poor fool knows nothing of the antagonist's true nature and has not the perception to read and learn by history and past events. In a nonviolent movement there must be a latent threat of eruption, a dormant possibility of sudden and violent action if concessions are to be won, respect gained and the established order altered. That nonviolent theory is practicable in civilized lands among civilized people, the Asians and the Africans, but a look at European history shows that anything of great value that ever changed hands was taken by force of arms."

Jackson, who educated himself during his years in prison, shows little awareness of the brutality and bitterness which, for example, was displayed by blacks against blacks in the Congo, and in the bitter war between Nigeria and Biafra. He seems unaware of the millions who were murdered by the Communist regime in China, about the policy of genocide practiced by that regime against their fellow Asians of Tibet, and of the rigid caste system which has existed for centuries in India, a caste system based upon color, with those of lighter skins finding themselves at the top of the scale, and those with darker skins at the bottom.

It is convenient to find all prejudice, hatred, and barbarity in Western or European civilization. That civilization, of which we in America are an intrinsic part, is certainly filled with examples of precisely the hatred and barbarity discussed by George Jackson. Who will deny that Hitler and Stalin have murdered millions of people, that America itself was the last civilized country in the world to outlaw human slavery? Yet the frailty of the human heart, the seeming need to draw lines between oneself and all those who are different, is as old as man. In *Hamlet,* Shakespeare writes, "There's a stranger, throw a rock at him!" Kipling noted that "Everyone like us is we, and everyone else is they." The fear of the stranger is not

[142]

a Western phenomenon, and not an Eastern one. It is not limited to men and women of any single race. It is a human weakness, and is universal.

What George Jackson seems not to have realized is that American society has been attempting, even if it has taken some years to begin this attempt, to make certain that the laws of society reject all distinctions based upon color or ethnic origin. It is interesting to note that Jackson did not write of the "racism" of American society at a time when segregation was in force, when racial intermarriage was illegal in many states, when discrimination was upheld by courts of law. Instead, he made his charges at a time when American society has made a commitment against all forms of discrimination, a commitment not equaled elsewhere in the world. How well blacks fare in Russia or in Cuba has been evident by the treatment accorded to African students in those countries. While all must applaud the efforts of this young man in a California prison to educate and inform himself, the result certainly indicates that he saw only one rather distorted part of the picture.

The relationship that developed between Angela Davis and George Jackson is particularly interesting in light of Jackson's frequently stated hostility for women. His letters indicate his view that women should not participate in any of the important work of the world, but should concentrate all of their energies upon supporting and encouraging their men—hardly a view which Angela would support. In a letter written July 15, 1967, Jackson expresses this view: "Women like to be dominated, love being strong-armed, need an overseer to supplement their weakness. So how could she really understand my feelings on self-determination? For this reason we should never allow women to express any opinions on the subject, but just to sit, listen to us, and attempt to understand. It is for them to obey and aid us, not to attempt to think."

Discussing a girl with whom he had been corresponding, Jackson explained that when he told ". . . her that she was not supposed to hold any opinions other than those of her menfolk, she stopped writing. Tell her that I feel no ill will toward her, but when she hears us debating method and policy, she is supposed to be silent, listen, and try to learn something."

[143]

Showing that he knew approximately the same amount about the Chinese as he did about women, Jackson saw not many-faceted human beings, but an image of perfection which may exist in some other world, but has never been seen in our own. He describes the Chinese this way: ". . . they are wonderful and aggressive, industrious people. They will make out. What I like most about them is their willingness to always help their brothers in Africa and Asia. They understand the need and power of ethnic solidarity. When they look in the mirror they see themselves, when they look at us they see their fathers and brothers. Brother, brother, is the way we'll call it. . . . Does it seem stupid of China to lend without interest, and build without taking over or capitalizing? Must be love."

These views show almost total ignorance of what is happening in the real world, and a willingness to completely romanticize history, to find all evil and all good just where you would ideally like it to be. Thus, the United States and Western Europe, representing white and, therefore, "alien" civilizations, are totally evil, and China, representing nonwhite, or black, civilizations is totally good and benevolent.

When George Jackson speaks of "ethnic solidarity" one wonders why his studies have not brought him to a consideration of China's invasion of India, genocide in Tibet, and attempted coups in Indonesia and throughout the African continent, resulting in the expulsion of Communist Chinese embassies from a number of African states. The fact is that George Jackson's political analysis is as unlearned and uninformed as might be expected of a young man who has spent most of his life in jail. Why people such as Tom Wicker consider it to be of real importance must tell us a great deal more about them than it does about George Jackson.

A great portion of George Jackson's hostility is reserved for those who call for positive change through nonviolent activity. He considers such individuals to be completely out of touch with history, and not to realize, as his own historical studies have apparently taught him, that violence is the best and, probably, the only means through which affirmative social change may be brought about. "The concept of nonviolence," he writes, "is a false ideal. It presupposes the existence of compassion and

[144]

a sense of justice on the part of one's adversary. When this adversary has everything to lose and nothing to gain by exercising justice and compassion, his reaction can only be negative."

Establishing this alleged adversary situation between all black Americans, on the one hand, and the remainder of the American society, on the other, Jackson declares: "Our response . . . must necessarily be negative when we consider that blacks in the U.S. have been subjected to the most thorough brainwashing of any people in history. Isolated as we were, or are, from our land, our roots, and our institutions, no group of men have been so thoroughly terrorized, dehumanized, and divested of those things that from birth make men strong."

What does Jackson think of his nonblack fellow citizens? He does not hesitate to vent his hatred and his view of the innate superiority of everything black. He writes: "People the world over are not the same but those that we meet here in the U.S. are generally of a single type. By and large they are all fools, intellectual non-persons, emotional half-wits. Status symbols, supervisory positions, and petty power motivate their every act. Personal, individual, financial success at any price is their social ethic, the only real standard upon which their conduct is built."

Black Americans, Jackson writes, are heir to a far different approach to life: "Black culture is a monumental subject that covers countless years. The first man and consequently the first culture was black." Writing to his younger brother Jon on December 28, 1969, he says this of Western religion: "Forget that Westernized backward stuff about god. I curse god, the whole idea of a benevolent supreme being is the product of a tortured, demented mind. It is a labored, mindless attempt to explain away ignorance, a tool to keep people of low mentality and no means of production in line."

In a letter written March 24, 1970, Jackson compares China and India and finds China far superior, an indication to him of the superiority of communism over Western forms of political and economic democracy. He notes, "They were both supposedly liberated at the same time. India may have had a year or more of what is loosely termed 'political self-determination.' China's problems in the late forties were ten times more severe, but today there is no one hungry in China. For the first time its population is united and organized under a government as decentralized and representative as a huge modern industrial-based society can be. China, land of the coolie, slave labor, open-door policies, floor mat of the West—they're vying for first place in every important economic sector today."

In making this statement Jackson once again exposes his own lack of familiarity with what is really happening in the world. He condemns his own country, the United States, not because it has failed to provide material well-being for its citizens. In fact, he condemns Americans precisely because they are concerned with such material well-being. His criticism of America is that it has kept his own minority group, the Negroes, from free and equal participation in society. Thus, he condemns America because of the quality of its life on a spiritual, political and social plane, not an economic one. Yet, he hails China because he argues that it is "vying for first place in every important economic sector today." He does not speak of China's spiritual, political and social virtues. This, of course, would be difficult. China forbids its citizens the freedom to travel, to speak freely, to pray as they choose, even to decide for themselves where to work, whom to marry, and when and how many children to have. Jackson condemns India, which has made major strides toward eliminating the ancient caste system of that society, while hailing China, which has exposed its own racism by the treatment it has inflicted upon the people of Tibet.

George Jackson's mind, being untrained, could probably see no distinction between applying different and contradictory standards of judgment to different societies. But even by Jackson's economic standard China would fail, when compared with the economic well-being of Asians in a free, capitalist country such as Japan. Reality and George Jackson's view of it had little relationship with one another.

Jackson had a kind of primitive attraction to powerful leaders, and his letters seem to indicate a man who would have been enamored of Hitler and Mussolini had he lived during the time in which they were alive. Today's versions, Castro, Ho and Mao, were, to him, great symbols of what man can achieve—

particularly nonwhite man. Discussing this point he writes: "The successes of China, Cuba, Vietnam and parts of Africa cannot be attributed to any innate, singular quality in the characters of their people. Men are social creatures, herd animals. We follow leaders. The success or failure of mass movements depends on their leadership and the method of their leadership. We must take our lessons from these people, reorganize our values, decide whether it is our personal desire to live long or to chance living right."

Comparing the challenge facing black Americans with the challenge which he imagined to be facing Chinese, Cubans, and Vietnamese, Jackson advances the view that what is needed to solve racial problems in America is a program of armed insurrection: "People's war, class struggle, war of liberation means armed struggle. . . . How can we deal with these men who have so much at stake, so much to defend. Honesty forces us to the conclusion that the only men who will successfully deal with the Hoovers, Helmses and Abramses will be armed men."

While he seemed intent upon making racial distinctions— seeing all virtue in what was nonwhite, whether it was black or yellow or red or some indeterminate color, and evil in all that was white—still his limited reading within the prison walls taught him that distinctions based upon race did not tell the whole story. There was something, he learned, beyond race, and that was economic class. This he learned from Karl Marx and if he had a difficult time keeping his hatred of whites and white society separate from his adoption of the essentially white and European Marxist philosophy, this seemed not to bother him very much.

"Our principal enemy," he wrote, "must be isolated and identified as capitalism. The slaver was and is the factory owner, the businessman of capitalist Amerika, the man responsible for employment, wages, prices, control of the nation's institutions and culture. It was the capitalist infrastructure of Europe and the United States which was responsible for the rape of Africa and Asia. Capitalism murdered those 30 million in the Congo."

Those black Americans who refused to share his view of the

[147]

enemy became, for him, simply a part of that enemy. One for whom Jackson had special wrath was comedian Bill Cosby. Using the rhetoric of his hero, Mao Tse-tung, he said this of Cosby: "Bill Cosby . . . this running dog in the company of a fascist with a cause, a flunky's flunky, was transmitting the credo of the slave to our youth, the mod version of the old house nigger. We can never learn to trust as long as we have them. They are as much a part of the repression, more even than the real live rat-informer-pig. Aren't they telling our kids that it is romantic to be a running dog?"

It is clear that Jackson's view was that any black man who did not seek to destroy the American society through the use of force, and who did not believe that communism would provide a better life for people, particularly minorities, was not in any sense an honorable man with whom he might disagree. That man had, of course, to be a "running dog" of the enemy. He had to be an "Uncle Tom," a "house nigger," or whatever other epithet came conveniently to hand.

One sad thing about all of this is that George Jackson does appear to have been a sensitive and thoughtful young man. He did try to educate himself while in prison, to come to grips with a complex world in which he had had few advantages. But his education was under the tutelage of people such as Angela Davis, as well as the left-wing attorneys who "assisted" him in his efforts to regain his freedom. He read the works of Marx and of Lenin, of Ho and Castro and Mao. But he seems to have read little else, and his image of reality is based not on reality itself but upon an ideological image of reality which served ideological purposes but bore no relationship to the real world. A young man who had not been beyond the inner cities of Chicago and Los Angeles, who had spent the better part of his adult life in prison, who had never read and studied, he was easily impressed with the propaganda presented to him.

It was because he was so impressionable, so much in need of something to believe in, that he could make a statement such as this: "Capitalism is the enemy. It must be destroyed. There is no other recourse. The system is not workable in view of the modern industrial city-based society. Men are born disenfranchised. The contract between ruler and ruled perpetuates this disenfranchisement. . . . Meaningful social roles, education, medical care, food, shelter and understanding should be guaranteed at birth. They have been part of all civilized human societies . . . until this one. . . . This world owes each of us a living the very day we are born. If not we can make no claims to civilization and we can stop recognizing the power of any administrator. Any man who stands up to speak in defense of capitalism must be slapped down."

It may or may not be true that the "world owes each of us a living the day we are born." This concept is one which George Jackson might accept and we might reject. It is, essentially, a matter of what our values are, and in a free society men may differ concerning such matters. What intelligent men who are seeking the truth may not justifiably differ about, however, are the facts of history. They may argue about what such facts really mean, they may draw contradictory messages from them, but the essential facts must remain undisputed. Whether we supported it or not, the Russian Revolution occurred in 1917. Whether we thought it a good or evil deed, the Japanese bombed Pearl Harbor in 1941. These things cannot be disputed. When George Jackson declares that all human societies until the United States have provided their citizens with "meaningful social roles, education, medical care, food, shelter and understanding," even those who might go so far as to sympathize with his Marxism and his desire for a revolution must admit that he is reflecting not any fact of history but only his lack of knowledge of the past.

Did Czarist Russia, or the Roman Empire, or those in ancient Sparta really provide their citizens with "meaningful social roles, education, medical care," etc.? The answer, of course, is that they did not. The Greeks and Romans had slaves, the czars had serfs. During the period of the Protestant Reformation, Protestants persecuted Catholics and Catholics persecuted Protestants. After the fall of the Roman Empire the armies of Islam swept across Europe. These various and diverse forces did not institute the "welfare state" that George Jackson seems to think represented the whole history of man until the development of the United States.

Beyond this, George Jackson failed to appreciate the fact that

[149]

free enterprise in his own country, the United States, had done more to provide medical care, food, shelter and understanding to all of its citizens than any nation or civilization that existed at any previous time in the world's history. This can be borne out in any statistical consideration, and makes Jackson's political thesis totally untenable. But, here again, his own lack of training and world experience may have led him to believe what professional Marxist propagandists declared in slogans which they expected no serious men to really take as being the truth. George Jackson was apparently sold a bill of goods, and it appears that the well-educated, white liberal press that hailed his political thinking must, somehow, have been sold this same bill of goods.

Jackson, in the course of his letters, also shows that the meaning he attaches to particular words is not necessarily the dictionary definition, or that definition accepted by the majority of literate men and women. When he states that black Americans are, in effect, "slaves," it is important to understand what he means by the term "slavery." He defines "slavery" in a letter written April 17, 1970, this way: "If you don't make any more in wages than you need to live you are a neoslave. You qualify if you cannot afford to leave California for New York. If you cannot visit Zanzibar, Havana, Peking, or even Paris when you get the urge you are a slave. If you're held in one spot on this earth because of your economic status, it is just the same as being held in one spot because you are the owner's property."

By this standard, that of mobility, many Americans would be slaves, Americans of all races. But by the standard of mobility, almost all Russians, Chinese, and Cubans would find themselves in this category. Jackson declares that those who are immobile are slaves, yet refuses to recognize the fact that he lives in the United States of America, the most mobile society in the world's history.

Between March, 1967, and March, 1968—in a single year—36,600,000 Americans (not counting children less than one year old) changed their place of residence. This, noted Alvin Toffler in his best-selling book *Future Shock*, "is more than the total population of Cambodia, Ghana, Guatemala, Honduras, Iraq, Israel, Mongolia, Nicaragua and Tunisia combined. It is as if the entire population of all these countries had suddenly been relocated."

Toffler points out, ". . . movement on this massive scale occurs every year in the United States. In each year since 1948 one out of five Americans changed his address, picking up his children, some household effects and starting life anew at a fresh place. Even the great migrations of history, the Mongol hordes, the westward movement of Europeans in the nineteenth century, seem puny in statistical comparison."

Jackson also seems notably unaware of the fact that around 1956 the United States became the first country in which more than 50 percent of the nonfarm labor force ceased to wear the blue collar of factory or manual labor. Blue collar workers were outnumbered by those in the white-collar occupations—in retail trade, administration, communications, research, education and other service categories. And within a single lifetime, agriculture, the original basis of civilization, has lost its dominance. In the United States, whose farms feed 200,000,000 Americans plus the equivalent of another 160,000,000 people around the world, this figure is already below 6 percent and is still shrinking rapidly. The USSR, Cuba, and Communist China —countries held out as examples by George Jackson—tell a far different story. There men and women spend most of their lives working at producing enough food, and each country must import such staples as wheat from the West, despite the fact that the majority of their workers and a small minority of our own are on the farms.

Beyond this, considering only the status of black men and women, those about whom George Jackson expresses ultimate concern, even a brief look at the comparative standards of living would show that black Americans live better than black people in any other country, and live better than the overwhelming majority of white people every place in the world.

Perhaps George Jackson's analysis would have been somewhat different if he had examined statistics such as these: Compared with a median annual income of $2,318 for Negro unrelated individuals in 1968, the per capita gross national product for that year was $91 in Haiti, $238 in Ghana, $298 in Zambia, and $304 in the Ivory Coast. In Chad, the Congo, Mali,

Niger, and Nigeria it ranged from a low of $63 to a high of $88. These figures are easily available in the *Statistical Abstract* of 1970, page 810.

Turning to European comparisons we find that in the early 1960s, when it was calculated, some 44 percent of America's nonwhite population was below the so-called poverty line of $3,000 a year. At the same time, 75 percent of Britain's entire, predominantly white population was also below that line. The $2,318 median income for American unrelated Negroes in 1968 compares with a per capita gross national product for that year of $1,544 in Austria, $2,154 in Belgium, $2,206 in West Germany, $1,418 in Italy, and $1,861 in the United Kingdom.

If he really knew the difference, in economic terms as well as in terms of individual freedom and dignity, between life in the United States and life in China, Cuba, or the USSR, we may well wonder whether or not George Jackson would have concluded that any Americans, white or black, really lived a life of "slavery."

George Jackson's seemingly warped view of reality led him to conclusions that logically followed from such a misapprehension about the society surrounding him. Thus, if black Americans really lived in slavery, the only way out was to destroy the slavemaster. Jackson's philosophy is inherently logical, but is based on a premise that is hopelessly false, a premise in which he had been carefully indoctrinated while in prison by those professional totalitarians who assumed for themselves the task of "revolutionizing" inmates in prisons across the country.

As a result, Jackson's analysis of the police, his reference to them as "pigs" who must be eliminated, follows from the rest of his worldview. In a letter written on April 17, 1970, he expresses this view: "The pig is protecting the right of a few private individuals to own public property. The pig is merely the gun, the tool, a mentally inanimate utensil. It is necessary to destroy the gun, but destroying the gun and sparing the hand that holds it will forever relegate us to a defensive action, hold our revolution in doldrums, ultimately defeat us. . . . Spare the hand that holds the gun and it will simply fashion another. The Viet soldier has attacked and destroyed the pigs and their guns,

[152]

but this alone has not solved his problems. If the Cong could get to the factories and the people who own and organize them, the war would end in a few months. All wars would end. The pigs who have descended upon the Vietnamese colony are the same who have come down on us."

For Jackson the struggle of the Vietcong and what he conceives of as the struggle of another "colonial" people, black Americans, is the same. Black Americans, however, have one opportunity lacked by the Vietcong. They exist within America, rather than outside of it, and the damage they are able to inflict could be fatal. He notes, "We are on the inside. We are the only ones (besides the very small white minority left) who can get at the monster's heart without subjecting the world to nuclear fire. We have a momentous historical role to act out if we will. The whole world for all time in the future will love us and remember us as the righteous people who made it possible for the world to live on."

As he began to read about Angela Davis and her exploits, George Jackson slowly changed some of his previous ideas about women. In a letter written April 18, 1970, he states: ". . . I've gone through some changes since then, I saw and read about Angie Davis and some other females of our kind, and I realized that perhaps it was possible that this country has produced some females like those of Cuba or Vietnam."

As Angela became more and more interested in the case of the Soledad Brothers she began corresponding with George Jackson, as well as working closely with his brother Jon in protest activities aimed at the defense of the Soledad Brothers. Writing to Angela Davis in May, 1970, George Jackson said the following:

"We've wasted many generations and oceans of blood trying to civilize these elements over here. It cannot be done in the manner we have attempted it in the past. Dialectics, understanding, love, passive resistance, they won't work on an activistic, maniacal, gory pig. It's going to grow much worse for the black male than it is already, much, much worse. We are going to have to be the vanguard, the catalyst, in any meaningful change. When generalizing about the black women I could never include you in any of it that is not complimentary.

[153]

"The blacks of slave society, U.S.A., have always been a matriarchal sub-society. The implication is clear, black mama is going to have to put a sword in that brother's hand and stop that 'Be a good boy' shit. Channel his spirit instead of break it, or help break it, I should say. Do you understand? All of the sisters I've ever known personally and through other brothers' accounts begged and bullied us to look for jobs instead of being satisfied with the candy-stick take. The strongest impetus a man will ever have, in an individual sense, will come from a woman he admires.

"As an individual, I am grateful for you. As a black male, I hope that since your inclination is to teach you will give serious consideration to redeeming this very next generation of black males by reaching for today's black female . . . we have altogether too many pimps and punks, and black capitalists (who want a piece of the putrescent pie). There's no way to predict. Sometimes people change fast. I've seen it happen to brothers overnight. But then they have to learn a whole new set of reflexes which can't be learned overnight. So cats like me who have no tomorrows have to provide examples.

"It's very contradictory for a man to teach about the murder in corporate capitalism, to isolate and expose the murderers behind it, to instruct that these madmen are completely without stops, are licentious—totally depraved—and then not make adequate preparations to defend himself from the madman's attack. Either they don't really believe their own spiel or they harbor some sort of subconscious death wish."

Writing to Angela Davis on May 21, 1970, Jackson expresses his view of those black spokesmen who have worked within the democratic system and have rejected the radical approach to solving the nation's racial problems: "There is an element of cowardice, great ignorance, and perhaps even treachery in blacks of his general type [Whitney Young]. And I agree with Eldridge and Malcolm, we are not protecting unity when we refrain from attacking them. Actually the reverse is true. We can never have unity as long as we have these idiots among us to confuse and frighten the people. It's not possible for anyone to still think that Western mechanized warfare is absolute, not after the experience of the Third World since World War II.

[154]

The French had tanks in Algeria, the United States had them in Cuba. Everything, I mean every trick and gadget in the manual of Western arms, has been thrown at the Vietcong and they have thrown them back, twisted, and ruined; and they have written books and pamphlets telling us how we could do the same. It's obvious that fighting ultimately depends upon men, not gadgets. So I must conclude that those who stand between us and the pigs, who protect the marketplace, are either cowards or traitors. Probably both."

Angela Davis was as enthusiastic about George Jackson as he was becoming about her. In her letters to him she referred to him as a "beautiful black warrior" with whom she wanted to fight "pigs." In the interim Angela Davis had become involved with Jackson's younger brother Jon in the shoot-out that occurred in the Marin County Courthouse and was subsequently arrested for murder, an aspect of the story to which we will shortly return. Many of Angela's letters to George Jackson were not delivered because of prison regulations. They were, however, later made public prior to her own trial.

Writing in the early morning on June 10, 1970, Angela told of her strong attraction for Jackson after seeing him in one of his court appearances. "The night after I saw you in court . . . ," she wrote, "I dreamt we were together fighting pigs, winning. We were learning to know each other."

In another letter, she disclosed the kinds of actions that should be taken when black militant leaders were killed. "Accepting the murder of a comrade in the struggle is not easy," she said. "Our first instinct is to rage, to return the attack, even if it be blind. We must learn how to plan the attack, gear it toward the total annihilation. . . ."

Angela wrote that black women "too must pick up the sword. Only a fighting woman can guide her son in a warrior direction." Black women, she said, have been overly protective and have tried to "dissuade our loved ones from accepting the burden of fighting this war which has been declared on us. We have to learn to rejoice when pig's blood is spilled . . . to learn how to set sights accurately, squeeze rather than jerk and not be overcome by damage."

On August 21, 1971, George Jackson was shot and killed and

[155]

five other persons died with slashed throats as Jackson tried to escape from San Quentin Prison. Jackson was shot by a guard, according to associate warden James Park. The bodies of three guards and two prison inmate trustees were found in pools of blood and locked in cells in the prison's maximum security section. Three other guards were wounded.

Park said that a visitor to Jackson had smuggled in a .38-caliber revolver and that the gun was found with Jackson's body. He reported that Jackson and some unidentified convicts began capturing officers in the maximum security wing at about 3 P.M. Death-row inmates and the most dangerous prisoners are confined in the wing.

According to Park, all the killings probably took place within thirty seconds. He said that Jackson was shot down by an officer when he "broke and ran out of the center." He said that Jackson was running toward a 20-foot wall with another convict who was identified only as Spain. "It was a carefully planned escape attempt," Park said. "They showed complete contempt for the lives of guards who didn't deserve to die and complete contempt for the lives of other inmates who also didn't deserve to die."

The death of George Jackson received extensive coverage in the national news media at least partially because he had become a propaganda favorite of the press. Few, however, considered the facts of the case. Tom Wicker, writing in the *New York Times,* declared that Jackson was ". . . not merely a victim of racism, although he was certainly that. He was a victim, too, of the poverty and hunger and disadvantage that are not the lot of blacks alone in this richest country on earth. Its schools treated him with contempt. He was shot at age 15 by its violent policemen. Its courts knew nothing better to do with him than to send him to its harsh prisons, where he spent a third of his life. There, and in his brief years on the streets of Chicago and Los Angeles—by his own account, he learned that 'the jungle is still the jungle, be it composed of trees or skyscrapers, and the law of the jungle is bite or be bitten.' "

That Jackson was a convicted burglar who was soon to be tried for murder seemed, for Mr. Wicker and others, essentially beside the point. They had established the fact that he was a "victim of racism," and his case fit their ideological preconceptions almost perfectly.

The fact is that, in many respects, George Jackson was indeed a victim, but he was victimized by something far more specific than the amorphous "racism" which allegedly led him to his illegal acts of violence. The background of the Jackson case indicates that members of the National Lawyers Guild, a cited Communist-front organization, had been manipulating Jackson and other inmates of California prisons to enhance the myth of the "political prisoner" and to create bitter strife, a "revolutionary atmosphere," behind the prison walls. In addition, the California Rural Legal Assistance program, an OEO-funded organization that had been embroiled in disputes with California Governor Ronald Reagan, had either wittingly or unwittingly abetted the National Lawyers Guild under the guise of protecting the "civil rights" of convicts.

To appreciate properly the forces at work in the California prisons we must also understand the astounding laxity of prison rules in that state, brought about partly by well-meaning "reformers," and partly by unrelenting propaganda and legal pressure from the left. Some law enforcement officials have expressed the view that it is not beyond the realm of possibility that many of those who have been speaking most vocally about the case of the Soledad Brothers may well have "set up" George Jackson in order to produce a badly needed martyr.

The National Lawyers Guild attorney who is suspected of having smuggled the gun in to Jackson, Stephen Mitchell Bingham, nephew of Congressman Jonathan Bingham (Democrat, New York) and grandson of the late Connecticut governor and U.S. Senator Hiram Bingham, is known as a fiery and intemperate radical who had been involved in the California grape pickers strike and several rent strikes in Berkeley. The case of Stephen Bingham is an interesting one. When viewed against his background, his career in social protest as a Berkeley storefront lawyer and migrant-labor organizer would appear to be a familiar episode in the revolt of the young against the conventional politics and conservative attitudes of their parents. Yet, a closer examination of the Bingham family tradition yields a strain not only of nonconformity, but also of outright radicalism.

Stephen's father, Alfred, became an outright revolutionary, breaking with his father, Hiram. Discussing this interesting facet of the Bingham family tradition, Professor Don Miller of Monmouth College in New Jersey, who wrote his doctoral thesis on Alfred Bingham, puts Stephen's radical activities with regard to the Soledad Brothers in some perspective. He writes:

"At Yale Law School, Alfred had served enthusiastically as president of the Hoover for President Club and aimed toward a career in law and Republican politics. But immediately after graduation, he took off on a two-year world tour that changed the course of his life . . . it was a three month visit to the Soviet Union that made the greatest impact on him. . . . By the time Bingham left Russia, he was calling himself a revolutionary. . . . He returned to America in the summer of 1932 with a burning determination to pursue a career in radical journalism as a public advocate of the coming revolution. But he rejected Marxism and the Marxist parties for an independent radicalism drawing on the American revolutionary tradition. . . ."

Alfred Bingham's career led him to the editorship of *Common Sense*, and to active participation in the League for Independent Political Action. Later on, however, he drifted away from his youthful radicalism. According to Professor Miller, "Alfred Bingham today is no longer a radical. For him, the present brand of radicalism is too pessimistic, too anarchistic. He still believes that man has the skills and resources to control his environment and end poverty and war. And he is still optimistic enough to think that it is the 'disparity between what a society says and what it does that is the major cause of social protest today.' Painfully, the radical movement, his son included, may have gone far beyond this optimism."

The Soledad Brothers had been the center of a vast fund-raising and propaganda campaign in California. National Lawyers Guild attorneys, particularly Berkeley attorney Fay Stender and San Jose radical lawyer John Thorne, had take a vigorous role in the affair. California law-enforcement officials believe that these attorneys, and others, abused their privilege of visiting inmates in the California prisons and used such

[158]

visits to smuggle weapons and inflammatory propaganda into the prisons, as well as to discuss escape plans and to transmit threats to "nonaligned" prisoners.

At 2 P.M. on the day George Jackson died, Saturday, August 21, 1971, he conferred with attorney Bingham, who had visited him at least twice before. They met in a loosely guarded visiting room at San Quentin, where there are no "dehumanizing" bars, screens, or windows to separate visitors from prisoners. Jackson, who reportedly was stripped and searched before he entered, was not in handcuffs.

Bingham had passed through the prison's metal detector without any alarm. Guards inspected his briefcase, which contained a small tape recorder. Recorders are not passed through the metal detector because it will erase tapes. Authorities believe that a Spanish-made 9-mm. automatic pistol and possibly a vial of powerful C-4 plastique explosive were inside the tape recorder.

After leaving the visiting room, Jackson was stopped by guards to submit to the routine strip and search that takes place each time a prisoner re-enters the prison's maximum security section. At that time a guard, possibly Officer Frank DeLeon, forty-four, discovered the pistol. Jackson then grabbed the gun, which had been hidden between his hair and an "Afro" wig. "We've got to do it now," he is reported to have said. It is, of course, not known whether Jackson planned to use the gun in an immediate and desperate escape attempt or whether he planned to hide it away, adding it to a building arsenal of weapons to be used at some future date in a riot or mass escape attempt. This question may never be fully answered, for the force of events rapidly took over.

The next few minutes, as far we can know from reports, were bloody chaos, ending in Jackson's sprint across an open area, trying to reach a low wall inside the prison. He was struck by two rifle bullets, one of which plowed through the top of his skull, down the length of his spine and out his lower back.

In the maximum security block behind him were two white prisoners, John Lynn and Donald Kane, dead, their throats slashed with a razor blade imbedded in a toothbrush handle. Three guards, DeLeon, Jere Graham and Paul Krasnes, were also dead, their uniforms stripped from their bodies. All three had been strangled and slashed at the throat. Two of them had also been shot in the back of the head. This was the deadliest day in San Quentin's 119-year-old history.

Jonathan Bingham immediately disapppeared, along with a twenty-three-year-old Negro girl, Vanitia Anderson, who gave her address as the Bobbie Seale Sickle Cell Anemia Clinic in Berkeley. She had accompanied Bingham to San Quentin when he visited Jackson, but she did not enter the visiting room.

Jackson was immediately made a martyr to the revolutionary left. In a memorial service conducted by the Black Panther Party, Jackson was eulogized as "a hero who died in a significant way."

"He showed us how to act," said Huey Newton, the founder and supreme commander of the Panthers, "and we will raise our children to be like him." Newton confirmed that Jackson had been a member of the Black Panther Party with the rank of field marshal. He described Jackson as "a strong man, determined, and full of love and strength." Newton, who himself faces a third trial on charges of killing an Oakland policeman, said that Jackson had been his hero and that he had left a standard for all "political prisoners."

The *New York Times* of August 29 includes the following report of the funeral: "The setting for the funeral was St. Augustine's Episcopal Church in the heart of West Oakland's sprawling black community. Crowds of the militant young, both black and white, began to gather hours before the services began, but it was the Panthers who were the most visible. There were dozens of them and they wore their familiar black uniforms over stiff blue shirts. Over the front door of the faded tan-colored church the party's official flag—a black panther mounted on a bright blue background—fluttered in the morning breeze."

The widow of one of the guards, Mrs. Vivian DeLeon, was bitter over the funeral and the general public support expressed for Jackson. "Every article we've picked up glorifies Jackson as a political prisoner," she said, "but nobody seems to care about the officers."

Many in California agree with columnist Tom Wicker that

George Jackson may indeed have been a "victim." They believe, however, that he had been a victim not of American "racism," but of the "revolution," and of the need of radical groups for a martyr who would serve their own propaganda purposes. "The big question on the minds of people out here," says a top intelligence source in the San Francisco Bay area, "is whether the National Lawyers Guild types sacrificed Jackson as part of a campaign to create a repressive atmosphere in California prisons."

Did "helpful" lawyers string Jackson along with promises of help in an elaborate escape plan? Or did Jackson develop such a plan on his own? Whichever the case, the role played by radical lawyers was certainly significant.

Even the events in the San Quentin yard did not signal an end to the left's legal assault on the penal system. National Lawyers Guild attorneys for the "surviving prisoners" in the maximum security section of San Quentin immediately filed a suit in San Francisco's federal district court calling for the dismissal of prison associate warden James W. L. Park, and asking, incredibly, that each prisoner be awarded $2 million in damages. A demonstration was quickly put together and about 500 screaming young people demonstrated outside the San Quentin gates yelling, "Three pigs is not enough," in reference to the slain prison guards.

Unfortunately, the difference between the old-fashioned criminal and the "revolutionary" criminal has confused many into believing that men such as George Jackson were indeed "political prisoners." This, however, is clearly not the case. Discussing this difference, Professor Murray Rothbard noted, "The old-fashioned criminal has always tended to be a 'right winger,' for he has generally acknowledged that his actions were morally wrong, that he had broken the moral law. Hence, while personally trying to keep out of prison as much as possible, the old-fashioned criminal does not challenge the correctness or propriety of the prison system per se. Hence, when sent to prison, he tries not to be a trouble-maker, tries to win privileges and early parole by good behavior, etc.

"But, in the last few decades, liberals and leftists have turned their mischievous attentions to the prison system, and to the concept of crime and punishment. They have promulgated the absurd theory, for example, that 'society' (i.e. everyone *except* the criminal, including his victim) is responsible for crime, and not the criminal himself. Criminals have of course become adept at using their increasing literacy to wrap themselves in left-wing justifications for their misdeeds. In the thirties and onward, it was sentimental liberalism that they clasped to their bosoms, whining that *they* were not responsible, but only the fact that not enough playgrounds had been provided for their childhood, or because their mother and father hated each other. In recent years, this liberal cop-out has been succeeded by revolutionary leftism. Now the murderer, the rapist, the mugger, can preen himself as a member of the vanguard of the 'revolution'; every time he knifes an old lady he can proudly label it a 'revolutionary act' against the Establishment."

George Jackson was not in prison for his political views; he was initially jailed for a number of crimes, including armed robbery, and most lately was accused of murder. He was shot in an attempted escape in which a number of guards were brutally murdered. It may serve the purposes of today's radicals to make a martyr of Jackson, but he was not a "political prisoner" by any objective standard, and his death resulted, it seems clear, not from his political activities but from his acts of violence.

Almost precisely the same arguments were used by the radical left concerning the riot at Attica Prison in New York as in the case of George Jackson. The aftermath of the riot at Attica has been a complex analysis of prison conditions and almost a reflex condemnation by the political left of Governor Rockefeller's decision to order the forced liberation of the prison and the hostages held by rebelling inmates. The criticism of Governor Rockefeller has not been based upon the fact that reports had it that a number of hostages had had their throats cut by rioting inmates, that this information was false, and that therefore the Governor's action was not called for by the facts. The criticism which has been most vocal, and most disturbing, is that which stated that *even if* the prisoners had in fact slit the throats of the hostages, still the Governor should not have acted.

We were told by such critics as radical attorney William

Kunstler that the Governor was guilty of murder, that prisoners riot because of oppressive prison conditions, and that our society itself is to blame for such disturbances, not those individuals who actually perpetrate them. Since it is society that is to blame, the Kunstler argument would seemingly have us alter society itself rather than take any particular action to free the hostages or bring order to the prison. This is only a consistent application of the idea that rapists and murderers are not guilty of their crimes but have become criminals because of a racist and harsh environment. Thus, Kunstler and others advance the view that Eldridge Cleaver is a "political criminal" even though he was sentenced for rape, and George Jackson is a "political criminal" even though he was sentenced for armed robbery. Previously we considered murder, rape, and armed robbery to be something other than "political crimes." But the radical analysis of today would disagree.

Commenting upon this view, Professor Daniel Glaser, of the University of Southern California, noted, "The concept 'political crime' as giving a special status to certain prisoners is alien to American legal philosophy. . . . American prisoners are sentenced for violations of criminal codes which make no references to political motivations, and are all sent to the same jails and prisons. Traditionally, most offenders approve laws against the kinds of acts—such as burglary, theft, or robbery—for which they are convicted, although many of them claim they are innocent or were victims of extenuating circumstances."

Professor Glaser points out, "This viewpoint has changed . . . almost everyone who is degraded by others strives to interpret his experience so as to view himself favorably. It is normal to excuse oneself by blaming others or by complaining about conditions." The fact is that nearly 100 million Americans saw representatives of the prisoners at Attica on television saying in clear and precise words that unless every one of their demands was granted they would proceed to execute hostages. The prisoners may have been bluffing. Still, Governor Rockefeller had to act on the possibility that they were not.

The simple fact of Attica was that a group of hardened criminals, stimulated by New Left rhetoric and ideas, held thirty-

[163]

eight hostages to the bitter end, beat them, killed at least one of them—the first hostage to get killed—and intended to murder them all unless their incredible, nonnegotiable demands were met by the state of New York. If the Governor erred, it may have been his hesitancy to act, not the action itself. *Washington Post* columnist Nicholas Von Hoffman, often a supporter of New Left causes, wrote, "Rule Number 1 in one of these joints is that you never bargain with inmates holding hostages. Never, not ever. The reason is that the jail guards—unless they're on the walls or in some other inaccessible place—must work unarmed. That's because they're always mixing with the prisoners and can be disarmed and made hostage too easily. Their one protection is making it absolutely, unshakably clear to the inmate population that grabbing a guard will do no good."

Discussing the situation at Attica, San Quentin, Soledad and other prisons, Fred T. Wilkinson, director of the Missouri State Department of Corrections and formerly deputy director of the U.S. Bureau of Prisons, stated: "We are reaping a harvest of the cult of permissiveness. Disciplines and controls in communities have been destroyed. And this has now reached our prisons, where so many militants and violence-oriented people from outside have been confined within the last year or two. They have carried with them hostility against any kind of law enforcement and order. You must have reasonable discipline—the kind of discipline we impose upon ourselves in a community. A prison is a community."

With regard to the question of outside influence, Mr. Wilkinson stated, "Trouble is being generated in many cases from outside sources. Aggressive militants in prison still have contacts outside. Many people engaged in law practice today are practicing barratry (the incitement of lawsuits). They are willing to create incidents. Some 85 percent of the people in prisons want nothing to do with this, but they fall under control of the militants through intimidation and violence."

Commenting on the statement by many militants, such as George Jackson and Angela Davis, that they are not only "political criminals" but are also, in effect, "prisoners of war," Professor Rothbard makes this observation: "One begins at least to sympathize with the exasperated Conservative Party

[164]

leader in Queens, who, after the umteenth justification by Black Panthers and others of themselves as 'political prisoners' or 'prisoners of war,' finally said: 'O.K., if these people are prisoners of war, let them be locked up until the 'war' is over.' For another curious aspect of this whole line of argument is this: Why do criminals expect, and often get, preferential treatment when they proclaim that they are 'revolutionaries' dedicated to overthrowing society and the existing system? If you knife a candy-store owner and then trumpet this as an 'act of the revolution,' why shouldn't you expect to be treated even *worse* than otherwise by authorities whose very task it is to protect existing society? Why expect 'acts of violent overthrow' to be treated especially gently by the very people who are being 'overthrown?' On the contrary, they should expect even harsher treatment as a result, for what kind of boobs are they who take threats of violence against themselves as passports for that violence? And yet, such boobs have obviously abounded in recent years. Once again, only firm and swift action against criminals, regardless of alibi, will restore proper perspective and end this latest form of 'revolutionary' cop-out for crime."

While George Jackson's mother has tended to side with the radicals in creating an image of her son as a martyr, his father, Lester Jackson, has expressed views which are far different. Lester Jackson and his wife did everything possible to provide a decent home for their children. In fact, because they did not find the public schools up to their own standards, they sent their children, including George, to parochial schools. When they became concerned about the atmosphere of their Chicago neighborhood, George's father, a postman, moved the family to California. As in the case of Angela Davis, George Jackson did not come from a broken home in which the children were mistreated or in which there was little concern for their education and well-being.

Lester Jackson, in his letters to George while in prison, and on his visits, disagreed with his son's growing militance and advocacy of violence. In an article in *Ebony* magazine, Lester Jackson writes, "The very idea of violence, I told him, is the same as suggesting (to use a prison analogy) that an inmate, hands handcuffed behind him, whose ankles have been firmly

[165]

shackled with irons, could defend himself in a locked prison cell against guards with pick handles, rifles and pistols. No, I couldn't buy this rhetoric for violence in the face of such obviously one-sided odds."

George, his father believed, had lost touch with reality and had been influenced by radicals to act against his own self-interest. He writes: "George, it must be remembered, spent much of his life in the junglelike environment of California prisons and had lost a certain touch with the realities on the street. Much of his reading had been theoretically weighted: Marx, Engels, Malcolm X, Cleaver. The purity of his notions and his expectations, I told him, had been achieved at the expense of a common-sense approach."

Discussing the atmosphere of the family, Lester Jackson recalls that "... no set of parents could have been more bourgeois than my wife, Georgia, and I were then. In an economic sense, we were not middle class. But for most of the 29 years of my marriage, I have labored under the yoke of simultaneous jobs (part-time jobs driving taxi-cabs, etc., in addition to daytime work at the Post Office). . . . It is clear, looking back, that we overprotected them [the children], and that we may often have stressed the more material side of life. The Jackson kids had to have the best clothing (at least to the extent that our income could afford it) and extra money in their pockets to spend. All of them went to parochial schools, as the public facilities available in the ghetto were seen by us as inferior in quality. Their every move was under constant surveillance, whether by Georgia, myself or one of our neighbors. The house rules which she and I had obeyed as children would certainly apply to our own children—or else."

Discussing his own attitude about public problems, Lester Jackson differs sharply from the radicalism adopted by his son. He writes, "My ideas on those subjects have been described as conservative. And deservedly. For I feel that blacks should spend a lot more time in attempting to build a more responsible black community. The welfare issue is a case in point. As I now reflect upon my days of hardship, I can certainly assure any black who will listen that the important factors in the salvation of blacks will be the old-fashioned qualities of responsibility and pride. I came to the conclusion very early in life that I would not like the idea of living my daily life in accordance with the dictates of the case worker. . . . Do not misunderstand me. Welfare is the best piece of legislation conceived as a measure against *emergency* human situations; and indeed the family assistance program was initially conceived as a temporary measure. But black men, for the most part, are playing a game with the program—and the game is a lot like Russian roulette. And women are going along with the game at a tragic price for their innocent children."

In his letters to George, Lester Jackson would occasionally report the comments of his white fellow-workers. He recalls, "In each of his letters for the next few months, he'd [George] rave at me for even bringing up 'Whitey.' 'He's no example to live by,' he'd write, 'Blacks and whites live in two different worlds.' "

Despite the fact that George Jackson has become a hero to the radical left, his father, if anything, seems to express the veiled belief that if it had not been for the radical left, his two sons, George and Jon, might be alive today. He writes, ". . . my basic ideology has remained unchanged. I still believe that the problems of this country can be adequately dealt with by working through the system—and that redress can be accomplished through the democratic process."

Those commentators who have spent so much time discussing the "tragedy" of George Jackson may have completely misunderstood the nature of the "tragedy." It may be that the real cause of his violent death was not the "white, racist society" against which they have launched their revolutionary crusade, but the radical movement itself. Unlettered, uneducated, little more than a street criminal, George Jackson's innate intelligence was used by the radical left for its own purposes, and not for his. He was as much a victim of the left as any of the "martyrs" to radical causes of the past. The tragedy is real indeed, but too many shed their tears in the wrong places.

The case of George Jackson and that of Angela Davis are inextricably entwined. One cannot be considered without the other, for it was Angela Davis' increasing concern with the case of the Soledad Brothers at the very time when her teaching contract at UCLA was not renewed that led to the violent actions at the Marin County Court House, actions in which Jon Jackson died and for which Angela Davis faced trial.

6

ON AUGUST 7, 1970, GEORGE JACKSON'S YOUNGER BROTHER, JONA-
than, walked into the San Rafael court of Judge Harold J. Haley
carrying four guns. Holding the courtroom at gunpoint, he
freed James McClain, thirty-seven, a San Quentin convict on
trial for assaulting a guard, and Ruchell Magee, thirty-one,
another convict waiting to testify. Magee went outside the
courtroom and freed another prisoner, William A. Christmas,
twenty-seven, also waiting to testify.

Wiring a shotgun to the neck of Judge Haley, they took him,
Assistant District Attorney Gary W. Thomas, and three women
jurors as hostages, intent on escaping in a rental van waiting
outside the courthouse. Officers opened fire. All the kidnapers
but Magee died. Haley's head was half blown off by the shotgun. Thomas was shot in the spine and permanently paralyzed.
One of the women jurors was shot but survived.

One week later, District Attorney Bruce B. Bales charged that
of the four guns brought into court by Jackson, three had been
"purchased by Angela Davis" in Los Angeles in January, 1968,
April, 1969, and July, 1970. The fourth, he alleged, had been
bought by her in San Francisco only two days before the shoot-
out.

According to *Newsweek* magazine, "She [Angela] told her
friends they were for self-protection; she had, indeed, received
a good many threats as a result of the UCLA hassle. She was

known to have gone target-practicing on weekends and she took to traveling in the company of bodyguards."

The last of her bodyguard companions was young Jonathan Jackson. He was often seen with her during the spring and summer, and it seems that they had become close friends. During this period Angela visited many times in the Jackson home. According to Lester Jackson, the father of George and Jonathan, "Angela, when we knew her, was a down-to-earth person. Many a night she even slept at our house, ate at out table and enjoyed our hospitality. She drank, smoked, wore mod-style clothing and generally behaved the way most women would. Except that she did a considerable amount of reading. (She'd sit at our table immersed in a book even with the television and record player going.) She took her turn with the household chores; cleaning, ironing, cooking, etc."

Shortly after the announcement that the guns used in the San Rafael courthouse had been "purchased by Angela Davis," Angela disappeared, and four days later was placed on the FBI's "Ten most wanted" fugitives list. Had she, in fact, masterminded the whole Marin County Courthouse affair? Many of her friends found it impossible to believe. They argued that she would hardly have suggested the use of weapons so easily traceable to her. In addition, even if she had come to espouse the philosophy of revolutionary violence, they could not imagine her devising so far-fetched a scheme as that which occurred at the courthouse. "It wouldn't be characteristic of Angela to let a seventeen-year-old walk into certain suicide," said one former colleague. A friend from San Diego added, "She's not a crazy romantic. She's a heavy, heavy, heavy rationalist. She believes things can be reasoned out and done scientifically."

Lester Jackson expressed this view: "The real state of affairs may have been just the reverse. Jon was an outgoing, persuasive kind of person, and it is not impossible, contrary to what has been thought, that he influenced Angela—not the other way around. It may have been that he involved her inadvertently without her being aware of what he may have planned to do."

Others suggested that Jackson may have had access to her guns because of his bodyguard status and had appropriated them for his own adventurous plan to save his brother. If that were the case, why then did Angela flee? One professor friend speculated that it might have been out of loyalty: "She would do anything, even risk killing during capture by the FBI, rather than dissociate herself from Jonny Jackson, when he had sacrificed his life." In addition, she gave vocal expression to the revolutionary conviction that fair trials for black radicals are impossible in today's courts.

On August 15, 1970, Federal fugitive warrants were issued to go with the state charges of murder and kidnap when Angela was not found in a raid on a San Francisco home and informants reported that she was seen in her home town of Birmingham, Alabama. Assistant United States Attorney Jerrold Lader said that he filed the complaint on the basis of the state warrants issued earlier in Marin County. District Attorney Bruce Bales said that Angela Davis was charged under a California law holding that anyone who aids or abets in a major crime is equally guilty with the direct participants. In the San Francisco raid, police found Angela's sister, Mrs. Fania Jordan of Los Angeles, but released her after questioning. The raided home was headquarters of defense activities for the Soledad Brothers.

Marin County authorities charged Angela Davis with first-degree murder and said that she was wanted as a "principal in the crime," not as a conspirator. The affidavit of District Attorney Bales said that Angela and Jonathan Jackson "were seen in the company of each other on several occasions during the two-week period preceding August 7, and were observed crossing the border from Tijuana, Mexico, into California on July 31 in an automobile registered to Angela Y. Davis." He added that shortly before the escape attempt they "jointly appeared in public and advocated the freeing from prison of the Soledad Brothers." The affidavit said that young Jackson visited his brother George at San Quentin on August 3, 4, 5, and 6, and that all four guns used in the escape attempt were purchased by Angela Davis—one of them only two days earlier.

With the disappearance of Angela Davis came a nationwide search and her placement on the FBI's "ten most wanted" list. She left San Francisco on a shuttle flight to Los Angeles; her companion during the following weeks was a man named Da-

[171]

vid Rudolph Poindexter, Jr. Little was known about Poindexter when his name was first brought to national attention. His father had been the Negro Communist Party candidate for Alderman in the second ward of Chicago in 1931. The elder Poindexter, now deceased, opened up a television repair shop which developed into a chain of record stores, and also owned a record shop. Poindexter's mother, Mrs. June Hunsinger, was a wealthy white woman.

Poindexter's record is a less than enviable one, totally aside from politics, which seems to have been only a peripheral interest for him. Some years before his association with Angela Davis, under the alias of Carl Davis, he paid a $31.50 fine on a misdemeanor conviction for carrying a concealed weapon. Later, in 1970, he had another involvement with the law, this time regarding the violent death of his wife, Lorean.

He and Lorean had been living in a nine-room home on South Crieger Street, in a middle-class black neighborhood of Chicago. The neighbors of the Poindexters have said that David drove a new Cadillac every year, and that they were among the more well to do people in the area. On May 3, 1970, Lorean Poindexter was found dead in their home with a bullet in her head. The coroner's jury, after two hours' deliberation, ruled the death a suicide. Chicago police said that she had left a suicide note saying that ". . . although I know you are opposed to fulfilling any of my requests, I'm going to make some anyway." The note asked that she be cremated, that her belongings be burned, and that she not be buried with her wedding ring.

Prior to the decision of the coroner's jury, Poindexter had been charged by Chicago police with failing to register a .32-caliber automatic pistol that was used by his wife, and three other weapons which they found in the house. The finding that Lorean's death was a suicide, however, caused the weapons charges against Poindexter to be dropped.

To add to his less than honorable facade, the police claim to have found mimeographed copies of phony transcripts and diplomas from the Illinois Institute of Technology, which showed Poindexter having a degree in mechanical engineering. The officials of the institute state they have never heard of Poindexter, a fact that tends to support the illegitimacy of the diplomas.

[172]

In one of the much publicized books favorable to Angela Davis, a volume entitled *Angela,* and written by a man who identifies himself only as "the Professor," there is no attempt made to portray Poindexter as anything more than he was. "The Professor" describes him in these terms: "Complicating the image of this man are the rumors that abound regarding him. One of Poindexter's hangouts was the Doghouse, a popular bar in the south side of Chicago. Several 'regulars' knew David, and said that he had told them he was a graduate of the University of Illinois, and that he was a pilot working for American Airlines. The university, and American Airlines, have never heard of David R. Poindexter, Jr. Numerous sources say that he served in the U.S. Air Force during the Korean war, but under a different name. However, Federal officials have been slow to either confirm or deny Poindexter's veteran status, under any name."

In addition, Poindexter was among those on a select list of presumably dangerous persons "to be watched" when the President of the United States would come to Chicago. Local police said that both they and the FBI had kept Poindexter under almost constant surveillance during those recent months.

A few days after Angela Davis had fled from California, it was claimed that Poindexter had taken $15,000 from the East Chicago Heights Sanitation Company, a company in which, allegedly, Poindexter is a partner. Following the disappearance of this money, Poindexter and Angela began their pose as Mr. and Mrs. George Gilbert. They spent only a short time in Chicago and then decided to go south. Available evidence indicates that Angela had gone with Poindexter and had stayed in his Chicago apartment from August 14 through August 16.

Why they went to Miami is not clear. At least two reasons have been considered—one, in order to escape to Cuba, and the other, to see Poindexter's mother, Mrs. Hunsinger, who lived there. By the time they arrived in Miami there was a nationwide search being conducted for Angela Davis. Despite this fact, the "Gilberts" on September 9 moved into the Golf View Apartments, and were given a new Toyota by Poindexter's mother. Angela signed in as "Lorean," the name of Poindexter's deceased wife.

The Golf View Apartments had been under twenty-four-hour surveillance of state troopers, sent there to provide protection for Dade County Deputy Charles Celona, who also resided at the Golf View Apartments. These state troopers, however, failed to make any connection between the "Gilberts" and Angela Davis.

On September 29 a report was circulated that Angela Davis and two male companions had been seen north of Miami. This report was stimulated by another report made by a boat captain, Warren Woods, who stated that a woman—whom he later identified from photographs as Angela Davis—and two men had attempted to force him, at gunpoint, to take them to Bimini shortly before midnight. This report turned out to be false, but it did put Florida officials on the alert and was soon followed by more accurate reports which then placed the FBI on Angela's trail.

An unidentified black pilot said that he had been contacted and that the preparations were under way to fly Angela to Cuba from a deserted airstrip. But due to the publicity and new rumors, she canceled these plans and left the Miami area. Angela, Poindexter, and the Toyota his mother had purchased all left Florida with great haste. Ironically, it was the Toyota that finally led to their capture when it was spotted in the parking garage of a downtown New York motel.

Very little is known about what happened to Angela and Poindexter between the time they left Miami and the time they were arrested in New York. "The Professor" relates, "There are only cold facts and bits and pieces of information volunteered by people in the Manhattan area at the same time that Angela and Poindexter were there. For instance, it is known that they went to a Holiday Inn first, but ended up at a Howard Johnson's where they were finally arrested. During the five days between October 8, 1970 (when "Mr. and Mrs. Gilbert" checked into the Howard Johnson's Motor Lodge), and October 13 when the FBI grabbed them at 6 P.M., they walked around the city as if nothing were wrong; just a happily married couple enjoying the sights. People have come forward swearing they were seen at two different motion-picture theaters on Broadway (including Radio City Music Hall); one usher at NBC claims they came in with a group to watch a television show. However, more reliable and calmer information indicates that David and Angela stuck rather close to the Howard Johnson Motel and frequented off-Broadway, predominantly white, areas when going out for food."

The FBI stated that it traced Angela Davis to the Howard Johnson's Motel through a car owned by Poindexter. Poindexter and Angela had been registered in Room 702 for five days. They are reported to have had two light blue suitcases, expensive cameras and other photographic equipment and "lots of new clothes," including pants, shirts, wigs and shoes. When arrested in their $30-a-day room, they were unarmed and offered no resistance, authorities said. "It was done very smoothly," said William Slevin, manager of the motel. "No one in the hotel even know they had been here."

Angela was arraigned on the California murder and kidnaping warrant and held without bail for a November 9 extradition hearing. At this time Angela decided upon which attorney she wanted for her defense. She chose John H. Abt, a leading Communist defense lawyer, to represent her at the New York proceedings. Even such a friendly observer of the Angela Davis case as "the Professor" had second thoughts about her choice of an attorney. He writes: "It could not have been a simple decision for her, especially if she intended to play the martyr role to the hilt; there are still a large number of black leaders in this country who absolutely refuse to align themselves—in any way—with the Communist Party. There was more than mild discontent among those leaders when Angela called on John H. Abt; and many of her supporters (those who based their support upon the principle of the matter and not upon any political motivation) were dubious about her choice."

"The Professor" describes John Abt in these terms: "In the late '40s, Abt was the chief counsel of the newly-formed Progressive Party, and was tireless in his efforts to elect the late Henry Wallace to the Presidency. He served as chairman at their party convention that election year in Philadelphia. Five years later, he represented the Communist Party before the

[175]

New York Board of Regents, which was trying to bar party members from holding jobs in the school system on the grounds that they were subversive. Then in 1957, he was back in the news when the Soviet spy, Colonel Rudolph Abel, asked him to defend him against the charges that he transmitted U.S. secrets to the Soviet Union. For whatever reasons Abt may have had, and they were never publicized, Abt turned Abel down. The day after President John Kennedy was assassinated in November, 1963, Lee Harvey Oswald asked to be allowed to hire John H. Abt to defend him. While the lawyer was considering the request, and before he could accept or reject the case, Oswald was shot and killed by Jack Ruby. (Intimates say that Abt was about to accept representation of the President's alleged assassin.)"

Angela was arraigned on a federal fugitive charge and ordered held on $250,000 bail by U.S. Commissioner Barle N. Bishop. When the California warrant arrived Angela was again brought before Bishop, who immediately revoked the bail and released Angela in her own recognizance. The move was only technical, however, because a city detective immediately stepped forward and said, "Miss Davis, you're under arrest."

The midnight arraignment was held before Criminal Court Judge Morton Tolleris, who in a brief hearing set November 9 as the hearing date for extradition. On October 21, Governor Nelson A. Rockefeller signed an extradition order for the return of Angela to California. On October 23 she was transferred from a normal cell to solitary confinement. At this time she filed suit asking that New York City be forced to release her from solitary and asked for a quarter of a million dollars in damages for mistreatment in the jail. Her lawyers in that case included Haywood Burns of the National Conference of Black Lawyers.

Burns told Federal Judge Walter Mansfield that Angela had been confined to a psychiatric ward from October 13 to October 22, and then put in a room where she had been denied any contact with other inmates. Her visitors were heavily screened, and Herbert Marcuse was turned away on October 23 when he attempted a visit.

In reply to the question of why Angela had been placed in solitary confinement, New York authorities stated, "she could possibly have a serious and destructive influence on the rest of the prison population. It's also for her own safety." Many supporters of Angela Davis argue that this makes little sense and that somehow placing Angela in solitary was a kind of retribution for her political ideas. Yet, the fact remains that Angela had repeatedly called for revolts within the nation's prisons. In her preface to the volume *If They Come in the Morning,* for example, Angela writes this: "The government's repression today has been met with substantial popular resistance—both spontaneous and organized. The revolt at San Rafael . . . must be seen as a response to the unrestrained brutality and the most severe forms of political repression in prisons. Even greater numbers of people are beginning to involve themselves in organized mass forms of struggle." This certainly sounds like a call to revolution to those in America's prisons. As such, authorities seem to have been provided with a substantial reason to isolate Angela from those to whom she might preach this gospel.

Angel was turned down by a New York State Supreme Court judge in her bid to avoid extradition to California. Judge Thomas Dickens denied her petition for a writ of habeas corpus and, finally, in December, 1970, the order to extradite Angela to California was issued. An appeal was then made to the United States Supreme Court to stay extradition. This was rejected and only twenty hours later Angela Davis was on her way back to California.

Angela was taken at 3:20 A.M. from the New York City jail and driven under a heavy police escort to the airfield, with decoy cars sent out in other directions. The flight from McGuire Air Force Base in New Jersey was listed as a "routine training flight" of the California National Guard. The plane was met by local authorities who handcuffed Angela and took her to the Marin County jail. She was booked on charges of murder, kidnaping and criminal conspiracy and was finger-printed and photographed at 3 P.M., only minutes from the scene of the violence that had taken the lives of Jonathan Jackson, the Superior Court judge, and the others a few months before.

The State Attorney General's office in San Francisco announced that Angela would be arraigned at the Marin County Courthouse at 9 A.M. on December 24. Spectators began lining up outside the building, shouting "Right on" and "Free Angela," seven hours before the hearing.

By this time, the trial of Angela Davis had been captured by the radical press and political movement as the international cause of the moment. Rallies were held in many cities, petitions were circulated, and a cause célèbre was being created.

Fourteen soviet scientists expressed concern for Angela Davis, and over the question of whether or not she would receive a fair trial. This came shortly after death sentences had been pronounced by a Soviet court on two Russian Jews who were charged with trying to hijack a plane and flee to Israel. When the Jews of Leningrad were first brought to trial a group of concerned Americans put together a large sum of money to send attorney Melvin Belli and a group of lawyers and law professors to Russia as observers. The Russians finally gave in to international pressure and set aside the death penalty.

In response to this, the Russians seemingly attempted to turn the tables on the United States by drawing attention to the Angela Davis case. In a letter to President Nixon, fourteen leading Russian scientists and intellectuals asked that Angela's life be safeguarded. President Nixon responded by inviting the whole group of fourteen to attend the trial as guests of the United States Government, to see justice in action. This offer, authorized personally by President Nixon, was contained in a letter from Assistant Secretary of State Martin Hillenbrand. The letter was a response to a December 25 cablegram sent to the President by the Soviet group. The Russian group was headed by Pyotr L. Kapitsa, dean of Soviet physicists. All of the Russians involved are members of the International Academy of Sciences, and some are members of the United States Academy of Sciences.

Discussing the Angela Davis trial in light of the plea made by the Soviet scientists, the *Washington Post* editorialized on January 5, 1971, that "An intriguing political sequence is revealed by the 14 Soviet scientists' expression of concern for Angela Davis, and by the American government's invitation in response to come and observe her trial. The 14 include not only distinguished academicians but leaders of the Soviet human rights movement. Limited by their own government in what

[178]

human rights work they can do at home, they found in America a case in which they could publicly advocate the very values—individual dissent, freedom from official persecution, open trial—for which even private advocacy is difficult and risky in their own country."

The *Post* noted, "The United States Government responded with admirable dispatch and sophistication. It acknowledged the genuine concern of the 14 and invited them to the trial to see for themselves whether justice is done. The offer is in nice keeping with the American tradition of an open society which affords its citizens due process in a court of law. It is also in keeping with the American tradition of judging a government by the way it handles its individual critics."

The *Post* concluded by doubting that the Soviet government would permit the scientists to attend the trial: "The granting of exit visas would imply a reciprocal Soviet willingness to let Americans attend 'political' trials in Russia—something that Soviet officialdom has opposed out of fear that outside observers might discover the trials are mere formalities. Observers' reports on the Davis trial could not fail to draw unflattering attention to the methods of Soviet trials and to the whole question of treatment of Soviet dissenters. There is some slight chance that the scientists might attend the trial and then dissemble in their public reports, as many Soviet visitors to the United States are forced to do in order to 'pay' for their trip and buy the next. Yet the integrity of the men involved argues against this possibility. We hope their government allows them to attend."

Speaking on January 5, 1971, Angela proclaimed herself innocent of the murder and kidnaping charges and declared that she was the victim of a "political frameup." She read her handwritten statement in a strong, clear voice amid repeated objections by the prosecution in the heavily guarded Marin County courtroom.

Angela spoke in support of a surprise motion to appear as co-counsel in her own behalf with her chief attorney, Howard Moore, Jr., a well known civil rights lawyer from Atlanta, and a battery of other attorneys.

Moore is thirty-seven years old, a graduate of Morehouse College in Atlanta, and of the Boston University Law School. He has been active for many years in civil rights work in the south and was aided in the case of Angela Davis by a number of other attorneys. Among them are Margaret Burnham, Dennis Roberts, and Michael Tigar.

Margaret Burnham is a young, black lawyer from Birmingham, Alabama, and has known Angela since they were children together. She was graduated from Tougaloo College in Mississippi and the University of Pennsylvania Law School and was made available to the Davis case by the National Conference of Black Lawyers in New York. There are rumors that Angela and Miss Burnham had periodic contact during the past few years, and that she gave legal advice during the UCLA controversy.

Dennis J. Roberts, thirty-three, is a University of California (Berkeley) Law School graduate and a personal friend of chief counsel Moore. He worked at a law center for constitutional rights in New York with radical attorney William Kunstler. After working at the center, Roberts returned to California to join a prominent San Francisco firm.

Perhaps best known among the lawyers who rallied around the case of Angela Davis is Michael E. Tigar, an honor graduate of the University of California Law School at Berkeley. Tigar teaches law at UCLA and first gained notoriety as a student leader in campus protests at Berkeley; he took a partial leave of absence from his teaching position to represent two of the "Seattle Seven," a group of young people accused of conspiracy in connection with disruptions at the Federal Courthouse in 1970. It was Tigar who agreed with Moore's suggestion that Angela should serve as co-counsel.

Speaking at the Marin County court, Angela stated: "I now declare publicly before this court and before the people of this country, that I am innocent of all charges which have been leveled against me by the state of California. I stand before the court as the target of a political frameup, which, far from pointing to my culpability, implicates the state of California as an agent of political repression."

At this point it appeared clear that the defense would take the position that Angela was being prosecuted for constitutionally protected political activities—such as her support for the defense of the Soledad Brothers. It was on the assumption that Angela herself is best qualified to address the political issue that she and her attorneys sought to include her as co-counsel. She declared, ". . . in order to insure that these political questions are not obscured, I feel compelled to play an active role in my own defense. As the defendant, as a black woman, and a Communist, it is my duty to assist all those directly involved in the proceedings as well as the people of this state and the American people in general to thoroughly comprehend the substantive issues at stake in my case. These have to do with my political affiliations, and my day-to-day efforts to fight all the conditions which have economically and politically paralyzed black America."

Angela added, ". . . a system of justice which virtually condemns to silence the one person who stands to lose most would seem to be self-defeating. . . . In order to enhance the possibility of being granted a fair trial, of which I am at present extremely doubtful, it is imperative that I be allowed to represent myself."

The co-counsel request was an unusual one. While it is common for defendants to ask to serve as their own attorney, there is little legal precedent for a joint defense. One such precedent, cited by defense attorney Michael Tigar, was when Clarence Darrow served as his own co-counsel in a jury-tampering case in Los Angeles.

At this same time a motion to dismiss the indictment for lack of evidence was made. The defense maintained that the transcript of the grand jury proceedings "is devoid of evidence that Miss Davis ever voluntarily gave these guns to Jackson or anybody, much less that she did so with a criminal purpose." The motion continued: "The court may take judicial notice, and evidence will later be adduced that Miss Davis was in fear of her life because of the atmosphere of hatred which had been generated against her by California public officials."

On July 28, Superior Judge Richard E. Arnason agreed that Angela would be permitted to act as co-counsel in the trial. In practical terms this meant that she would not be restricted to passing notes to her lawyers with suggested questions, or speaking only when she was on the stand. As co-counsel she could participate fully in the trial. Judge Arnason granted the request to have Angela act as co-counsel because he believed her participation would serve the cause of justice and would not interfere with orderly procedure. The judge warned that he might revoke the permission if Angela abused her right or if it appeared "to impede the administration of justice."

In the January 5 motion to set aside the indictment, Angela's lawyers admitted that Angela did seek official leave to visit George Jackson at both San Quentin and Soledad prisons. They also admitted that there was evidence that she accompanied George Jackson's brother Jonathan on his visits to his brother at San Quentin and that she purchased four weapons, and registered them according to the California law. The defense contended, however, that the grand jury proceedings had no evidence that Angela voluntarily gave these guns to either Jackson or anyone else. In addition, the defense challenged the entire institution of the grand jury. The defense was given until February 15 to submit the motions, and the prosecution fifteen days from then to argue them.

The defense's pretrial motions were submitted to the Marin County Court on February 5. Briefly, they were as follows:

1. Dismissal of the indictment on grounds of insufficient evidence.
2. That Angela be released on bail.
3. That Angela be granted permission to act as co-counsel in her own defense.
4. Dismissal of the indictment on grounds that the grand jury which handed it down was illegally selected.
5. Discovery motions: aimed at getting the state to issue names of witnesses and other evidence which they were planning to use.
6. Dismissal of the indictment on grounds that Angela could not receive a fair trial due to pretrial prejudicial treatment by media and government officials.
7. That illegally obtained state's evidence be suppressed.

Prior to this, on January 16, the 127 pages of the grand jury's testimony were made public by court order. The testimony showed that Superior Court Judge Harold J. Haley, San Quentin prison convicts James McClain and William Arthur Christmas, and seventeen-year-old Jonathan Jackson were killed in a rented yellow van during the escape attempt. Peter D. Fleming, a service station attendant, testified before the grand jury that he had helped Jackson and a woman resembling Angela Davis start a rented yellow van with battery trouble in the Civic Center parking lot the day before the shoot-out.

Fleming said that several photographs of Angela looked "a lot like" the woman he saw with Jackson. "This looks like her," he said at one point. "But I can't remember the teeth." There is a noticeable space between two of Angela's front teeth.

Testimony identified Angela as the purchaser of four guns found inside the van. David Lifsen and Frank Blumenthal, both clerks, testified that Angela bought a 12-gauge shotgun on August 5, two days before the shoot-out. Lifsen said he recognized Angela at the time from news photos and got her autograph. Both Lifsen and Blumenthal worked at a shop in San Francisco.

Nancy Conrad, a clerk in the Western Surplus Store in Los Angeles, testified that Angela bought an M1 carbine and 200 rounds of ammunition on July 25.

John E. Plimpton, assistant manager of the Brass Rail Gun Shop in Hollywood, testified that on January 12, 1968, Angela purchased from him a Browning semiautomatic pistol. He identified the gun found after the shoot-out as the same one.

Owen Swisher, a salesman at Western Surplus, testified that on April 7, 1969, Angela bought from him a .30-caliber carbine and 100 rounds of ammunition. He also identified the weapon shown him as the one he had sold to Angela.

Jonathan Jackson was identified in testimony as the man accompanying Angela during the purchase of one gun, and possibly a second. In addition, San Quentin Prison Lt. Robert H. West testified that Angela accompanied Jonathan on two visits to his brother George, on August 4 and August 5. Angela remained in a waiting room while Jonathan visited his brother.

A Pacific Southwest Airline employee testified that he sold, near flight time, a Los Angeles ticket at San Francisco International Airport to Angela Davis at 2 P.M., August 7, three hours after the shoot-out. "She was terribly rushed, very rushed, realizing that it was the last minute and she was terribly worried that she wouldn't make it because she had this check to write out," Marcia Brewer, a PSA ticket agent, testified.

Sixteen pages of the grand jury testimony were withheld from the public. These pages were primarily from Gary W. Thomas, Marin County assistant district attorney, who was taken hostage during the shoot-out and was shot in the spine. He is now paralyzed from the waist down.

Dr. John H. Manwaring, who performed the autopsy on Judge Haley's body, testified that the judge was shot in the chest by a pistol or rifle and in the face by a sawed-off shotgun that had been taped to his neck. Manwaring said that it was impossible to establish which caused death, but said either wound could have been responsible.

In the midst of Angela Davis' pretrial preparations, a surprising headline was found in the newspapers of April 13, 1971. The *Washington Evening Star* put it this way: "Poindexter Is Cleared in Angela Davis Case." The *Chicago Daily News* service issued this report: "Neither David Poindexter, his bride Jane, the defense attorney nor even some of the jurors expected the verdict: Not guilty. 'Sweet day, sweet day,' crooned Poindexter, after the foreman read the jury's decision yesterday on Federal charges that Poindexter had harbored and concealed black militant Angela Davis during a two-month flight from justice last year."

Poindexter declared, "We proved the government can't foist just any charge on the people. Maybe this will help put an end to the question of jailing people for what they think rather than what they do." Poindexter said, "This is just a minor skirmish in a big war," and added that, politically, he is a "Marxist-Leninist." He said, "I want to go to the coast now to see Miss Angela. But I won't be taking any vacations until she is free. . . ."

The jury deliberated only two and one half hours before emerging with its decision. This followed four days of testimony and forty-two prosecution witnesses who appeared in the U.S. District Court in New York. The crux of the case against Poindexter, as Judge John M. Cannella pointed out to the jurors, was not whether Poindexter knew of the California murder and kidnap charges against Angela, but whether he knew that Federal warrants had been issued.

Angela's pretrial hearings began on March 16 with Judge John McMurray presiding. Immediately, Ruchell Magee, Angela's co-defendant, charged that Judge McMurray was prejudiced and could not judge fairly and introduced a challenge for cause in his efforts to disqualify Judge McMurray. The hearings were postponed pending Judge McMurray's answer to the challenge and on March 18, Judge McMurray disqualified himself from hearing the pretrial motions.

On March 23, in an unusually speedy action, the California Judicial Council named Judge Alan Lindsay of the Alameda County Superior Court to hear pretrial motions. On April 1, the pretrial hearings were reconvened, presided over by the newly appointed Judge Lindsay. At the outset, Angela's defense attorneys introduced a motion to disqualify Judge Lindsay on the basis of an alleged history of "racist" practices and his lack of experience in trying felony cases. Judge Lindsay responded by stating that he could, in fact, judge fairly and objectively.

Angela's co-defendant, Ruchell Magee, stalled the case again on May 10 when he disqualified Judge Lindsay on a peremptory challenge. A United Press International report for that date notes that "Under California law, Lindsay had no choice but to withdraw from the case. Magee had one peremptory challenge and his attorney, Ernest L. Graves, joined in filing the challenge although he advised Magee not to exercise it 'at this time.' 'But I am not going to stand in his way,' the Los Angeles attorney told the judge."

The disqualification-for-cause motion filed by Angela during the previous month, charging him with "racism," was rejected in a special hearing which ruled Lindsay qualified to hear the case. The California State Supreme Court later upheld the decision.

Three judges from the Marin County bench previously had withdrawn from the case because of their friendship for the deceased Judge Haley. Thus, a sixth judge was sought for the case, making somewhat dubious the charge leveled by Angela and her supporters that something less than due process was being used in the state's legal conduct of the judicial proceedings.

In a statement to the Court on May 5, Ruchell Magee set forth the reasons why he rejected the court-appointed attorneys and wished to conduct his own case. He said, "I cannot accept an attorney, an attorney appointed by a state judge nor federal judge at this particular time due to the fact that I'm aware, and fully aware of a conspiracy that exists from President Nixon down to prison guards in this case, out to hide and conceal evidence in this case, evidence that will prove and show that the entire State of California, the American judicial system, prison system, is practicing slavery under the color of law, without legal power or authority. One would have to be very naive to believe that any court could appoint one attorney to whip themselves, or expose themselves. This is the reason that I constantly refused attorneys. . . ."

Reading Magee's impassioned statement it is easy to forget the violent murders which occurred at San Rafael. In fact, the larger purpose of setting forth the idea that the trial of Magee and Angela was, in fact, a "political" trial was to focus attention on the area where the strongest case could be made, namely their right to hold dissenting and unpopular political opinions, and downgrade the only thing the trial was really about, namely the facts of the case of the shoot-out at the Marin County Courthouse.

Neither Angela nor Magee, despite their protestations, were being tried for their political opinions. They would, of course, have preferred to be tried for their opinions for, in that event, the defense they were using at this time would be both relevant and deserving of support. In law it has often been said that when an attorney has the facts of a case on his side he argues the facts, and that when he has the law on his side, he argues the law. When neither the facts nor the law support his case, he argues about politics and personalities, he protests and pleads and demonstrates. In this sense, the Angela Davis case seemed to fit a familiar pattern.

In setting forth the reasons why she should be permitted to defend herself in court, Angela was eloquent about the plight of the black Americans, attempting thereby to transform her

[186]

trial into one in which she was accused of being black rather than one in which she was accused of murder. In her presentation to the court, she stated: "From the pre-Civil War slave codes and the equally pernicious Black codes of the postwar period to the overt, codified racism of the South and the more institutionalized racism of the country as a whole, Black people have consistently been the victims of what is supposed to be 'justice.' In a courtroom situation, the white prosecutor, the white witnesses, especially white policemen are given far more credence by the jury—usually overwhelmingly white—than the Black defendant. In the event that the Black defendant has been previously convicted of a crime, his chances of acquittal are virtually nonexistent. He is therefore generally advised by his white court-appointed lawyer to enter a guilty plea even when he is manifestly innocent."

Angela continued: "The political character of this case gives my request to represent myself all the more validity and force. . . . It cannot be denied that I am a Black woman, member of the Communist Party, active in the Black Liberation struggle and the larger revolutionary movement for socialism. This is directly relevant to the case against me."

Angela, in a veiled threat to the court, declared, "It should be of interest to the court that some of the most serious courtroom disruptions of this period have proceeded from the failure of the court to permit defendants in political trials to represent themselves. This is to say, the disruptions were provoked in part by the presiding judges. The outrages which occurred during the Chicago Eight conspiracy trial—the chaining and gagging of Brother Bobby Seale—followed as a result of the court's denial of his right to defend himself. I ask the court to consider the proposition that when formal considerations of order are placed above justice, it is usually disorder which prevails. On the other hand, out of a true and sincere respect for justice, order naturally flows."

Angela Davis was, of course, not the only one who had been attempting to place the question of the murder charge in the background and transform her trial into a political confrontation which radicals could then turn to a propaganda advantage in their continuing efforts to foment internal disorder. The National Conference of Black Lawyers announced that a panel of twelve black law professors from eleven colleges would provide advice and counsel to the defense of Angela Davis in California. In an article in the *Washington Evening Star,* Dean Paul E. Miller of the Howard University Law School presented the reasons for this unprecedented move.

Dean Miller argued that the black law professors joined together in this effort not because they supported Angela's political views, but simply because they were dedicated to the proposition that all Americans should receive fair trials. He wrote: "We have not joined together to champion ideology. This has not been a consideration at all. I neither know nor care what political views other members of the panel hold. To me, and, I hope, to each of the individual panel members, what Miss Davis espouses, what political 'bag' she is in, and what and who her associates are, are irrelevant. What is relevant and important is our deep belief in the soundness and sanctity of the principle that any American citizen, irrespective of color, political belief, race, class or economic station, is entitled to all the privileges, rights and immunities incident to that citizenship. We are determined to live by that principle and in the practice of law to honor it."

Dean Miller proceeded to say a good deal about what he considers to be "various pieces of legislation which seriously threaten individual freedom." Among such pieces of legislation he listed the Organized Crime Control Act, the Comprehensive Drug Abuse Prevention and Control Act, and the District of Columbia Court Reform Act. Without spelling out what they are, or even mentioning their substance, he declared that all of these acts "carry provisions which are sinister threats to rights guaranteed individuals by our Constitution."

Whatever the case may be with regard to these various pieces of legislation, their relationship to the case of Angela Davis is difficult to discern. Dean Miller, however, did return to the subject of his article. He stated, "We cannot allow capricious and arbitrary acts by governmental officials to deprive any individual of his dignity—and as long as one human being, be it Angela Davis or anyone else, is deprived of the social justice that is guaranteed under our Constitution, no citizen is safe.

The time is gone forever when middle-class blacks who have a certain expertise will sit back and allow their leadership to be destroyed by those who believe that a contrary opinion is a dangerous force."

These are, of course, sentiments which few men of good will, either white or black, would challenge. How they apply to the case of Angela Davis remains questionable. Dean Miller's article was published on February 14, 1971. At that time pretrial hearings in the Angela Davis case had not yet begun. The defense's pretrial motions had been submitted to the Marin County Court on February 5. In no sense had Angela Davis' rights been violated in any way. She had been arrested not for her political views but for murder. She had been indicted by a grand jury, and extradited from New York to California after fleeing from that state, according to the proper legal processes.

Dean Miller's statement, as well as most similar statements which have been made concerning Angela Davis, bear little relationship to the facts of the case. They are, instead, generalized statements about American society and the racial problems and tensions that exist within it. In an article entitled "In Defense of the Rights of Angela Davis," Dean Miller said almost nothing about the murder charge, or about the violence that occurred at the San Rafael courthouse. Instead, he discussed the demands that black militants are making of American society.

In this vein, he wrote: "The blacks of today as well as the youth, Chicanos and brown Americans are, indeed, making certain demands of government. They are in fact demanding power to deal with the various political and legislative forces that repress them. They are demanding respect not at the expense of another individual's dignity but respect as human beings. They are demanding enlightenment so as to achieve freedom of thought, liberty of association and liberty to believe in one political ideology over another. They are demanding the right to participate fully in the wealth of this nation, to share this nation's destiny. . . . We have formed this panel and with these aims we intend to actively participate in Angela Davis' defense."

We understand all too well why the Communist Party, the

[189]

Black Panthers and other violent and revolutionary organizations sought to transform the murder trial of Angela Davis into a political trial, to make it appear that Angela was being tried for her opinions and thoughts rather than for her actions. They hoped to create a martyr, to create the impression within our own country and in the world that political and intellectual freedom has ceased to exist in America, that the American judicial system provides something other than justice to blacks and to those who hold unpopular and dissenting viewpoints. This is transparent—it has happened before and will happen as long as revolutionary movements exist.

It is more difficult to understand why seemingly thoughtful men such as Dean Miller, men whose role it is to teach the law and practice and support it, adopted the same tactic. Perhaps the militants have succeeded in intimidating those black Americans who are not Communists or radicals into believing that they must adopt such a stance in order not to be accused of being an "Uncle Tom." What is doubly unfortunate is that those who adopt such a posture are probably more guilty of being "uncle Toms" than are any others. They are, after all, engaged in what Tom Wolfe so accurately described as "radical chic" and "Mau Mauing" the white liberals. The Panthers, in reality, are not attacking white society. They are, in a larger sense, saying and doing the kinds of things that masochistic white liberal intellectuals want to hear and see. As a result, such white liberals have seen fit to contribute large sums of money to the very black militants who threaten most vocally to tear down the society. It is an interesting and dangerous game. It is too bad that the National Conference of Black Lawyers seems to have failed to understand its real meaning.

Many recall an example of this process. In January, 1970, ninety people, including individuals such as Leonard Bernstein, Otto Preminger, Peter Duchin and Mrs. August Hecksher, the wife of one of New York Mayor John Lindsay's leading appointees, attended a meeting held in the apartment of Leonard Bernstein. There they heard Donald Cox, the field marshal of the Black Panther Party.

Cox told the group that if full employment is not available, "then we must take the means of production and put them in

[190]

the hands of the people." Cox called America "the most oppressive country in the world." The result was: checks totaling $3,-000 presented to the Panthers, including a $1,000 check from film producer Otto Preminger.

The Panthers are clearly a violence-prone, revolutionary, Marxist organization. Founded in 1966, its platform states: "We want an end to the robbery by the capitalist of our black community . . . education for our people that exposes the true nature of the decadent American society . . . an immediate end to the police brutality and murder of black people . . . a United Nations-supervised plebiscite to be held throughout the black colony in which only black colonial subjects will be allowed to participate. . . ." Required reading for Panthers are the works of Marx and Engels, Lenin, Mao and Che Guevara.

The Panthers' abstract principles translate into such calls to action as "Dynamite! Black Power! Use the Gun! Kill The Pig Everywhere!" and "In order to stop the slaughter of the people we must accelerate the slaughter of the pigs." Children who receive the much-discussed free breakfasts from the Panthers are taught to chant "Kill the Pigs! Kill the Pigs!" In Illinois all Panthers had to attend three "political orientation classes" weekly, sell a quota of party newspapers, and own and know how to use at least two guns. David Hilliard, the Party's Chief of Staff, is under arrest for threatening the life of President Nixon. What he said was: "We will kill Richard Nixon. We will kill any ___ that stands in the way of our freedom."

The day after the meeting at Leonard Bernstein's apartment, the *New York Times* criticized those who had participated in this masochistic session of hate for America: "Emergence of the Black Panthers as the romanticized darlings of the politico-cultural jet set is an affront to the majority of black Americans. This so-called party, with its confusion of Mao-Marxist ideology and fascist para-militarism, is fully entitled to protection of its members' constitutional rights . . . the group therapy plus fund-raising soiree at the home of Leonard Bernstein . . . represents the sort of elegant slumming that degrades patrons and patronized alike."

The *Times* noted, "It might be dismissed as guilt-relieving fun spiked with social consciousness, except for its impact on

[191]

those blacks and whites seriously working for complete equality and social justice. . . . Responsible black leadership is not likely to cheer as the Beautiful People create a new myth that Black Panther is beautiful."

The Panthers, of course, do not deny their violence, but proclaim it. At the very moment when the Bernstein meeting was taking place, *The Black Panther* newspaper proclaimed that "last year [1969] 167 pigs were thinned out by liberation fighters and this year looks as though it will surpass last year." This, most observers believe, is far in excess of the real figures. The real figures are bad enough: in 11 cities, 5 dead and 42 wounded in 26 months, including 4 dead and 23 wounded in the 6 months preceding the Bernstein affair.

Despite all of this, the white liberals proceeded with their plans to lionize the Panthers. Nearly a dozen more parties for the Panthers were held. They ranged from 5 to 7 P.M. cocktail parties to buffet dinners with speakers. One East Side meeting in New York involved more than one hundred people. Show business people as well as Panthers agreed to participate in a large benefit in New Rochelle.

Panther leader Hilliard at this time declared, "We advocate the very direct overthrow of the government by way of force and violence, by picking up guns and moving against it because we recognize it as being oppressive and . . . we know that the only solution to it is armed struggle." It is sentiments such as these which have produced such a positive response from so many self-proclaimed liberals. It is the same people, for the same confused motives, who were in the forefront of the movement in behalf of Angela Davis.

An argument used by political extremists both in the case of the Panthers and in the case of Angela Davis is that it is not possible for black radicals to receive a fair trial in American society as it is constituted at this time. Such individuals, they argue, are prisoners of a repressive society, a society that seeks to eliminate them as examples to any others who might have ideas of dissent or rebellion.

Setting forth this view, Negro author James Baldwin states, "Only a handful of the millions of people in this vast place are aware that the fate intended for you, Sister Angela, and for

[192]

George Jackson, and for the numberless prisoners in our concentration camps—for that is what they are—is a fate which is
about to engulf them too. . . . We know that we, the Blacks, and
not only we, the Blacks, have been, and are, the victims of a
system whose only fuel is profits, whose only god is profit. We
know that the fruits of this system have been ignorance, despair, and death, and we know that the system is doomed because the world can no longer afford it. . . . If we know, then we
must fight for your life as though it were our own—which it is
—and render impassable with our bodies the corridor to the gas
chamber. For, if they take you in the morning, they will be
coming for us in the night."

The impassioned statements of men such as James Baldwin
have had a significant impact, but the fact is that they are based
far more on passion than on reality. A look at the facts shows
that the claim that black radicals cannot receive fair trials is
totally at variance with the record.

Over the past several years many in the Black Panther Party
have been on trial for crimes ranging from bombing to conspiracy to murder. In case after case the jury has come back
with a quick verdict of not guilty. The trials may have been
unfair, in the sense that they were weighted *in favor* of the
Panthers. They were, however, clearly not unfair in the direction claimed by black militants.

An Associated Press dispatch from New Orleans, dated August 7, 1971, includes the following: "All twelve Black Panthers
on trial for attempted murder in a shoot-out with police last
September were found innocent by a unanimous vote of a
criminal court jury Friday after a 30-minute deliberation. The
case went to the twelve-man jury, of which ten were black and
two white in late afternoon. Only nine jurors had to agree on
a verdict, but each stood in turn and said, 'Not guilty.' "

The report continued: "Assistant District Attorney Numa
Bertel had told the jury earlier that the twelve Black Panthers
were dedicated militants who made their own law. 'You must
decide whether their law or the law you and I live by is the right
one,' he said in closing arguments of the one-week trial."

According to this story, "One of the two white jurors said most
of the half-hour deliberation was spent trying to decide not on

[193]

the guilt or innocence of the defendants, but whether to make a statement with the verdict. He said some jurors wanted to include a statement that the defendants were not acquitted because they were Panthers, but only in the interest of justice. However, they decided the two best words would be 'not guilty.' "

At least two things are clear from this brief report: all twelve jurors had already decided that they would vote not guilty, and they did not use even the short half-hour to deliberate on the verdict.

The Panthers, far from being unable to receive a fair trial, are using the American legal system to subvert justice. By skillful maneuvering and by using their challenges, the Panther defense attorneys are able to eliminate from a jury those who might not be friendly to their cause, while ensuring the inclusion of Panther sympathizers.

Of greater frequency is the Panther strategy of controlling juries by sheer terror. How many men or women are willing to stand up in open court to pronounce a guilty verdict against the Black Panthers and then return to his or her home in the black community? Just one of many examples of this fear and terror is shown in connection with one of the Black Panther trials in New York. On Page 42 of the *New York Times* of January 14, 1971 was a story by Edith Evans Asbury that was headlined: "Panther Aided the Police Despite Fear, Trial Is Told." It began this way:

"Joan Bird was afraid 'her blood would be spilled and her family's blood would be spilled if she cooperated with the police' following her arrest after an alleged Black Panther-police shoot-out, a detective testified yesterday.

"Miss Bird did decide to cooperate, however, Detective Delvar Watson said, and explained that she had been at the scene of the shoot-out because she had been sent 'to prove herself as a Black Panther'. . . .

"He conceded that Miss Bird cried and sobbed now and then, and was very frightened. This, he said, was primarily because she was worried about her mother who, Miss Bird told him, 'is a very excitable woman' and had 'worked too hard to put her through school.' "

[194]

In addition to this example of persons in the black community terrified by the Panthers, a number of additional points of interest were brought out in the same article. The defendant told how she joined the Black Panther Party and had taken courses in guerrilla warfare at Panther headquarters and at apartments of other members. She told how the goal of the party was the violent overthrow of the government and "breaking the back of the law by explosions in public places which would cause mad chaos."

When asked how this group on Seventh Avenue in New York could hope to accomplish all this, she replied that there were other such groups in almost every city and a national headquarters in California.

In this particular trial in New York City the charge was conspiracy to bomb public places—department stores, railroad terminals, police stations. The plan for the police stations, it was alleged, was to bomb them and then shoot the police as they ran from the building.

The trial took many months. Weapons and explosives were found in the homes of the defendants and presented as evidence. Three undercover police informants who had infiltrated the Panthers gave details of the elaborate plans that had been laid. Despite all this, the New York jury reached its verdict quickly and unanimously. All the defendants were declared not guilty on all counts—not guilty even of possessing the very weapons that had been shown in the courtroom.

In this trial, there had originally been twenty-two defendants. The number was later reduced to thirteen. Three of them, Michael Tabor, Richard Moore, and Edward Josephs, had disappeared and were presumed to have fled to Algeria.

An interesting footnote to this case appears in an Associated Press story of June, 1971: "Two Black Panthers arrested in a mass holdup at a black social club were held without bail Sunday after police connected them to the May 19 machine-gunning of two policemen. A prosecutor said facts in the case related also to the May 21 murder of two other officers. The two men, Richard Moore and Edward Josephs, had been missing since last February when they jumped bail as defendants in the Black Panther bomb conspiracy case here."

[195]

A submachine gun used in the holdup had been positively identified as the one that riddled the two policemen on May 19. Yet, these men were among those who had been declared innocent in the bomb conspiracy trial. This certainly does not appear to be a legal system "stacked against" the Panthers.

It is not only black militants, however, who argue that a black radical cannot receive a fair trial. Yale University President Kingman Brewster, for example, declared that he did not believe that Black Panthers could receive a fair trial anyplace in the country. The particular case that had prompted Mr. Brewster's statement was that of Bobby Seale and Mrs. Ericka Huggins. Seale, national chairman of the Black Panthers, and Mrs. Huggins were accused of ordering the murder of Alex Rackley, whom they suspected of being an informant for the police.

One of the pieces of evidence in the case was a tape recording, made by Mrs. Huggins, vividly describing the torture of Rackley in Black Panther headquarters. Then there was the mutilated body of Rackley found in a Middlefield, Connecticut, swamp. But the jury could not agree on a verdict. Two voted for conviction; ten voted for complete acquittal. This is, of course, a hung jury, and the usual procedure is for a new trial to take place with a new jury.

The judge in this case, however, came up with the opinion that an impartial jury would be impossible to find, and he dismissed the case against both Seale and Mrs. Huggins. They were, thus, free to proceed with the Panther's business of fomenting violence, disorder, and revolution.

This allegedly "unfair" legal system spent four months and called 1,500 prospective jurors before the final panel of seven whites and five blacks was chosen. After the verdict, two of the jurors were in the front ranks of those cheering Bobby Seale.

Another Panther leader, David Hilliard, was freed from serious charges, this time with the judge clearly showing a bias not against him, but in his behalf. Hilliard had told an antiwar rally on November 15, 1969, "We will kill Richard Nixon." Threatening the life of the President is a crime, and Hilliard was so charged.

There had, however, been wiretap surveillance on Hilliard's other allegedly subversive activities. Even though they had no bearing on this case, the defense asked that it be allowed to hear all of the wiretaps that the government had on Hilliard. This could clearly have endangered national security, but U. S. District Judge William P. Gray ruled that either the government must disclose the information to Hilliard or the case would be dismissed. As a result, Hilliard went free. Here again, it is difficult to see any bias *against* Panther defendants. The bias seems to be almost uniformly in the other direction.

The argument that Angela Davis could not receive a fair trial was, of course, simply a replay of the same arguments that were passionately presented with regard to the Panthers. The fact that they were not true with regard to the Panthers, and not true with regard to Angela Davis, has had little effect, for these arguments are presented for political and not legal purposes. The purpose, again, is to discredit the American judicial system and to create political martyrs. In such an instance, the facts of any given case are irrelevant.

When Angela was captured she was accompanied by David Poindexter. He was, at that time, charged with aiding and harboring a fugitive. Poindexter simply contended that he was innocent because he did not know that Angela was a fugitive. It was brought out that this fact was well publicized by newspapers, radio and television, yet Poindexter claimed that he did not read the papers or hear the broadcasts. The judge accepted his response, and he went free. Once again, where is the bias against black radicals which the world is being told is inherent in the American legal system? The fact is that it is no place to be found.

This fact, however, had little to do with stemming the tide or impact of the growing "Free Angela" movement which rose throughout the world—in Europe, Latin America and Asia, in Communist as well as in Western countries. The question of whether or not she was guilty of the charges against her was obscured by those who had purposes of their own in adopting the case of Angela Davis.

7

THE CASE OF ANGELA DAVIS HAS DIVIDED MANY AMERICANS, FOR A variety of reasons. Few, however, have fought more bitterly over this case than have members of the United Presbyterian Church.

The Presbyterian Council on Church and Race allocated $10,-000 from its Emergency Legal Defense Fund to Angela's defense. The money was paid May 18 and the disclosure of the gift was made at the denomination's general assembly in Rochester, New York on May 24, 1971.

Presbyterian Life magazine, in its issue of July 15, 1971, noted, "Four weeks after the General Assembly adjourned, the officials of the United Presbyterian Church were still hearing from United Presbyterians about the decisions reached by the commissioners in Rochester. Some actions were criticized. Some were praised. Nothing else, however, stirred as much comment as the announcement at the General Assembly that the Council on Church and Race had made a grant of $10,000 from the Emergency Fund for Legal Aid for the defense of Miss Angela Davis. The volume of mail reaching the Moderator, the Stated Clerk, *Presbyterian Life,* and others was altogether without precedent. The correspondence was overwhelmingly negative about the grant, a fact that cannot be entirely dismissed with the observation that most people who are pleased with a development do not bother to write about it."

The Session of the First United Presbyterian Church of Abilene, Kansas, registered its opposition to the church's involvement in the Angela Davis case. It stated: "We question the propriety of this action for the following reasons: (a) that such a gift does not assure a 'fair trial' nor any appreciable movement in this direction; (b) that because of the self-stated objectives of the Marin County defendants any gift is subject to gross misinterpretation; (c) that such a gift does not represent any adequate evangelistic or missionary effort toward the Marin County defendants in behalf of Jesus Christ; and (4) that such a gift does not represent an adequate ordering of priorities by our boards and agencies when our other mission efforts are being curtailed. . . ."

Writing in *Presbyterian Life*, a church member, Judge Martin De Vries of Long Beach, California, declared, "Our laws and constitutional provisions already give Angela Davis more legal protection than she would receive in any other country in the world. The doctrines of reasonable doubt, presumption of innocence, self-incrimination, her right to a jury trial, appeals, and the right to be represented by able attorneys make the award of $10,000 an unwise and absurd use of church funds. In approving this action, the United Presbyterian Church, U.S.A., sets a precedent for all future criminal cases that must be avoided by rescinding the action it has taken. . . ."

A letter from the prestigious National Presbyterian Church of Washington, D.C., was critical of the grant to Angela Davis. Signed by the Rev. Edward L. R. Elson, moderator of the church and chaplain of the United States Senate, and Ervin N. Chapman, clerk of the church, the letter states the following:

"Nothing we heard or read concerning the gift of Presbyterian money by the Council on Church and Race to the defense of Angela Davis mitigates our feeling of disappointment, revulsion, and for many persons outright indignation. We note that the General Assembly itself held 'serious questions concerning the propriety' of this grant. Long ago it was said that 'Church Councils do err.' We regret that the Moderator of the General Assembly in her first message to church sessions has been placed under the burden of attempting to explain what is not explainable.

[199]

"Can it be that Church people have been seized by such exaggerated guilt feelings about race, and such an intense desire to avoid the slightest accusation of being 'anti-Communist' that there remains no longer a proper sense of responsibility, rationality, or perspective?

"Whatever else is known about Angela Davis, she is a self-confessed Communist who openly taught atheism, Marxism, and anti-Americanism in an honored university position.

"Even so, Miss Davis *is not* under indictment for her *ideas* but for murder or as an accomplice in murder.

"Being a self-confessed and widely advertised member of the Communist Party, she gave no intention of making a Christian witness in any sense.

"Moreover, as a self-confessed Communist, unlimited funds are surely available to her as they were to the Rosenbergs in the nineteen fifties—the resources of the whole world Communist apparatus. To provide Miss Davis with Church funds from any source seems to us to be an immoral squandering of dedicated dollars which on any basis is indefensible."

Briefly, this is the way the grant to Angela Davis' defense came about. In 1970 the Presbyterian Church set up its Emergency Fund for Legal Aid to be administered by its Council on Church and Race. The Board of Missions made $100,000 available, not from general mission funds, but from unrestricted gifts, legacies and individual bequests. The Council established guidelines for the use of the fund and the staff of the council, or Division of Church and Race of the Board of National Missions, administered it.

St. Andrew Presbyterian Church, in Marin County, California, whose court had Angela Davis in custody, expressed concern for a fair trial for her, and in February, 1971, submitted the statement to the Council on Church and Race, which concurred in it.

Later, the Office of Ethnic Affairs of the Golden Gate Synod, to which St. Andrew Church belongs, asked about a grant from the fund. The staff investigated and made the grant, and it was revealed a few days later to the General Assembly.

At this time, the uproar broke out. Delegates talked about doing away with the fund, restricting grants to $1,000 and barring any further grants to Angela Davis. The assembly turned down all of these proposals and continued the fund, but let the council know that it had "serious questions" about the Davis grant.

Upset by the protests, a group called the Black United Presbyterians donated $10,000 to the church's emergency legal aid fund, the fund from which the money was being drawn for Angela Davis' defense. In a letter dated June 7, six black Presbyterian ministers wrote:

"We the undersigned Black United Presbyterians concerned about the continuing reaction and alarm among some United Presbyterians over the church and race [committee] grant to the Angela Davis Marin County Legal Defense Fund, met on Saturday, June 5, and have come to the conclusion that it is our moral obligation to take some appropriate action on this issue.

"As a result of the meeting on June 5, a group of Black United Presbyterians are contributing the sum of $10,000 to the United Presbyterian Church, designated to the emergency legal aid fund. In this way we assume personal responsibility, as Black Presbyterians, for the United Presbyterian grant to the Angela Davis Defense Fund."

It is clear that the decision of the Presbyterian Church to contribute the money it did to the Angela Davis defense fund is based on a critique of the American society which holds that, somehow, that society has become repressive and that the likelihood of a fair trial for one with unpopular views is questionable. This decision, of course, has been reached despite the overwhelming burden of proof available to dispute it.

The document *Racism and Repression,* received for study by the church assembly, makes its position clear. It states: "We face today a future characterized not merely by the normal reluctance to change, but by a growing conservatism that is ready to apply inhibiting political and judicial sanctions against dissent and to bait militant groups into open confrontation in order to destroy them with an overwhelming application of force and violence. Such action on the part of the state, when directed against whole communities of minority persons, borders on genocide."

Discussing a society as far from the reality of present-day

[201]

America as any could be, this document declares that "We face today a future characterized . . . by huge systems of police surveillance and secret files; no-knock laws, anti-riot laws, and other legislation that can be broadly interpreted and used against minorities; unpunished violence by whites, as in Cairo, Illinois; and the repression of silence, in which the church participates."

Overlooking the vast resources at her disposal, and the judicial record of dismissal after dismissal in the case of black militants on trial in recent days, the Rev. Edler G. Hawkins, who in 1964 became the first black pastor to win election as United Presbyterian moderator, stated, "Our hope is that no one will confuse the issue in a discussion of Miss Davis' political affiliation. . . . We made the grant because we knew this black woman needed help in securing an adequate defense just because she was black, and a woman, and because she, too, must be treated as 'innocent' until proven guilty."

The Rev. Lester Kinsolving, an Episcopal minister and syndicated newspaper columnist, devoted one of his columns to the Rev. Cecil A. Williams, pastor of Glide Memorial Methodist Church in San Francisco. Williams, who has been widely publicized as the spiritual adviser of Angela Davis, presides over a church which the Rev. Kinsolving describes in these terms: "There are three red hot combos, with which Williams has displaced the church's mighty organ. A psychedelic light show diverts anyone's memory from the magnificent choir which Williams dismissed en masse, two years ago. The giant cross . . . has also been removed by Williams, who is now the center of the stage—where he delivers a sort of stylized ranting, which is obediently punctuated (on cue) by shouts of 'right on!' from an adoring interracial flock, whose vesture runs a wide gamut from Brooks Brothers to Omar the Tentmaker."

Another clergyman, the Rev. Earl Neil of Oakland, California, presided over the funeral of George Jackson, and shares with the Rev. Williams a passionate dedication to the cause of black militancy. Discussing this situation, the Rev. Kinsolving notes that ". . . why it is any less scandalous for an Episcopal priest to chaplain to this violent, bigoted, segregated band of hustlers than for Baptist ministers to have served as chaplains

('Kleagles') for the Ku Klux Klan, has not yet been explained by Episcopal authorities."

An editorial in the *Presbyterian Layman* stated, "It is hard to understand how and why . . . our United Presbyterian Church could provide $100,000 for legal defense . . . and yet grant only $86,000 for evangelism; why $10,000 could be given for Angela Davis . . . and yet was hard pressed to provide only $350,000 in support of each church-related college—and all when the church has been forced to recall missionaries and cut back on other valid work because of lack of funds."

The *Presbyterian Layman* expressed the view that individuals, ministers and laymen are encouraged to involve themselves in any political, social or economic cause they choose, but that "The Committee . . . questions the right and authority of official church bodies to take such actions on behalf of the church, especially where their competence to speak has not been clearly established, and where both sides have not been thoroughly heard and considered in advance of the action."

Regardless of where their sympathies lie, 3.1 million Presbyterians will not soon forget the controversy over Angela Davis which rocked their church. Unfortunately, the involvement of religious organizations with radical politics is not an isolated phenomenon. It is one which we have been witnessing for many years, and on the part of most major denominations.

The World Council of Churches, for example, has moved from an advocacy of peaceful change to vocal and financial support for revolution. This became clear at a "World Conference on Church and Society," which it sponsored in Geneva in 1966. This meeting included 420 participants representing 164 churches in 80 countries. The usual clergymen and theologians were there. In addition were a number of economists and "political experts," all on the ideological far left.

Speakers called for a fundamental "restructuring of the world economy," a shifting of millions of employed workers from developed countries to those in the developing stage, even though such forced migration would "necessarily imply temporary dislocation and possible suffering for a large number of people." This project was to be financed by an "international

[203]

tax" levied on the "have" nations, of at least two percent of their gross national product.

Writing in the *Reader's Digest,* Clarence W. Hall notes, "The methods used to engineer acceptance of the Program to Combat Racism provide sharp insight into the World Council. First, the Council's secretariat submitted a summons to action at the 1968 General Assembly in Uppsala, Sweden. Heavy emphasis was put on what WCC staffer Baldwin Sjollema (now the Program's director) called 'the church's complicity in benefiting from and furthering white oppression.' Though nobody explained how the church had so benefited, the assembly contritely agreed to the development of a 'crash program' of unspecified nature."

With this mandate, the World Council's staff and a "committee on race" sponsored a "consultation" at London's Notting Hill in May, 1969. Its purpose: "To advise the WCC on an ecumenical program of action to eradicate racism." Its chairman: Senator George McGovern. Participants included a number of black power militants. A Negro identified as George Black leaped to the platform to demand from white churches millions of dollars in "reparations" for ills done to Negroes— $12 million to defend such "political prisoners" as Huey P. Newton, Eldridge Cleaver, and H. Rap Brown; $77 million to support various "liberation" movements; and $48 million to establish a propaganda publishing house dedicated to Malcolm X and Che Guevara. Quoting Mao Tse-tung—"Political power grows out of the barrel of a gun"—Black ended: "We shall have our freedom, or your Christian society, your Christian banks, your Christian factories, your Christian universities, and your fine churches will be leveled forever."

Clarence Hall reports, "Amazingly, this bombastic attempt at blackmail was taken seriously. The delegates spent nine hours discussing it, finally putting to the WCC a recommendation that it 'support the principle of reparations as a way of producing a more favorable balance of economic power throughout the world.' Another recommendation by the 'consultation' included the demand that the WCC and member churches apply economic boycotts against corporations and institutions doing business in countries considered racist (such as South Africa)

[204]

and that, 'all else failing, the churches should support resistance movements, including revolutions.' "

This, for better or worse, is the atmosphere in which the United Presbyterian Church decided to contribute to the defense of Angela Davis. In a sense, it represents a misunderstanding of the nature of the Christian commitment. In a greater sense, it appears to be a masochistic display of self-hatred on the part of white liberals who feel the need to bear a guilt which, in fact, may not be theirs at all.

One thing that seems clear upon a careful examination of the matter is that it is not black Americans who have chosen individuals such as Angela Davis, Bobby Seale or Huey Newton as their heroes. It is, for a variety of reasons, the white liberal establishment that has heralded such militants who, in fact, do not represent any large number of black Americans at all. In large measure, the Angela Davises and Huey Newtons are the black men and women hailed as leaders by white men, but not by members of their own race—much the same situation which was true of those to whom they refer as "uncle Toms" in past eras.

Part of this point was made by Negro columnist William Raspberry writing in the *Washington Post* of November 10, 1971. He noted, "Among the first casualties of the new black consciousness of the 1960s were the white-appointed black leaders and heroes. Whether it was Booker T. Washington or Whitney Young, the easiest way to knock a black man off his hero's pedestal was to have white people say nice things about him. Let white folk describe you as 'a credit to your race,' and blacks automatically put you down as an Uncle Tom or worse."

Thus, according to Raspberry, the axiom became "white people can't choose black people's heroes." Despite this new axiom, the fact which columnist Raspberry and many others have discovered is that today's situation is precisely that: white people are, in reality, choosing the "heroes" of black people. He notes that "Angela Davis, Bobby Seale, Eldridge Cleaver, George Jackson—all are heroes, particularly among young blacks, even though not one in ten can tell you what they have done to merit heroism. They represented no superior philosophy, like Dr. King's; they had no national movement, like Stokely Carmichael or Rap Brown; they put together no comprehensive program like the Nation of Islam; they evidenced no unusual prowess on the order of Willie Mays' or Muhammed Ali's."

The fact is, declares this writer, "They became heroes not because of their own actions but because of the actions of white people. They were jailed, shot, exiled and hated by whites, and that was enough to make them the heroes of young blacks. . . . It is one thing to understand that black people cannot afford to remain silent when a black man is 'convicted' of the crime of thinking wrong thoughts. It is quite another to respond by draping the hero's mantle on any black man so 'convicted.' For what it means is that the FBI, or any county sheriff for that matter, can decide on his own who the next black hero will be."

Part of the reason for the "heroism" and popularity of militant black activists who preach violence, destruction and revolution, is that the mass media of America have raised them to a position of prominence which they could not have achieved in any other manner.

Why is it that we hear so much about the alleged "racism" of American society and so little about the real meaning of our history and the dramatic progress of recent years? News commentator Howard K. Smith noted, "There is a substantial and successful Negro middle class. But the newsmen are not interested in the Negro who succeeds—they are interested in the one who fails and makes loud noises. They have ignored the developments in the South. The South has an increasing number of integrated schools. A large part of the South has accepted integration. We've had a President's Cabinet with a Negro in it, a Supreme Court with a Negro on it—but more important we have 500 Negroes elected to local offices in the deep South. This is a tremendous achievement. But the achievement isn't what we see on the screen."

One of the chief conformist patterns in the news media, states this prize-winning reporter, is the automatic obedience to a convention of negativism in journalism itself. "As reporters," he says, "we have always been falsifying issues by reporting on what goes wrong in a nation where, historically, most has gone right. That is how you get on page one, that is how you win a Pulitzer Prize. This gears the reporter's mind to the negative, even when it is not justified."

For too long, extremists have been permitted to appear as the spokesmen for the aspirations of black Americans. This has led to a situation in which white people accept the militants as legitimate black spokesmen, and since the general society accepts this to be the case, blacks themselves eventually adopt the same view.

Columnist William Raspberry laments this fact. He says, "The problem is that no one believes the eccentrics or the wayward priest to be representative members of their groups. But when a handful of Negroes express radical views, there is the tendency to believe that these views are held by most Negroes ... the militants and radicals have learned how to dramatize their views, how to make them newsworthy. Moderate opinions by their very nature are harder to dramatize, and neither the holders of these opinions nor the media which want to report them have learned how to do it successfully."

The disputes to which the Angela Davis case have given rise within such organizations as the United Presbyterian Church have been overshadowed by the massive campaign being mounted on Angela's behalf by the world Communist movement. That campaign, which is being pursued not only in the United States but throughout the world, both in the East and West, makes the $10,000 Presbyterian contribution seem miniscule by comparision. It tends to prove erroneous the view advanced by Presbyterian advocates of the grant, as well as by the groups of black lawyers who have declared that, somehow, Angela is "in need" of assistance in preparing her defense. It appears that Angela has all of the assistance she needs and may, in fact, have a great deal of "assistance" which she does not need—assistance which, in fact, will harm rather than help her case.

In an article distributed by the North American Newspaper Alliance in November, 1970, Martin Arundel notes, "The U.S. Communist Party hopes to make as much money out of Angela Davis as it did out of the Scottsboro boys in the '30s. The party leaders also expect that, by championing Miss Davis, they will

[207]

lure blacks into the party in record numbers. 'We are committed to building the largest, most comprehensive movement this country has every seen to free Angela Davis,' says James Tormey, the party's Defense Commission chairman."

U.S. Communist Party leader Gus Hall has denounced the charges against Angela Davis as "a Nixon-Reagan frame-up" and insists that "she couldn't get a fair trial in California, because Governor Ronald Reagan has made her an issue in his campaign for re-election."

Hall added: "It is imperative that a movement of national proportions fighting to free this heroic black woman be immediately organized."

Arundel reports, "The party evidently thinks it has another cause célèbre in the Davis Case. She is black, young, and very attractive. To the Communist bosses, she apparently is a symbol of academic freedom, and of the youth, black and women's liberation movements rolled into one."

Party spokesman Tormey made it plain that the Communists intend to fully exploit each one of these areas. He mentioned "black communities," "college campuses," and "Women's Liberation" groups as areas where the Party will concentrate its efforts. He said that money had already started to come into the committee as early as the fall of 1970, and noted $470 had been raised at one "Free Angela Davis" rally in Los Angeles shortly after she had been arrested in New York on October 13.

In its half-century of existence, the U.S. Communist Party has exploited many causes in which it gained a large number of recruits (most of whom soon left the party in disillusionment) and collected large sums of money. The charge has frequently been made by ex-party leaders and members that much of the money raised in these various campaigns had been diverted to the party treasury and used to pay party expenses —salaries, rent, etc.—and also to finance clandestine revolutionary activities.

"One of the most famous cases in which the party stands accused of profiting financially," reports Martin Arundel, "is that of the Scottsboro boys, which took place back in the 1930s and lasted for more than ten years."

In that case nine young blacks were convicted in the Alabama courts and sentenced to death for allegedly raping two white girls on a freight train. The U.S. Supreme Court upset their convictions, and ordered new trials. They were again convicted and most of them served prison sentences, though one of the girls in the case later testified that the rapes never occurred.

According to Arundel "The Communist-dominated International Labor Defense (ILD) took up the defense of the Scottsboro boys and made it a worldwide issue. The ILD was then headed by William Patterson, long one of the most prominent black Communists in the United States. Patterson, now in his mid-70s, is reported to be in on the planning of the Davis campaign. Patterson placed ILD Scottsboro Defense Fund (SDF) collection cans at the doors of every left wing rally in the country. The ILD is rumored to have collected 'millions.' Some former Reds connected with the campaign insist that close to $3 million was collected, but a more conservative figure, which is believed to be more accurate, is $1.5 million. Several ex-Communists maintain that close to 75 percent of the money collected by the ILD in the Scottsboro campaign found its way into the party coffers."

The campaign on behalf of Angela Davis has received official encouragement and support from the Soviet Union. In what appeared to be an official Soviet campaign in her support, the government press agency TASS issued a long commentary on her case early in 1971. Angela was described as a young Communist and "courageous fighter for freedom." The charges against her, said Tass, were groundless and came against a background of a campaign of hounding and intimidation of those who press for social change.

Soviet intellectuals, including composer Dmitri Shostakovich and Aram Kachiturian and the ballerina Maya Plisetskya, wrote to President Nixon requesting clemency for Angela Davis. The letter was signed December 30, 1970, five days after a similar message was sent to the President by fourteen Soviet scientists. In the latter case, the President responded promptly by inviting the fourteen to attend the trial as observers.

The *Daily World*, official paper of the Communist Party of the United States, continually granted front-page coverage to Angela and claimed that a "Free Angela campaign sweeps

Sovietland." According to the *World*, workers of the Moscow tire factory, the Soviet Women's Committee, the Soviet Teachers Union, Patrice Lumumba University, and the Pioneers and Komsomols (young Communists) are mounting a major campaign to free her. The *World's* Moscow correspondent, Mike Davidow, reported that "In the Tadjik and Turkmen republics, schoolchildren have written letters to President Nixon and Governor Reagan demanding her freedom."

The national coordinator of the "Free Angela" movement is Franklin Alexander, who operates the group's national headquarters in Los Angeles. A 1968 report by the House Committee on Un-American Activities states clearly that "Alexander is a member of the Communist Party, U.S.A." and was a leader in the W. E. B. Du Bois Clubs. The Du Bois clubs have served as the youth arm of the Communist Party and in 1968 were charged with being a "Communist front" organization by Attorney General Nicholas deB. Katzenbach. Alexander's sister, according to sworn testimony, is Charlene Mitchell, a member of the National Committee of the Communist Party, U.S.A. On March 9, 1970, Gerald Wayne Kirk, who worked as an undercover source for the FBI for several years, testified before the Senate Internal Security Subcommittee that Alexander told him personally that he was acting as an agent of the Communist Party. There is, it seems, little doubt about who is orchestrating the "Free Angela" movement.

Only two days after Angela was captured by the FBI in New York, October 15, 1970, a press conference was called in Los Angeles by the Communist Party to announce that it was going to build "the largest, broadest, most all-encompassing people's movement the country has ever seen to free our comrade, Angela Davis—political prisoner." The speaker was Franklin Alexander. The National United Committee was formed shortly thereafter, with Alexander and Fania Davis Jordan, Angela's younger sister, as national coordinators.

According to Alexander, there were, during the summer of 1971, sixty fully functioning local committees in operation around the country. The national committee staff coordinated the work of the local committees, supplying them with literature, posters and speakers, and, in conjunction with the legal staff, set the over-all political strategy.

Writing in the *New York Times Magazine*, Sol Stern, a contributing editor of *Ramparts Magazine*, reported that "The money that pays the salaries comes in steadily from a variety of sources: from people on traditionally liberal mailing lists who have been sent letters; from collection cans set up outside supermarkets; from spontaneous, unsolicited donations, such as the $10,000 given by an affiliate of the United Presbyterian Church, and from the profits of extravanganzas such as the birthday celebration for Angela attended by about 5,000 people at the Manhatten Center in New York last February, with the Rev. Ralph Abernathy, chairman of the Southern Christian Leadership Conference, as speaker."

Mr. Stern notes, "It is not to belittle the seriousness of her situation to say that she has the best-organized, most broadbased defense effort in the recent history of radical political trials—more potent than that afforded to any of the Panther leaders or the Chicago seven. Much of the strength is due to the considerable resources which the Communist Party, U.S.A., still alive and kicking after many lean years, is putting into the struggle. And, as one Bay Area radical put it: 'If there's one thing the Communist Party does well, it's organizing a legal defense.' "

Many other black radicals have been critical of Angela's close ties with the Communist Party. The Black Panther newspaper of January 23, 1971, published a statement by Eldridge Cleaver from Algiers. Cleaver made the charge that the Free Angela movement was started by the "Communist Party in collusion with the U.S. fascists," in order to divert attention, resources and support away from the trial of Bobby Seale in New Haven. Despite such criticisms, the Communist Party remained in firm control of the prospering Free Angela movement.

One of Angela's attorneys, Margaret Burnham, frankly proclaimed the leadership being exercised by the Communist Party. She stated, "The party is playing a major role. Angela is a member and it is incumbent on the party to come to her defense. I say that because we want to be up front about it. There is no 'infiltration' in the case—they are there."

Despite the fact of Communist leadership and support, the Free Angela movement has the support of many non-Communists, for a variety of reasons. The committee has a long list of support from such prominent blacks as Coretta King, Ralph Abernathy and Aretha Franklin. Miss Franklin offered to post Angela's bail, ". . . not because I believe in communism but because she is a black woman and she wants freedom for black people." Organizations supporting Angela range from the Urban League to the Black Panthers.

In fact, Washington, D.C.'s nonvoting delegate, Walter Fauntroy, endorsed a Free Angela rally held at the Frederick Douglass Home in that city. He said that Angela is a "political prisoner" and that her incarceration was the result of her being an avowed Communist. Fauntroy declared, "I am fearful that our country is moving at a fast pace toward a more repressive and police oriented society" and added that he would urge the congressional black caucus to hold its own hearings on the Davis case.

Despite the involvement of such non-Communists as Rep. Fauntroy, the fact remains, states Sol Stern, that ". . . it is clear that the Communist Party people on the committee are making the key decisions about how this broad front is to be used in the legal battle."

The Communist Party's connections seem even more significant in the Free Angela demonstrations overseas. A recent sampling of protest activities included the following: In Ceylon, a three-day vigil by 2,500 women in front of the American embassy; in Sydney, Australia, a march by 700 women; a telegram demanding Angela's freedom signed by the entire cast and crew of the film "Z," including Yves Montand, Simone Signoret, director Costa Gavras and composer Mikis Theodorakis.

"We have received 100,000 pieces of mail from East Germany alone," states Rob Baker, the publicity director who is the only white on the national staff. "They're lying around in hundreds of mail bags unopened—because we don't have a big enough staff to do the work."

[212]

Communist party-oriented groups such as the Women's International Democratic Federation, with headquarters in East Berlin, have set up Free Angela Committees in scores of countries. In the committee files is a letter from the World Federation of Democratic Youth, based in Budapest, telling the committee that "huge solidarity actions were and are undertaken by all our member organizations in support of Angela Davis."

"In some countries—in Italy, for instance—the party has taken a heavy responsibility," says Baker. "They have printed up thousands of postcards for people to send to Angela, with copies to Reagan, or Hoover, or Nixon. On the other hand, we get things like a letter from a woman who runs a coffee shop in Utrecht and wants to print up thousands of copies of Angela's statement to the court. I would say it is a mixture of party support and nonparty support in every country."

Angela Davis wrote a statement for delivery by William L. Patterson, member of the Communist Party's Political Committee and co-chairman of its Black Liberation Commission, at a symposium in East Berlin, in honor of Paul Robeson's seventy-third birthday. The symposium, held April 13–14, 1971, was under the auspices of the Paul Robeson Committee of East Germany, which has established the Paul Robeson Museum, containing the world's largest collection of Robeson documents, correspondence, books, articles, photographs and paintings.

Angela wrote the following:

"Dear Comrades, Of the innumerable messages of support and solidarity from abroad, the most impressive have been the tens of thousands of letters from the GDR [German Democratic Republic]. The letters and especially the drawings from the schoolchildren of your country attest to the truth of José Martí's comment on youth: 'Los ninos son la esperanza del mundo.' You have given me and my captive comrades a tremendous reservoir of strength and courage. Having experienced the most formidable eruption of fascism yourselves you, more than anyone, are aware of the dangers we face in the U.S.A.

"The savage aggression against the peoples of Indochina is reflected inside our country by the growing suppression of revolutionaries. As larger sections of the Black, Chicano, and Puerto

Rican communities attain higher levels of political maturity and follow in the tradition of such great men as Paul Robeson and W. E. B. Du Bois by refusing to acquiesce in the government's monstrous deeds, we become the targets of ever-increasing official repression.

"Behind the walls of America's prisons—key instruments, along with the judicial system, in carrying out that repression — political consciousness is developing at an accelerated pace. Prisoners, from 30 percent to 50 percent of whom are Black and Brown in the major cities across this country, are swiftly realizing that their individual 'criminal' acts are inadequate responses to a complex system of monopoly capitalism and that, therefore, they must involve themselves in a collective movement for liberation. The works of Marx, Engels, Lenin, and other revolutionaries are smuggled into prisons and radical political groupings have been formed in virtually every major penal institution.

"There can be no doubt that the blatantly totalitarian structure of the prison renders it by far the most hazardous terrain for struggle. Yet, despite the perils, many of our brothers and sisters have continued to courageously educate and enlighten their imprisoned companions. George Jackson, for example, who has long been a Marxist-Leninist, did not permit his indeterminate life sentence of one year to life to deter him from his political tasks. As a direct consequence of his politics, he had already spent eleven years in prison for a crime which usually brings two and a half years at the very most."

Discussing the shoot-out at San Rafael, which she describes as an "insurrection," Angela continued to state the following:

"The insurrection spearheaded by George Jackson's brother, Jonathan, which occurred August 7, 1970, at San Rafael, must be seen against the background of the unrestrained brutality and political repression rampant in the prsions. Jonathan, James McClain and William Christmas lost their lives in an heroic attempt to compel the people of this country to look through the concrete walls and iron bars of California's prisons and to begin to demand changes.

"Because of my efforts to build a mass movement around the issue of prison repression, the August 7 insurrection was seized

[214]

upon as an excuse to falsely charge me with three capital offenses. . . . Our movement is rapidly achieving the consciousness that a primary target of our struggles against incipient fascism must be the penal system (according to Engels, the chief instrument, together with the army and the police, in maintaining class domination). Paramount among our demands must be the release of all political prisoners—the Soledad Brothers, Black Panther leaders Bobby Seale and Ericka Huggins, Ruchell Magee, myself and all the thousands of brothers and sisters whose names have not been learned as yet. . . . There is no doubt in our minds that the people of the German Democratic Republic will continue to support us in our struggles as we must consider every imperialist attack on your country and its accomplishments an attack against all people fighting for Socialism and peace."

For Angela Davis to speak about "political prisoners" in the same statement in which she is hailing the Communist government of East Germany as a fighter for "Socialism and peace," is the utmost hypocrisy. In an uneducated and unlettered man such as George Jackson such statements can be attributed to his unfamiliarity with what is really occurring within Communist countries. When Angela Davis makes such statements, however, it is clear that she is misleading her non-Communist supporters and that rather than advocating freedom, she is advocating a real system of political repression—with herself and her fellow Communists as the agents of that repression.

It is the East German government, Angela forgets to tell her supporters, which presides over the Berlin Wall which keeps an entire nation enslaved. Were the brave men and women who were killed by East German border guards in their attempts to achieve freedom really "agents of imperialism and fascism"? Is the government which holds its citizens prisoner and refuses to give them the elementary human right to travel freely a model which Angela suggests for America? When Angela denounces her own country as being "repressive" while hailing a truly totalitarian society as being "free," we are reminded once again of the fact that Communists use words such as "repression" and "freedom" to stand for different concepts than are understood by the remainder of the world. When, for example, did East Germany last have free elections? Where in East Germany can *Time* or *The Economist* or *Der Spiegel* be purchased? Angela knows very well where *Pravda* or the *Peking Review* can be obtained in Los Angeles or New York. She fails, however, to acknowledge the difference and very real distinction.

Henry Winston, National Chairman of the U.S. Communist Party, visited Angela Davis in the New York Women's House of Detention on the evening of December 7, 1970. It was the first time that the two Communists had met face to face, and the Communist *Daily World* of January 9, 1971, contains an interview by Gene Tournour with Mr. Winston.

Asked about Angela's morale, Winston replied:

"It couldn't have been higher. She said that she received at least 100 letters a day. Some days the number was as large as 400 letters. She said the letters not only came from all sections of the U.S. but from all the socialist countries, from Asia, Europe, Africa and Latin America.

"In my lifetime I can remember no case of a political prisoner receiving the support that Angela Davis has received. ... Angela was especially moved by the demonstrations of support for her and other political prisoners in communities across the south, and especially in Birmingham, where Black and white were brought together in common cause. She paused a moment before stating in an emotion-charged voice, 'The pigs will rue the day they ever attempted this.'"

Asked how he viewed the case of Angela Davis in the "long history of political persecution in the U.S.," Winston stated:

"In the case of the Rosenbergs this country saw an example of courage and dedication to principle rare in U.S. history. They were the victims of rampant McCarthyism. The guiding spirit of that wave of repression was anti-Sovietism and anti-communism. The show trial of Ethel and Julius Rosenberg saw the highwater mark of the drive of the U.S. ruling class to whip up cold war hysteria and to dismantle the Black Liberation movement, the labor movement and the Communist Party. They sought to behead every form of struggle by the American people for a better and more human society. During that period

[216]

both the Black Liberation movement and the labor movement were put on the defensive."

Winston continued: "Today the attempt to 'get Angela Davis' by the Nixon-Reagan-Rockefeller forces in this country is a foredoomed plan to push the mass movements of the people back into the dark night of McCarthyism. This plan will not work. Every day we see new signs that the leading sections of the Black Liberation movement, the labor movement, the peace movement, the student movement see the attack on Angela Davis as an attack on them."

Rather than discussing any of the facts of the case, such as the origin of the weapons which were used in the violence at the San Rafael Courthouse, Henry Winston follows the pattern of other Communist and non-Communist defenders of Angela Davis. He proceeds to make her a martyr, rather than proclaiming her innocence of the specific charges against her.

He writes, "Angela Davis was chosen for this frameup because in this one courageous woman they had the chance to strike at the upsurge of Black Americans in the community and in the ranks of labor, the rising tide of dissent on the campuses, the growing outcry for peace and radical social change."

Winston concludes by declaring, "We will turn into its opposite this campaign to silence and crush Angela and the causes which she represents."

The Communist effort has resulted in mass demonstrations on behalf of Angela in the United States as well as in many other countries. As in previous Communist "defense" efforts, many non-Communists have willingly and enthusiastically participated. Some, of course, were unaware of the real sponsorship of the events involved. Others knew the facts, but participated nevertheless.

In October, 1971, an "Angela Davis Day" rally was held in New York's Central Park Mall. The crowd, estimated at 5,000 by the far left *National Guardian*, gave a standing ovation to Angela's mother, Mrs. Sallye Davis, and to Henry Winston, chairman of the Communist Party. Among the speakers were actor-writer-director Ossie Davis; Prentice Williams of the Fortune Society, an association of former convicts; Jarvis Tyner, head of the Young Workers Liberation League; Rep. Ronald Dellums (D.-Calif.); New York State Assemblyman Arthur Eve from Buffalo; Haywood Burns of the National Conference of Black Lawyers; and David Livingston, head of District 65 of the Distributive Workers of America.

According to the *National Guardian*, "Livingston said he had not come as an individual to speak for the freedom of Angela Davis, but with a mandate from the 30,000 workers in his union. He said genocide against black and Puerto Rican people has been going on 'for hundreds of years' in the U.S. and white people should know that they are not free from persecution as long as there is any oppressed group under attack and discrimination by the government."

A message from Angela Davis was read by Louise Patterson of the national committee. Her message said that the "murder" of George Jackson and the "massacre" at Attica were "indisputable signposts that the U.S. is on the way to fascism. Attica is Mylai revisited on home territory."

To appreciate the importance that the world Communist movement places upon the case of Angela Davis it is interesting to review the comments about the case that have appeared in the Soviet press. The following is by no means a complete rundown of such commentary, but it does give an indication of the interest which has been shown:

Pravda, Number 78, page 4: A photo with a banner reading, "Freiheit fur Angela Davis!" or "Freedom for Angela Davis" is identified as being a photo from the newspaper *Daily World*. The caption says, "Progressive Forces of the USA and all the world are actively fighting for the liberation of Angela Davis." The defense of Angela Davis, the *Daily World* is quoted as saying, "is defense from repression of all black Americans. It is defense of the women's liberation movement. It is defense of the right to be a Communist." In the picture, representatives of a West German public group meet in protest against the "persecution" of Angela Davis.

Pravda, Number 67, page 5: A picture is shown of Angela Davis at her indictment, accompanied by an article, "Behind the Facade of the Free World." The caption ends with the claim that working people, scientists, creative artists, and others are working for Angela and finally, "Millions say, 'Angela must be set free!'"

Krokodil [*Crocodile*], Number 1, 1971, back page: A portrait of the Statue of Liberty with the face of Angela Davis. The upper right-hand caption says, "Progressive mankind is indignant at the reprisals against Angela Davis by American authorities." The caption is "Liberties!" The tablet in Angela's left hand is, "The Constitution of the USA."

Pravda, Number 26, page 4: A cut of Angela and an accompanying article entitled, "For you, tomorrow, Angela!" The "you" is in the familiar form of that word. This is an article of tribute to Angela on her twenty-seventh birthday. It tells how Soviet women dedicate themselves to accomplishing the goals for which Angela has given so much. The final sentence says, "People are fighting for your life, Angela, because they know that they fight for tomorrow, for you, and for your freedom." Communist attorney John Abt is also lauded in the article.

Pravda, Number 20, page 5: A cut of Angela is shown before a symbolic presentation of Themis, the goddess of Justice, in a Ku Klux Klan costume, complete with burning cross. This is reprinted from the *Daily World.*

Pravda, Number 8, page 5: A picture of Angela in her Afro is shown with her lawyers under an article entitled "Stop the Reprisals! Millions Demand." The sub-headline is, "The persecution of Angela Davis takes on a political character."

Pravda, Number 7, page 5: Another picture of Angela in her Afro under an article with the title, "Halt the Reprisals Against Angela Davis." The article includes dispatches from New York, Budapest, Sofia, Paris, Rome, Geneva, Leningrad, Kiev, and Sverdlovsk telling how all progressive mankind has the message.

Pravda, Number 5, page 5: A cartoon of Themis, the goddess of justice, entitled "The Scales of the American Themis." Themis is holding a paper which says, "The Case of Angela Davis." The upper caption says, "The case of Angela Davis, fabricated by American Okhranka [secret police], is considered by the judicial powers from an openly racist, Black Hundreds [a czarist group] viewpoint." The reprisals against Angela Davis, states the paper, have taken on a purely political charac-

[219]

ter, spilling over into a hunt for "those who are different," which "recalls the worst days of McCarthyism."

This brief selection of articles from the Soviet press indicates the level of interest that has been stimulated in the Angela Davis case by the world Communist movement. The message is always the same: Angela is a political prisoner, being persecuted because she is black, a woman, and a Communist. Little, if anything, is said about the facts of the case, the major fact being that she is on trial for murder and kidnaping, not for her race, her sex, or her opinions.

The approach taken by the propaganda machines of world communism is the same approach as the one being taken by Angela's attorneys. The fact that Angela Davis' trial is being made into a political one by her supporters, and that she may find herself victimized by her self-proclaimed "friends," is virtually guaranteed by the radical lawyers who are in charge of her defense. "We have an obligation to our client," admits one of her attorneys. "But just as important, we have an obligation to fight a racist, repressive society. It is not Angela Davis who is on trial. It is America."

At least three of the lawyers connected with Angela's defense —Allen Brotsky, Dennis Roberts and John Thorne—have been active in the National Lawyers Guild, often cited as a Communist front. As far back as 1950 the House Committee on Un-American Activities (now the House Internal Security Committee) labeled the National Lawyers Guild "the foremost legal bulwark of the Communist Party."

Brotsky is the law partner of Charles Garry and Benjamin Dreyfus, both identified in congressional testimony in 1957 as Communist Party members. Given an opportunity to rebut the allegation, both men took the Fifth Amendment.

It was Garry, chief counsel and spokesman for the Black Panther Party, who charged that twenty-eight Panthers had been killed by the police and that the deaths were "part and package of a national scheme by various agencies of the government to destroy and commit genocide upon members of the Black Panther Party."

Garry's assertion that twenty-eight members of the Panthers had been killed by the police was widely reported. On December 7 and December 9, 1969, the *New York Times* reported as an established fact, without giving any source for the figure or qualifying it in any way, that twenty-eight Panthers had been killed by police since January, 1968. On December 9, 1969, the *Washington Post* stated, "A total of twenty-eight Panthers have died in clashes with police since January 1, 1968." In a later article, the *Post* declared, "Between a dozen and thirty Panthers have been killed in these confrontations."

On the basis of these reports, many public figures issued statements. Roy Innis, director of the Congress for Racial Equality, called for an immediate investigation of "the death of twenty-eight Black Panther members killed in clashes with the police since January, 1968." Ralph Abernathy, who succeeded Martin Luther King, Jr., as the chairman of the Southern Christian Leadership Conference, attributed the death of Panther leaders to "a calculated design of genocide in this country." Julian Bond, a member of the Georgia state legislature, said, "The Black Panthers are being decimated by political assassination arranged by the Federal police apparatus."

The newsmagazines further amplified the sketchy reports. *Time* reported on December 12, 1969, that "a series of gun battles between Panthers and police throughout the nation" amounted to a "lethal undeclared war," and concluded, "Whether or not there is a concerted police campaign, the ranks of Panther leadership have been decimated in the past two years." *Newsweek* began a news report entitled "Too Late for the Panthers?" with the same question: "Is there some sort of government conspiracy afoot to exterminate the Black Panthers?" The article then proceeded to portray a "guerrilla war between the gun-toting Panthers and the police," in which the Panther "hierarchy around the country has been all but decimated over the past year," and concluded that "there is no doubt that the police around the nation have made the Panthers a prime target in the past two years. . . ."

Finally, someone investigated each of the twenty-eight names provided by attorney Garry. Writing in *The New Yorker* magazine, Edward Jay Epstein showed clearly that of the twenty-eight, eighteen died of causes totally unrelated to police action. In the ten remaining cases, those in which police action did apparently result in the death of Panthers, Epstein notes that "In all of the ten cases to which Garry's list has been reduced, at least some of the Panthers involved were armed and presented a threat to police. Six of the ten Panthers were killed by seriously wounded policemen who clearly had reason to believe that their own lives were in jeopardy. In none of these cases, moreover, is there any positive evidence to support a belief that the wounded policemen knew they had been shot by Black Panthers. According to the evidence that *is* available, Bartholomew, Lawrence and Lewis were stopped as burglary suspects; Pope approached a robbery stakeout at night; Winters opened fire when two policemen entered an abandoned building to investigate a citizen's complaint; and although it is agreed that Robertson took it upon himself to challenge the behavior of the police investigating the burglary of a fruit stand, it is not reported that he identified himself as a Black Panther."

In the four remaining cases, Epstein points out, the fatal shots were fired by policemen who had not themselves been wounded. In two of those deaths, those of Armstead and Clark, the police state that in each instance they were confronted by an adversary with a lethal weapon and had reason to presume that their own lives were endangered. Epstein notes, "In any event, there are two cases in which Black Panthers were killed by policemen whose lives were not being directly threatened by those men. These are the cases of Hutton, who was shot while allegedly running from the scene of a ninety-minute gun battle in which three policemen had been wounded, and Hampton, who was apparently hit by stray bullets in a reckless and uncontrolled fusillade."

Epstein concluded by stating, "The idea that the police have declared a sort of open season on Black Panthers is based, principally, as far as I can determine, on the assumption that all the Panther deaths cited by Garry—twenty-eight or twenty or ten —occurred under circumstances that were similar to the Hampton-Clark raid. This is an assumption that proves, on examination, to be false."

The news media saw no reason to investigate the facts in this case, but were eager and willing to accept as fact Charles Gar-

[222]

ry's extreme charges. Similarly, many seem eager and willing to accept the allegation that, somehow, Angela Davis is on trial for her views, her sex, or her race rather than the actions of which she is accused.

Angela's other attorneys have records that are similar to those of Mr. Brotsky. Dennis Roberts, a self-proclaimed "radical lawyer," has been active in the antiwar effort, defending draft dodgers and aiding the War Resisters League. He has worked closely with "Chicago Seven" attorney William Kunstler. John Thorne, an attorney from San Jose, has been active in the Soledad Brothers case.

The man who is known as the leader of the Angela Davis defense team is Howard Moore, Jr., an Atlanta lawyer who has made a name for himself defending such prominent black revolutionaries as H. Rap Brown and Stokely Carmichael. Moore does not hesitate to admit that the trial has more to do with Angela as a symbol than it does with an effort to find out the truth and the real facts with regard to the violence which occurred at San Rafael.

In an article, "Angela—Symbol of Resistance," which appears in the book *If They Come in the Morning,* Moore states that, "As incredible as the charges against Angela are, they must be met at both the legal and political levels. It is not enough to meet them on just one level. That would be only a partial defense. The objective of the prosecution is not just to lynch Angela but to lynch her as a symbol of resistance. Angela, as a political prisoner soon to be tried for her life, is a tool in the hands of the reactionary white racist American ruling class. Angela is a symbol of what that ruling class would do to all Blacks if the chance presented itself. The objective of the prosecution is not merely to murder Angela, under color of law as they bomb and ravage the heroic people of Vietnam in quest of a peace only they prevent, but also to provide a ghastly example to all Blacks and people of revolutionary sentiments. To use Angela as a symbol—a sort of latter day Harriet Tubman leading her people through the ideological thicket of decadent bourgeois democracy—is a manifestation of the long struggle in the United States between Black-led progressive forces and white-led forces of reaction. If Angela is a symbol to those forces which would willingly destroy her, she is equally a symbol to Black people and all oppressed people inside the United States."

Moore concludes by arguing that "Angela is a symbol of the People's resistance to tyranny and oppression. The people will win without a doubt, because they know that their resistance is not just in defense of a symbol, but in defense of a real live and courageous human being. They give life for life, not for death. The humanity of the people will triumph over the callous inhumanity of the ruling class. Right on Kojo! Free Angela and all political prisoners without a doubt!"

With regard to actual courtroom tactics, Moore declares, "We are going to raise the question of the national status of blacks in the courtroom. When we say that Angela should be judged by her peers, we mean by other blacks. What was significant and critical about the New Haven and New York cases was the number of blacks on the jury. It prevented the prosecutor from making openly racist appeals in court and it prevented white jurors from making racist arguments in the jury room."

Another of Angela's attorneys is Michael Tigar, a young movement lawyer who directed the defense of the "Seattle Seven." Tigar has been affiliated with the Castro-financed Fair Play for Cuba Committee, served as a delegate to the Communist-sponsored World Youth Festival in Helsinki, and has written for official Communist publications.

The activities of the National Lawyers Guild have increased during the past year. Close to 1,000 lawyers, many of whom were involved in the Angela Davis and George Jackson cases, met at the University of Colorado in the summer of 1971 for the convention of the National Lawyers Guild. Not hesitating to express his real goal, attorney William Kunstler stated, "I want to bring down the system through the system. I have no faith in the ability of the system to produce a just result." Guild members also discussed the swaying of juries with such ploys as that used by Barry Balis, a Golden, Colorado, lawyer, who hides his flowing locks under a wig to impress the jury. "I want to be a freak," Balis told his peers, "but it's rough, especially when it jeopardizes your client." Kunstler told the convention to use the press to the utmost in manipulating trials. "You have

[224]

an obligation to work the media for all it's worth," said Kunstler.

The main purpose of the meeting, as described by Doris Walker of Oakland, California, the Guild's president, was "to keep the road clear of legal roadblocks" for revolutionaries and "to preserve the freedom won by the first American Revolution to make possible the second American Revolution."

Founded in 1937, the Guild began to fade after it was labeled a Communist front in 1950. But with the rise of radical groups in recent years it has begun to grow slowly and now has some 3,000 members in chapters across the nation and thrives in several law schools. The Guild's budget is now approaching the quarter-million-dollar mark. At least three members of Congress, Rep. Robert F. Drinan (D-Mass.), Rep. Bella Abzug (D-N.Y.), and Rep. John Conyers (D-Mich.), have belonged to the group.

The Guild once occupied itself primarily with the filing of amicus curiae briefs and pressuring bar associations. Now this practice has been augmented with the politicizing of the courts by organized demonstrations both in and out of the courtrooms, the setting up of the People's Law Schools to radicalize young attorneys, instituting legal defense committees to represent "political" defendants, as was done preceding the violence-marred Chicago Democratic Convention in 1968, and raising issues as a means of organizing entire communities around civil and criminal cases.

Kunstler, speaking at Boulder, declared, "This is a partnership with the Movement. You have to identify with your client —live and die with your client."

The Angela Davis case, to the attorneys who are defending her and to the national and international committees that are agitating in her behalf, is far more than the case of a single individual on trial for murder. They have made it into a political trial, and they seek to create a martyr as a result. Whether Angela Davis would serve their purposes better dead than alive is a question that Angela and her family should spend a good deal of time considering.

[225]

8

IT BECOMES CLEAR, AS WE REVIEW THE ARTICLES, SPEECHES, AND editorials written in defense of Angela Davis that this defense is not based upon a claim to her innocence of the particular charges against her, namely her involvement in the violence that occurred at the San Rafael Courthouse. The defense of Angela Davis is based more on the notion that she is being persecuted for her race, her political opinions, even her sex, than that she is being tried for murder. Since, in the opinion of her defenders, this is the case, it is only natural that her defense is based not upon the idea that she is innocent but is based, instead, on the passionately held belief that she is a scapegoat and a victim. Thus, the facts of the case become far less important than the view that is held of American society at large.

Yet, even when the defenders of Angela Davis ignore the question of her guilt or innocence of the charges and turn their attention to the alleged "fact" of America's repressive nature, they fail to provide very convincing evidence.

Writing in *The Nation* magazine of July 19, 1971, Jerome H. Skolnick, a professor of criminology at the University of California, and Steven A. Brick, a law student at the University of California and research editor of the *California Law Review,* declare, in effect, that neither Angela Davis nor other black militants—such as Bobby Seale and Huey Newton—can hope to receive a fair trial.

They conclude their article with this assessment: "A model 'fair trial' suggests a proceeding that is procedurally correct, with an intelligent judge sensitive to his own prejudices. The ultimate decision of guilt or innocence should be left to a jury that can comprehend the testimony given in behalf of the accused, whether it chooses to believe it or not. Miss Davis is now receiving a 'fair' trial only in the sense that she employs a team of able attorneys who will vigorously assert her rights. But they are operating within a social and legal structure that is stacked against her."

How, exactly, is the social system "stacked" against her? The authors explain what they mean: "In predominantly white middle-class Marin County, communism and black militancy are anathema. The much publicized rise in the tax rate attributed to this trial can hardly fail to influence the county's taxpayers, from whose ranks the jury will be drawn. Accordingly, an analysis of the fairness of the Angela Davis trial cannot proceed on a purely legal level. It must also examine the community and racial aspects of the trial, and the peculiar but no longer unique combination of race and politics influencing the atmosphere of the trial in and out of the courtroom. Both the state and the accused have an interest in obtaining the fairest trial possible. In reality, fairness can only be approximated; we come closest to it when, while operating in an imperfect system, we strive to remedy imperfections. The worst we can do is deny their existence."

This is the level of thinking on the part of those who advance the idea that America is a repressive society and that black militants cannot receive fair trials in American courtrooms. Such arguments are filled with invective, but tend too often to overlook the facts.

The authors of the *Nation* article argue that the trial of Angela Davis will almost certainly be unfair because the predominantly white citizens of Marin County will "hardly fail" to be influenced by the rise in the tax rate somehow caused by the trial itself. They tell us that we cannot discuss the fairness of this trial, or of any trial, by concerning ourselves only with legal matters, but must take other factors into consideration as well. These other factors, however, tend to be highly subjective.

These very authors, however, have overlooked the major "other" factor to be taken into consideration—the trials of black militants that have already taken place, before the article was written, and subsequent to it. We have reviewed several of these, including the case of Bobby Seale in New Haven, Connecticut, a case which provoked Kingman Brewster's charge that a black man could not receive a fair trial any place in the United States. Seale, of course, was acquitted, even though the burden of the evidence pointed to his guilt. If the trial was "unfair," it erred in a direction different from the one feared by Mr. Brewster.

Another example of how the courts have acted in questions such as this was observed in December, 1971, when two black militants were acquitted of assault and burglary charges brought by a medical records librarian who said that she was tortured for crossing a picket line. In this case, an all-white San Mateo County Superior Court jury acquitted Leo Bazile, twenty-eight, a former Stanford University student and president of the Stanford Black Student Union, now a law student, and Christopher Laury, twenty-two, of Palo Alto, a member of the Third World Liberation Front.

An article in the *Los Angeles Times* of December 10, 1971, included the following report: "Jury foreman Gordon H. Bannerman, a retired engineer, said the acquittal was based for the most part on failure of Miss Mary Jane Schmidt, forty-one, fully to identify her assailants. There was 'considerable reasonable doubt and there wasn't sufficient evidence,' Bannerman said. Miss Schmidt, who is white, said that she was beaten and burned in her East Palo Alto apartment May 2 after she refused to honor a picket line at Stanford University Medical Center. The pickets were protesting the discharge of a black janitor."

No law professors have pronounced this trial "unfair." In fact, the clamor with regard to the question of the fairness of the trial of Angela Davis is based upon a political judgment that her trial "will be" unfair, not upon an observation that the trials of Bobby Seal, or other black militants, "have been" unfair. The proponents of this view have not seen fit to provide any evidence of past unfairness in the trials of black militant spokesmen. They are not arguing logically, but dogmatically and ideologically. They "believe" that trials will be unfair in the same sense that Christians and Jews believe in God, namely on faith. When men believe things to be true which factually and logically can be disproven, and continue in this belief regardless of the facts, they may only be called, as Eric Hoffer has called them, "true believers" in political ideologies which may bear no resemblance to reality.

Let us consider one final case in the area of jury trials of black militants, that of Black Panther leader Huey Newton.

On October 28, 1967, Huey P. Newton, minister of defense of the Black Panther Party, allegedly shot and killed one police officer and wounded a second officer in Oakland, California. Newton was wounded in the shoot-out and was sent to San Quentin State Prison hospital.

At the time of the incident *The Black Panther* newspaper was published intermittently, and it was not until November 23, 1967, that Panther statements concerning the incident appeared. In that issue, the Panther minister of information, identified only as "underground," made a statement. This is the "showdown case," he declared. "We have reached the point in history where we must claim that a black man . . . has a right to defend himself—even if this means picking up a gun and blowing that cop away."

In September, 1968, the jury returned a verdict of guilty of voluntary manslaughter. The September 14, 1968, issue of *The Black Panther* carried Newton's statement on the verdict. He denounced it as a reflection of the "racism that exists here in America."

A summary of the trial appears in the same issue. It acknowledges that witness "Henry Grier had testified that he clearly saw Huey Newton shoot and kill patrolman Frey in the beams of the bus headlights. He said the bus stopped with the men and cars in front of it and he could see everything through the front window and door to his right."

Despite that acknowledgment, the summary emphasized a verbal exchange between defense attorney Charles Garry and the presiding judge, and declared: "Now the whole world knows that Huey P. Newton, Minister of Defense, Black Panther Party, did not receive a fair impartial trial."

The following month a California-based political organization—the Peace and Freedom Party—nominated Huey Newton as its candidate for the United States Congress in the 7th Congressional District, Alameda County, California, according to the October 26, 1968, issue of *The Black Panther*.

On August 5, 1970, Huey Newton was released from prison. He was freed on $50,000 bail pending a new trial. On August 21, *The Black Panther* published a "Letter from Huey to the Revolutionary Brothers and Sisters about the Women's Liberation and Gay Liberation Movements." It was accompanied by a photograph of Newton with the title "SUPREME COMMANDER, Black Panther Party."

Huey Newton was brought to trial for the third time in the Fall of 1971, and in December, 1971, he walked away from the courthouse a free man. The charge that he had killed an Oakland policeman, despite the preponderance of the evidence, had been dismissed due to a third hung jury.

Once again we have observed a case in which a black militant leader has been accused of murder, with the evidence pointing clearly to his guilt, and his supporters launching nationwide and worldwide protests against the alleged "racism" and "repressiveness" of the court system in which the case was being adjudicated. Once again, we have seen a black radical free on bail continuing to preach violence and revolution and once again we have seen a jury refuse to find him guilty of the crime for which he was being tried. The experiences of Bobby Seale, Ericka Huggins, and Huey Newton would lead the observer to believe that, if anything, the American court system has gone far out of its way to avoid even the appearance of "racism" or "repression." Yet, despite these facts, the radical rhetoric continues. Had all three of these black militants been executed, the cries of "unfairness" with regard to the case of Angela Davis could not be more vehement.

A certain degree of irony may be seen in the pamphlet "The Meaning of San Rafael," by Henry Winston, black National Chairman of the Communist Party, U.S.A, since 1966. In this pamphlet, published by the Communist Party, Winston declares, "Today, the need to build a mass movement to free Angela Davis, Bobby Seale, Ericka Huggins, the Berrigan Brothers and Arnold Johnson—Catholic and Communist peace leaders, the Soledad Brothers, Ruchell Magee and all political prisoners is a vital starting point for speeding the formation of a great, popular movement to turn back the forces aiming to push the country into fascism."

Winston thus freely admits that the real purpose of the campaign to free Angela Davis has nothing to do with the merits of her case but is, instead, "a vital starting point for speeding the formation of a great, popular movement to turn back the forces aiming to push the country into fascism." Angela's case, for the Communists, is clearly a means to other ends.

Nevertheless, at the end of the paragraph just quoted from Winston's pamphlet, an asterisk appears. It directs the reader to the bottom of the page where the following sentence is found: "This was written prior to the dismissal of charges against Bobby Seale and Ericka Huggins in New Haven on May 25, 1971." In the very pamphlet in which our court system is attacked for "racism" and "repression," the author is forced to admit that two of his most prominent examples, Bobby Seale and Ericka Huggins, were, in fact, released and the charges against them dismissed.

The Communist Party, Winston states, does not advocate reckless and "adventurous" acts of violence such as occurred at San Rafael. Immediately after the San Rafael incident, the Communist Party's Political Committee declared:

"The violent scene played out to its deadly end in the shadow of the San Rafael courthouse is an American tragedy which arouses profound concern and deep sorrow in all people of conscience throughout the nation.

"Behind the desperate deed of the imprisoned men and their youthful would-be liberator are the goading realities of a bestial prison system, brutal police handling, and a cynical and ruthless courtroom pattern devoid of justice or any touch of humanity or concern for the dignity, lives and liberty of arrested men and women; especially so when they are Black people.

"The Communist Party has always made clear its opposition

[231]

to acts of desperation or resort to gunplay on the part of individuals, no matter how awful the provocation or lofty the
ideal. Communists reject the concept of revolutionary suicide
or revolutionary superman-ism.

"Communists always stand for the extension and enrichment
of life, and commit their lives to the cause of helping the
masses to struggle in a winning way for a social system devoid
of such tragedies and worthy of mankind.

"We are confident that Communists and all honest leaders of
the people will be vigilant against reaction's efforts to exploit
the tragedy of San Rafael and to undertake diversionary assaults upon the Communist Party."

While Mr. Winston decries the acts of violence which occurred at San Rafael as "suicide" and "superman-ism," he proceeds to declare: "Those who rule this country are doing all in
their power to prevent militant fighters from learning the real
meaning of these [Marxist-Leninist] principles. They know
they will be unable to hold on to their barbarous prison system
or their system of class and national oppression when the Black
liberation movement and all working people are led by fighters
like Jonathan Jackson. . . ." On the one hand, the events at San
Rafael are criticized. On the other hand, the man who carried
out the event is hailed.

It is clear that the Communist Party is interested in the
events at San Rafael and in the Angela Davis case only as a
means to further its own revolutionary ends. Neither Mr. Winston nor other commentators on the case seem to support the
violence that occurred at San Rafael. None argue that it was a
good and virtuous thing. They argue only that conditions in
America are so brutal and repressive that misguided young
idealists such as Jonathan Jackson, and, we must suppose, Angela Davis, are to be excused for errors of "superman-ism."
Even though such efforts harm the revolution, their own expression of revolutionary zeal is to be viewed only as a lag in
their education in the principles of Marxism-Leninism.

Lenin himself discussed situations such as that which occurred at San Rafael. In his *Collected Works,* he writes: "The
greatest, perhaps the only danger to the genuine revolutionary
is that of exaggerated revolutionism, ignoring the limits and

[232]

conditions in which revolutionary methods are appropriate and can be successfully employed."

"True revolutionaries," Lenin adds, "have mostly come a cropper when they began to write 'revolution' with a Capital R, to elevate 'revolution' to something almost divine, to lose their heads, to lose the ability to reflect, weigh and ascertain in the coolest and most dispassionate manner at what moment, under what circumstances and in which sphere of action you must act in a revolutionary manner, and at what moment, under what circumstances and in which sphere you must turn to reformist action. True revolutionaries will perish (not that they will be defeated from outside, but that their work will suffer internal collapse) only if they abandon their sober outlook and take it into their heads that the 'great, victorious world' revolution can and must solve all problems in a revolutionary manner under all circumstances and in all spheres of action."

The Communist Party itself does not, in effect, deny that Jonathan Jackson and the others involved in the incident at San Rafael were engaged in violent and illegal actions. From a tactical view, the Communist Party does not deny that such reckless action will tend to be harmful to their own goals of revolution. What the Party does seem to be saying is that, despite the fact that those involved in San Rafael were both guilty and foolish, nevertheless their own guilt and foolishness may be turned to the Party's tactical advantage by painting Angela Davis as a "political prisoner," as a victim of racism and repression, as a symbol of the "revolution" which is, they believe, really waiting in the wings of the American society.

Whether or not Angela Davis is guilty of the charges against her is, thus, essentially beside the point for the Communists and others who have launched the "Free Angela" movement. Their purpose is not to defend an innocent young woman falsely charged. Their clearly stated purpose is to bring about a revolution in America. Everything that aids them in this purpose they consider to be moral. Everything that does not assist them is, accordingly, immoral.

Our own standards with regard to telling the truth, with establishing the real facts of a case, are considered by them to be irrelevant. Angela Davis is, as a result, a political prisoner not

[233]

necessarily because she is *really* a political prisoner, but because it serves the purposes of the Communist Party and other radicals to provide the naive and uninformed with an image of America as a repressive society. Once that picture is painted, it is more possible to enlist recruits for the revolution. Many, of course, would be willing to assist in destroying a racist and repressive society. Few would be so willing in the case of an open, tolerant, and free society. In this sense, Angela Davis may be, as the protest song of recent years had it, "only a pawn in their game." Whether she is a willing or unwilling pawn is difficult to tell.

The defense and prosecution in the case of Angela Davis will differ on many points, the most important of which is exactly what her trial is really about.

The prosecution's effort was to prove that Angela did, in fact, purchase the guns used in the shoot-out at San Rafael and knowingly turned them over to Jonathan Jackson for this purpose. The defense effort did not deal with this crucial question except in a peripheral sense. Prior to the trial, defense attorney Howard Moore declared, "This case will show whether a black person can hold unpopular beliefs and unflinchingly admit her connection with what is considered a subversive organization. The political and legal aspects of this case converge in a very precise way. . . . There is no way you can separate them."

After the results of the trials of Bobby Seale, Ericka Huggins, and Huey Newton there is no doubt that a "black person can hold unpopular beliefs and unflinchingly admit her connection with what is considered a subversive organization." What is doubtful is whether real justice can ever be achieved in cases of criminal violence in which the perpetrator of such violence interposes his or her race, sex, or political beliefs as a barrier to prosecution. The defense effort in the trial of Angela Davis moved the center of consideration and focus as far away from the facts of the case as possible. In doing this, the press was an enthusiastic vehicle for support. And by doing precisely what the defense wanted it to do, namely give Angela and the "Free Angela" movement maximum coverage, it provided the defense with still another argument against the "fairness" of the trial, namely that as a result of press coverage a "fair" trial was no longer possible.

Attorney Moore, for example, claimed throughout the case that there had been so many pictures of Angela on television, and in the newspapers and magazines, that any of the witnesses who identified her were probably responding to suggestions rather than their actual memory. The argument seemed to be that since the radical left had been able to create a national furor over the case of Angela Davis, therefore Angela should be set free for the resulting publicity had made it impossible to achieve a fair trial.

If such a concept were accepted as valid, any individual seeking to escape trial would only have to become a public figure to avoid his day in court. This is, of course, a gratuitous argument, and one designed to prevent and not assist in implementing a system of equal justice for all.

Even so pro-Angela an observer as "The Professor" finds this argument with regard to fairness difficult to accept. In his book *Angela*, he discusses this question: ". . . one of the defense claims is her inability to get a fair trial because of publicity throughout California. At the same time a good deal of that publicity has been pro-Angela and is being pushed by the Communist Party. Some political observers (and they make a lot of sense) have reasoned that the Communists would like nothing better than to see Angela convicted so they can have a beautiful martyr . . . the Communists are gloating over the fact that they're now beginning to gain some attention. For too long that organization that still seeks to change the form of government in the United States had to take a back seat among militant Black Panthers and other liberation groups. Now Angela and the charges against her are bringing about strange bedfellows, who are making a lot of noise on behalf of her innocence but who, on their federally subsidized radio stations (e.g. Pacifica), are helping create a climate for conviction."

Thus, even some who support the concept of Angela's innocence, but who are not Communists, can see that the Communist propaganda apparatus is not, in reality, helping Angela, but is using her for political propaganda purposes—purposes which, in the long run, would be better served by a finding of her guilt rather than her innocence.

Angela's sincere supporters—those Americans, black and white, who really think that, somehow, she is being persecuted because of her race, her sex, or her political beliefs—should carefully consider the possibility that Angela is being used, either knowingly or unwittingly, by the world Communist movement to create an image of a repressive America, something that is not the reality of American society, but which it is necessary to create in order for world communism to carry forth its propaganda assault against free institutions with greater effectiveness.

Many who are not Communists, both at home and abroad, seem to have been influenced by this tactic. The German weekly newsmagazine *Der Spiegel* produced a cover story about the Angela Davis case and asked the question: "Is America becoming a Fascist society?" The burden of the article is a description of how this is, in fact, becoming the case. The article overlooks, to a large degree, the real charges against Angela Davis. It overlooks the fact that the court has permitted her to act as her own attorney, that the man with whom she traveled to escape from the law was released, and that other black militants, rather than being railroaded into unfair courts, have been released in instances in which the preponderant evidence pointed to their guilt. *Der Spiegel,* along with too many others, seems to have been strongly influenced by the propaganda mechanism surrounding the Angela Davis case, even to the point of overlooking reality in its presentation.

The very term "political prisoner" used so often by critics with regard to the case of Angela Davis is little understood. Traditionally, it refers to someone who is prosecuted or arrested not for crimes in the ordinary sense, but for holding or expressing views that are in opposition to an established order of government. Discussing the question of "Who and What Is a Political Prisoner?" Lance Morrow noted in *Time* magazine that ". . . a profligate inclusiveness tends to drain the phrase 'political prisoner' of its specific (and still valid) meaning. To accept the idea that all black prisoners are political is to condemn implicitly laws that sent them to prison and to suggest

[236]

that they all be freed. But since an overwhelming majority of the victims of black crime are black, and since most blacks, in or out of ghettos, obey the law, the release of all black prisoners might strike law-abiding Negroes as a subtle kind of redoubled racism. Moreover in demanding Angela's freedom, radicals forget that by their own definition there are all manner of political prisoners in the U.S. who are not black. If all political prisoners are to be released, what about James Earl Ray, the convicted assassin of Martin Luther King, Jr.?"

Stanford law professor John Kaplan bluntly answers, "If someone has committed a crime of violence because of his political views, he damn well belongs in jail." Harvard sociologist Seymour Martin Lipset, in answering the question of whether or not George Jackson was a political prisoner, replied that Jackson was "politicized" rather than a political prisoner.

Commenting on the Jackson case, Lance Morrow notes, "Initially he was held in prison for his defiant intransigence. Eventually, it could be argued, parole boards may have kept him locked up because to them his radical political views were evidence that he had not been rehabilitated. For his part, Jackson rejected the entire notion of rehabilitation. He saw it as the prison system's conspiracy to turn him into a subservient 'good nigger.' It is easy to understand a parole board's collective bafflement as it tried to decide what to do about this unabashed advocate of revolution who, like a 19th-century anarchist bomb thrower, denied the legitimacy of all laws ('white, fascist, capitalist') and regarded himself as virtually a prisoner of war."

The fact remains that George Jackson was not being kept in prison for his opinions, but for illegal acts—acts which are illegal in every society. Many other radicals today advocate the violent overthrow of the American system. Yet they have not been, and properly cannot be, prosecuted until they act upon their beliefs in some overt way that violates the law.

When radicals, such as Yippies Jerry Rubin and Abbie Hoffman, advocate shoplifting and the destruction of property as justified ideologically as "ripping off the Establishment," they are not discussing what has been traditionally known as "political crime." And these same radicals are strangely silent about the Communist societies which do imprison people strictly for

[237]

political reasons. Not a word has been said by such radicals, for example, about the refusal of the Soviet Union to permit the Nobel Prize-winning author Aleksandr Solzhenitsyn to accept his award in Sweden, virtually keeping him under house arrest, only for his opinions. It is the United States that must meet a "utopian" standard, and even when it tries its best to adhere to proper legal standards, radicals find this not to be sufficient.

Commenting upon the false double standard inherent in much of the radical rhetoric to which we are subjected, Professor Edward Bloomberg of the University of California wrote the following in his book, *Student Violence:* "Unlike radicals of the thirties who compared our miserable existence to the idyllic life in Russia, today's radicals use no culture, past or present, as a point of comparison. When asked to what they are comparing American institutions, radicals have no answer. It is to their dreams that they are comparing them."

Professor Bloomberg points out, "Here we see an obvious contradiction, for they insist on the one hand that if the United States is not perfect, it is perfectly corrupt while demanding no such perfection for themselves. . . . One cannot penetrate radical 'thought' without understanding that it applies relative—and extremely lenient—moral standards to radicals, but absolute—and intransigent—ones to society. Radicals generally couch their complaints in Marxist terms. . . . This explains the amusing references to the exploited workers, supposed allies of the students in the revolution. There is of course no group less revolutionary, or less exploited, than American workers, but when you accept a dogma you cannot make an exception of its fundamental thesis."

Carrying the recently revised concept of "political crime" to its ultimate degree of unreality, exiled Black Panther leader Eldridge Cleaver explained that he used to rape white women because he was so incensed by "the white-racist American system." *Time* magazine, discussing this notion, declared, "The rationale may be metaphorically interesting, but it is one that no free society can accept if it hopes to survive. A democracy —or a dictatorship, for that matter—obviously could not function under the radical assumption that a crime ceases to be a crime if the perpetrator can persuade himself that it has politi-

[238]

cal intent. The revolutionary's aim is to destroy the system, but a society naturally protects itself against those who want to overthrow it. The problem is how to avoid repression while achieving social stability and liberty even for would-be revolutionaries."

The facts seem unimportant to those who have rallied to George Jackson and Angela Davis. Many who mourn Jackson and lament Angela's condition are oblivious of the fact that in the San Quentin incident three guards and two other convicts died with Jackson. They seem equally unconcerned with the fact that, regardless of Angela's innocence or guilt, four people, including a judge, Jonathan Jackson and two convicts, died in the Marin County Courthouse gun battle. Why, they fail to answer, should anyone accused of supplying weapons that were ultimately used for the murder at the courthouse not be brought to trial? Their position would certainly be far different were we dealing with a white racist group that had done violence to black inmates awaiting trial. In a free society, doing its best to achieve a system of justice that is colorblind, the differences should be irrelevant.

The charges of political crime overlook almost completely the fact that various anti-Establishment radicals have been able to use the legal system they decry as "repressive" to defend themselves, often with success. Not only the cases of Bobby Seale, Ericka Huggins, and Huey Newton bear this out. There are many more. Dr. Benjamin Spock, to cite the case of another radical brought to trial, had his conviction for conspiring to counsel young men in draft evasion reversed. He is now busy traveling across the country doing exactly what he was doing before the charges were brought against him. Even Angela Davis herself has written, "We will not infer that fascism in its full maturity has descended upon us. We must continue to make use of the legal channels to which we have access, which, of course, does not mean that we operate exclusively on a legal basis."

Discussing the question of whether or not George Jackson was, in fact, a political prisoner, Malcolm Braly, who served time in San Quentin for burglary and is the author of *On the Yard* and other novels, notes, "It is being said that Jackson was a political prisoner because he was sentenced on a charge for which a white man of nineteen would have received probation. I'm inclined to agree that there are areas in California where blacks are not treated impartially, but the suggestion of systematic political prejudice is absurd. Probation is always a desperate gamble and robbery, even second-degree, is treated gingerly. Further, Jackson had an extensive juvenile record, and for robbery, and had already served time in the California Youth Authority."

Writing in the *New York Times,* Braly states, "The second leg of the political-prisoner hypothesis is the abnormal length of Jackson's confinement. Jackson would have been eligible for parole within a year, and, if his prison record had been simply average, would have been paroled at the end of three years, possibly four. He could have been something of a disciplinary problem and still been out in five."

Such, however, was not the case with George Jackson. Braly points out that if Jackson's actions were, as he proclaimed them to be, "revolutionary" then ". . . what were the prison officials supposed to do—permit his protest? Permit him to kill? . . . why isn't it considered that those men who rose up to demand their rights at Attica had never been so delicate about the rights, the property, and even the lives of others? Why isn't it noted that their play-acting and posturing, the immediate formation of a military organization in their ranks, looks nothing so much as an attempt to copy that which they so bitterly protested?"

It is often said by radicals that black Americans, precisely because they are black, have some obligation to defend and support the violent actions of self-proclaimed black militants. In advancing this view, such spokesmen totally ignore the fact that the violence perpetrated by black militants, and by blacks who may only be criminals, is aimed primarily at the black community itself, not at the so-called "white establishment." A black American is more than twenty times as likely to be the victim of a crime of violence than a white. The statistics show that though whites outnumber blacks about nine to one, seven out of ten crimes committed against blacks are by blacks.

Why many allegedly "responsible" and "moderate" black spokesmen speak favorably of men such as George Jackson is difficult to understand. Roy Wilkins is a case in point. After the San Quentin incident Wilkins wrote, "The cry has already been raised, whether in angry vocalizing or in silent stares, that 'law-abiding' Negro Americans would do well to join in condemning George Jackson, the San Quentin inmate who was killed in a prison break. Black Americans in overwhelming numbers hate crime and criminals. They are preyed upon, they are robbed, beaten, raped, cheated in a multitude of ways, terrorized and often killed by criminals, black and white. The vast majority of them do not gloat over the brutally murdered white San Quentin guards."

Mr. Wilkins proceeds, however, to declare that "As bad as he might have been considered by some in authority, George Jackson did not deserve to have his life snuffed out by a rifle bullet." In making such a statement, Roy Wilkins overlooks the fact that George Jackson was killed in a felonious prison break in which he committed murder personally and was intent upon committing more. The authorities did not initiate the onslaught. Jackson did. Wilkins states that "Negro Americans cannot join in the denunciation of Jackson."

Where Mr. Wilkins receives his authority to speak in the name of more than twenty million black Americans is not clear. The reasons he gives to justify his statement that "Negro Americans cannot join in the denunciation of Jackson" are worth considering.

Jackson, he says, "was a brother in his tribulations under our system of justice. He was a member of that great nonwhite fraternity whose brothers have suffered a wide variety of deprivations because the law has looked first at their skins." He continues, "It is a violation of a statute to hold up a bank. Is it a worse crime for Negroes to rob a bank?" The answer, of course, is that the crime is neither better nor worse depending upon the race of the criminal. Yet, on what basis should black Americans refuse to condemn the bank robberies committed by criminals who happen to be black?

The NAACP leader concludes, "The black American population, like any race or color, includes hardened and consciousless criminals of all kinds, not omitting killers. These, regardless of newspaper headlines and TV pictures, constitute but a small minority. . . . The great majority understand the George Jacksons and are angered by a court system which they are convinced is stacked against black men. Poor people, whatever their race, generally have more run-ins with the law than affluent persons. This may help to account for a black prison population twice that of whites, but how does one account for the unbelievable ratios to a state's black population?"

What Mr. Wilkins tends to overlook is the fact that though the whites outnumber blacks about 9 to 1, black criminals commit nearly 3 out of 4 violent crimes against black Americans. Black Americans complain that it is 25 times more dangerous for them to take a walk at night than it is for a citizen in a white area—and in this statement they are completely correct. As a matter of fact, the complaint of black communities has not been that they have been harassed and brutalized by the police, although too many examples of such harassment and brutalization have occurred and continue to occur today. The major complaint of the black communities after the Detroit and Newark riots was that they were deprived of the equal protection of the laws because there weren't enough police to protect them, and what few there were arrived late.

The rhetorical acrobatics engaged in by Roy Wilkins and other black leaders who are hailed as "moderates" by the press may be self-serving, but it is hardly serving the needs and interests of black Americans. It may be the case that men such as Roy Wilkins believe that unless they use the flamboyant and excessive rhetoric characteristic of the self-proclaimed militants, they will be labeled "Uncle Toms" and dismissed from any position of black leadership.

As many spokesmen, both black and white, have made clear, the militants do not represent anyone but themselves. It is because their own rhetoric is precisely what white liberals and leftists want to hear that they have been elevated to prominent positions and given extraordinary press coverage. In this sense, it is they who are the "Uncle Toms," if by the term "Uncle Tom" we mean someone who is black doing what he thinks will please someone who is white in order to receive the rewards that may await him as a result.

Men such as Roy Wilkins violate their own integrity when

[242]

they say things which they know are not true. How can the American court system, as he charged, be "stacked against the Negro," when it is his own organization, the NAACP, which has won court case after court case, including the famous 1954 decision in *Brown* v. *Board of Education?* Mr. Wilkins evidently feels that he must not be "left behind" as the militants escalate their attacks upon American society. The previous NAACP goal of integrating into a free and open society is, as a result, in danger of being abandoned in favor of a radical and separatist critique of the nation's social structure. It is ironic indeed that the NAACP threatens to turn its back on its own principles at the very time when real equality has been achieved in so many areas of American life. It is a high price to pay indeed in order to escape the name-calling of the radicals.

A black American who seeks to integrate peacefully into American society is no more an "Uncle Tom" than is the American society a "fascistic" one, or the American court system "stacked" and "repressive." Mr. Wilkins may use the rhetoric, but his previous career is testimony to the fact of its unreality and irrelevance to our real situation. His attitude, and the attitude of too many other black "moderates," is similar to the attitude of white "moderates" who for so long looked the other way at racism, at the Ku Klux Klan, and at other manifestations of bigotry and hatred. Once again, it cannot be wrong for white men but proper for black men. This is the very racism Negroes have been trying for so long to overcome. Now it seems to be preached most vocally by their own self-appointed spokesmen.

It has been said that black Americans do not and cannot hold the opinions expressed here, that somehow any who do have not suffered poverty and discrimination, have somehow escaped the reality of black experience in America. This writer is a black American, totally familiar with the reality of life in America's inner-city areas, aware of the discrimination and hatred that Negroes have faced.

My own experience and my own life have convinced me that the approach used by black militants is dangerous and is based upon a false view of reality, and it is important to add the fact that I am by no means alone. I do not doubt that the overwhelming majority of black Americans share the view that the militants have misrepresented both American society and the needs and desires of its black citizens.

It is this black silent majority which for too long has been without a voice, and without any interest on the part of the white press and media establishment. At the very moment when the press was highlighting the efforts of black militants, the majority of black Americans were expressing their desire for additional police protection. Consider the results of a poll, reported in the *New York Times* of September 4, 1966. "A survey of Negro attitudes in Harlem and Watts," wrote *Times* reporter Robert B. Semple, Jr., "suggests that ghetto dwellers are concerned more about police protection than about police brutality. Although the survey found considerable evidence of hostility among Negroes toward the police, it also discovered that many Negroes sympathized with police problems and wanted more instead of fewer policemen in the neighborhoods."

These were among the conclusions arrived at by John F. Kraft, Inc., an independent public opinon research organization. The concern conducted 527 interviews in the Watts area of Los Angeles one month after the riots there in August, 1966. The Harlem survey involved interviews with 1,200 persons. The polls were released by Senator Abraham Ribicoff of Connecticut, whose subcommittee on executive reorganization held public hearings on urban problems. Noting that many polls are flawed because the interviews are conducted by "outsiders," Mr. Ribicoff said, "the Kraft polls surmounted this communication barrier." They went into the neighborhoods themselves and selected and trained residents to interview their neighbors.

The people of Harlem were asked about the biggest problems on their block. The results: Crime in the streets, 28 percent; the need for better police protection, 15 percent; and murders and drunks in the hallways of buildings, 3 percent each. "Problems of police brutality are conspicuous by their absence," the report said. "It appears that police malpractice is an issue in Harlem only insofar as the police are inadequate in doing their jobs. Police brutality as such was not a volunteered problem of concern for the people of Harlem."

It has not only been the black "man on the street" who has expressed such views. Many prominent black Americans have vocally criticized the militants, yet their voices have gone all but unreported to the majority of Americans—of both races.

The "black power" approach to the Nation's racial problems was denounced in an inportant speech at the University of Iowa by Negro columnist Carl Rowan, former head of the U.S. Information Agency. He stated that talk of separatism was "a scheme of recklessness, of desperation." He blamed the nation's press for giving "irresponsibles" large play as Negro leaders.

Meeting in Chicago, some 250 Negro ministers representing 12 million black Americans unanimously adopted a manifesto repudiating the concept of "black power." It said: "The black power quest must not be condoned or followed for it is divisive and is an expression of discrimination from the Negroes' point of view when used as a separatist movement among Negroes against white people. . . . We cannot build by destroying and we cannot win the struggle of freedom with weapons of hate and confusion." The meeting was called by Bishop Joseph Gomez of the African Methodist Episcopal Church, with attendance of ministers from 45 states.

Even the "father" of the March on Washington Movement has come to believe that the effort for civil rights has been subverted by those who do not, in fact, seek civil rights but are calling for violent revolution and upheaval. Speaking before the United Steel Workers' convention, A. Philip Randolph deplored "lawlessness of any kind," and warned that "the time has come when the street marches and demonstrations have about run their course . . . the strategy now in order is to shift from the streets to the conference room for the purpose of discussion of the problems in the interest of finding an answer."

Much of the truth about black Americans was stated by the then U.S. Ambassador to Luxembourg, Patricia Roberts Harris, before a Howard University audience in Washington, D.C.

Mrs. Harris, a 1945 graduate of Howard College of Liberal Arts, declared that most Negro Americans are now "politically and economically conservative, with all that term conveys." She explained that Negroes want to conserve the good in

American society and do not seek radical solutions "as the failure of every far right and far left institution to recruit significant numbers of Negroes attests."

Mrs. Harris, chairwoman of the credentials committee of the 1972 Democratic National Convention, stated, "We must never minimize the fact that freedom of speech, petition, and the press as guaranteed by the Federal Constitution, not guns and bombs, have been the weapons with which the Negro minority, with its friends in the majority, have assailed the walls of segregation."

She reminded her audience that "Our fortunes as Negroes cannot be separated from the fortunes of the United States. Therefore self-interest requires that we, as Americans, use all our resources to improve the position of this nation."

Still another black leader to reject the radical critique of violence and revolution is Bayard Rustin, executive director of the A. Philip Randolph Institute. He has said, "We are in a society where young people—particularly young Negroes—are being systematically taught that unless they resort to violence there is no future for them." He called for "political action" and argued, "We have simply got to get people in action politically. We have got to do the education job that is required. . . . Negroes only want a piece of the existing pie. They are not revolutionaries."

The statements by these and countless other Negroes in prominent positions in American life have been all but overlooked as the press tends to glorify the Stokely Carmichaels, Rap Browns and, today, the Angela Davises, Bobby Seales and Huey Newtons. The tragedy this misrepresentation holds for our society has already been witnessed by the violence we have seen.

Many young blacks on our college and university campuses feel that, somehow, the prevailing attitude or our academic and intellectual community is irrelevant to the situation they face. Yet they see few black leaders with whom they can identify, except those portrayed as "leaders" by the white press. My own background and experience, and my present identification with those Americans seeking to preserve a free society, may be instructive in this regard.

[246]

I was not born into a family with a political philosophy of belief in free enterprise, limited government, and the other elements of a free society advocated by those who in recent days in the American political arena have been called conservatives. My early life was like that of many American Negroes. Reared in a "ghetto" in South Philadelphia, with all of the struggles that went along with it, I delivered grocery orders at the local supermarket, junked scrap paper, cleaned basements, carried out ashes, and ran errands for the neighbors. In short, my family needed the money, so we boys did our best to assist by attempting to defray somewhat the cost or our personal expenditures in the family budget, and also so that we would have money for movies, candy, and other assorted "luxuries."

My brothers and I did what was necessary as youngsters to improve our lot, augment our status, and thereby detonate the solidified myth that people are the products of their environment. Then as now, and even more so now, there are many ways for an individual to accomplish a goal in America. Not all objectives are fully dependent on "timing" and "breaks."

Although my life was greatly influenced by two of the late John Gresham Machen's books, *Christianity and Liberalism* and *What Is Faith,* I believe and have always believed in the private enterprise system, primarily because I am convinced that this system is not only the best available and the best developed by man, but that it has the important ingredient of recognizing man's true nature. Empirical evidence suggests that rewards usually follow imagination, initiative, and ingenuity, thereby causing the individual to continue to think about improvement, constantly recognizing the proposition that "there is always a better way to do it."

Being black presented a greater challenge to me. I grew older and I developed additional motivation, which was destined to carry me perhaps farther than a nonblack with similar potential and ability, who finds comfort in complacency, with neither inner drive nor circumstance to activate dormant talents.

It is unfortunate that there are so few young black Americans who have been made aware of the moral and intellectual alternatives to the collectivist philosophy which so dominates our academic, intellectual, and media circles. I have, for example,

[247]

too often been the only Negro in a great many situations. In spite of the view that black Americans are solidly ensconced in the liberal camp, I have found from my own observation and conversations over the years that Negroes, of all economic and educational levels, are far more conservative than the public is led to believe. In addition, distinguished Negro conservatives such as George Schuyler and Max Yergan are rarely publicized, and remain unknown to large numbers of young people who might emulate them were they aware of their very real contribution.

The vast majority of black Americans are disturbed by taxes, inflation, and the lack of fiscal responsibility on the part of the local, state, and federal government. More than this, many are alarmed at the power and abuse of labor unions. The unions have been one of the classic examples of the duplicity of the prevailing liberal Establishment and its handicraft. Long a vocal proponent of "equality," the labor union movement has discriminated against the Negro. On the one hand, trade unions have systematically barred blacks from membership, with the use of "grandfather" clauses and a variety of other subtle and not-so-subtle techniques. On the other, they have lured unskilled Negroes with the herd instinct into the ranks of the labor unions as a cure-all, which proved to be a myth. To be sure, there were many black individuals who rose to substantial positions in the labor movement, and in some cases, admittedly at the expense of the black membership. This, of course, made it possible for the AFL-CIO's Committee on Political Education to further exercise its influence in the black community. Few blacks, of whatever viewpoint, will argue that the labor movement has treated them fairly. Most will admit that it has erected major barriers to their achievement of equal job opportunities. Yet, the very spokesmen who claim most to befriend black Americans are also the most vocal supporters of organized labor. The inconsistency and double standard is becoming more and more evident to more and more black Americans.

What I object to most is the categorization of people as members of collective units rather than as individuals. It is on the basis of this kind of classification that it is possible to argue that blacks must have a particular position with regard to the case of Angela Davis. There is, as a result, not a valid or invalid position, not a logical or illogical one, not one that is right and one that is wrong. Instead, there is a position for blacks, and one for whites. The only way racism can be eliminated is if each individual begins by eliminating the racism that exists in his own heart and in his own mind. Only when all of us, black and white together, can view reality without racial blinders can we hope to come to any degree of truth.

I have mingled with old and young conservatives and have found that they basically believe that the individual is supreme. The pitfall of much of the civil rights movement was that it attempted to move along or elevate the entire race, even those who did not want to be disturbed. The fallacy of this approach was, and is, that we can approach people only on an individual basis in that we must recognize innate individuality as opposed to "environmental determinism." We must reward or penalize citizens as individuals and not as units. The liberals have for years promised so much that they could not deliver, and now they are very much suspect in the black community. Many conservatives recognize that the time is ripe to demonstrate to members of the black community that they will be received and respected on the basis of their competence, intellect, and ability gainfully to perform and produce, rather than as subordinates.

Many people commit the error of thinking in stereotyped opinions. For instance, the white man may hold the following stereotyped opinions of the Negro:

1. The Negro is lazy.
2. The Negro is particularly fond of watermelon, fried chicken, fried fish, and corn pone.
3. The Negro is violent.
4. The Negro has rhythm.
5. The Negro is capable of thinking only in a simple fashion.

On the other hand, we find that the Negro may often hold the following stereotyped opinions of the white man:

1. The white man wants to keep the Negro down.
2. The white power structure is against the Negro.
3. The white power structure will not accept the Negro.
4. The white man hates the Negro.
5. The white man has everything he needs in bountiful supply.

The stereotyped opinion must be replaced with judgments of individuals, if we are to communicate, and if we intend to achieve social progress and economic growth. The Negro must necessarily communicate with the white man and the white man with the Negro.

Many Negroes have rebelled against the liberal attempt to view them not as individuals but as racial representatives. In an article in *The New Guard,* the magazine of Young Americans for Freedom, Jerome Tuccille wrote an article entitled "Emerging Black Conservatism." He noted, "The current demand in the black community for stronger local control and the restructuring of public schools along the lines of smaller, privately-run institutions is consistent with the traditional conservative principle of individual freedom and decentralized government."

Tuccille pointed out, "Suddenly, across the entire country, a young, strong, sometimes militant conservative voice is emerging from the black community. It is no surprise that it is sometimes loudest in New York City where the liberal trend has already gone as far to the left as it can possibly go without degenerating into undisguised socialism."

It is high time that black Americans rejected the kind of collectivistic thinking that argues that each black American is responsible for the acts of each other black American. Actions must be judged in a manner that separates them from the actors. Murder is murder, regardless of the race of the murderer. The same is true concerning all other crimes of violence. As a Negro I have no moral, legal, political, or racial obligation to defend others who happen to be Negroes in their commission

[250]

of illegal or immoral acts. The same, of course, is true for white Americans and for members of other races. Law must be color-blind, and the violator of law must be treated in the same manner, be he black or white, rich or poor, educated or uneducated. We may often fall short of this goal, but this is a valid goal toward which to strive.

Angela Davis and her supporters have attempted to make this case a test of racial solidarity. Negroes, as a result, are asked to defend Angela not because she is innocent, but because she is black. In a letter written by Angela Davis to her supporters, requesting funds to assist her in her legal battle, she states: "My life is at stake but as I have repeatedly said, not simply the life of a lone individual, but a life which belongs to Black people and all who are tired of poverty and racism and the unjust imprisonment of tens of thousands."

I, for one, am tired of racism, do not believe in the unjust imprisonment of one person, let alone tens of thousands of persons, and am black. Yet, I do not identify with Angela Davis. If she were, in fact, being railroaded, my feeling would be different. Were she, in fact, being tried because of her race and opinions, or were she not being given fair and equitable treatment by the courts, my feeling would be different.

In her letter Angela reports that she has been denied bail: "We have long considered my release on bail as a basic condition of judicial fairness." That is only one of the reasons advanced as a basis for the conclusion that she is scheduled for a "legal lynching."

California authorities, she explains, are "intent on maintaining and intensifying the racist hysteria which is inherent in the prosecution itself." She states that California officials "have created an atmosphere of military occupation in the Marin Civic Center." And, as for witnesses, she declares, "George Jackson, who would have played an important role in my defense, has been killed."

What Angela has contended, essentially, is that the United States is far gone in repression and that "tens of thousands" of Americans are unjustly imprisoned; that she is a special victim of American oppressors, primarily because she is black, a Communist, and a woman; that the courts in California have no

[251]

intention of giving her the rights commonly given to other defendants in like circumstances; and that the state of California is going so far as to contrive the murder of critical witnesses.

What Angela does not state in her letter is that several people, including a California judge, are dead as a result of the courtroom kidnaping to which she is linked by the circumstance of the lethal weapon having been issued in her name. She does not explain that bail is seldom given to defendants who have been guilty of attempting to flee the state, as she did, successfully, for several months during which her answers were being sought to several questions.

Another factor Angela does not mention is that one of the reasons for the elaborate preparations being taken in connection with her custody is the obvious need to protect her, and to protect her protectors. Similar precautions were taken to protect Sirhan Sirhan, and no one at that time drew the inference that the state of California was anti-Arab.

It is clear that American society is not guilty of the charges leveled against it by Angela Davis and her supporters. Other black militants have been released after long trials in which the preponderant evidence was against them. In Angela's own case, the judge agreed to permit her to act as counsel in her own defense. It was clear that due process was being followed in every particular, and it was also clear that Angela is and remains a Communist, dedicated to the overthrow of our democratic system.

What this means is that no matter how fair the court process was, Angela had a vested interest in opposing and denouncing it. No matter how the racial passions of past years had abated, Angela had a vested interest in proclaiming racial bigotry to be ingrained and hopeless in a democratic and capitalist society. She had made a commitment to the idea that only revolution, violent if necessary, can bring racial amity.

What Angela and her supporters, some purposefully and some naively, have done is to turn their backs upon all of the evidence of racial progress in American society. Today, for example, Southern political leaders would not even think of

[252]

trying to defend the segregationist ideas that were considered an unnegotiable code just a few years ago. The reason is made clear by a study released in 1971. Dr. Angus Campbell of the University of Michigan, a long-time researcher in the field of race relations, wrote a book on white attitudes toward black people. And the National Opinion Research Center, which is affiliated with the University of Chicago, has released a study showing a steady decline in white prejudice against blacks, and a tremendous drop in white resistance to the concept of desegregation.

The study shows that about half of Southern whites now express support of school integration, compared to two percent in 1940's. Nationwide, it is favored by nearly 75 percent of the white people, compared to 30 percent three decades ago. More than 70 percent of whites are favorable to integration of all facilities that serve the public, and again the favorable response has been climbing steadily in recent years.

All of the racial tumult of the sixties, according to the study, "has not impeded the steady increase in the proportion of white Americans willing to endorse integration."

The study also showed that black attitudes have not remained static. With the increase of vocal anger and impatience, however, the extremists have won relatively few converts. The goal of the great majority of black citizens is to share fully in the American system, in an integrated society.

The Angela Davis case must inevitably produce a feeling of sadness. Here is a bright, well-educated young woman who had all the advantages American society had to offer. She hardly suffered from the racism and poverty about which she speaks so much today. Yet, from the very beginning of her life, Angela seemed to be the target of white radicals. They brought her from Birmingham to New York, they indoctrinated her. They sent her from Brandeis to the Marxist academies of Europe, they turned her from a French major and devotee of literature to a hardened revolutionary.

Angela may be in the position of one who has used the extremist rhetoric so often and so vehemently that she now believes it herself. She may really believe that American society is racist and repressive, and that the only chance blacks have for a decent life lies in violent revolution. If she does believe all of this, it is testimony to the excellent job the Communist "underground railroad" of today has done.

9

THE TRIAL OF ANGELA DAVIS BROUGHT TOGETHER A GOOD DEAL OF circumstantial evidence leading to the conclusion that she was, in fact, deeply involved in the events which occurred at San Rafael.

The defense at no time disputed the state's contention that all of the private weapons used in the Marin County escape attempt—two pistols, a carbine with a collapsible stock and a sawed-off shotgun—were Angela Davis' property. It was admitted that she had purchased each weapon, but it was argued that they were stolen from her by Jonathan Jackson.

A San Diego police officer on patrol at the Mexican border the night of July 30, 1970, testified he saw Angela and Jonathan Jackson at the U.S. inspection station that night. They told him they were cousins, and had been shopping in Mexico. They were riding in her blue rambler when they were stopped. Officer Jerry Hoover's testimony underscored the close and continuing relationship between the pair in the days immediately preceding the shootout.

Another state witness, Lt. Robert H. West of San Quentin, discussed the days immediately before the shooting. He testified that he was in charge of mail and visitors at San Quentin and saw Angela Davis and Jonathan Jackson together just two days before the violent events, and that Jonathan held a long conference with his brother while Angela waited outside the visitor's room, registered under a false name.

West said that on August 5, Jonathan appeared at the prison and signed in to visit his brother at 11:50 a.m. He also signed stating that his companion was "Diane Robinson." Asked who accompanied Jackson that day, West replied, "the lady sitting over there with the purple clothes on," meaning Angela Davis.

A United Air Lines passenger agent testified that he sold an airline ticket to Angela Davis in Los Angeles on August 3, 1970, for an 8:30 flight to San Fransisco. Asked how he could identify her as Miss Davis, he noted one of her outstanding personal markings—"the split in her teeth was something that stuck in my mind."

Four witnesses placed Angela Davis with Jonathan Jackson in the vicinity of the Marin County Civic Center on the day before the shootout, Wednesday. That August 6 was possibly the originally scheduled time for the kidnapping, but the court was recessed early on that date.

Alden Fleming, who runs a Mobil gas station across San Pedro Avenue from the Marin Civic Center, said that on August 6 at about 10 a.m. "a colored man and a colored girl" came to his station. The young man reported he had a rented Hertz van and it wouldn't start. He didn't seem positive about what he should do, Fleming said. "I wondered why she did not come inside. He didn't know what to do. I had to do everything for him. He gave me the impression he wanted some help from her, wanted the authority to do things."

Fleming said he suggested calling Hertz and getting authorization to run a bill for repairs up to at least $6. Then Fleming sent his son, Peter, over in a station wagon to jump start the stalled truck. It was the next day, when he heard about the shootout that involved a rented yellow van, that he phoned the sheriff's office to provide the identification he had, Fleming said. Asked to identify Angela Davis, Fleming approached her at the counsel table. "It's the lady here."

Two witnesses, Frank Blumenthal and David E. Lifson, employes of the Eagle Loan Company on San Francisco's 3rd Street, testified that Angela Davis, accompanied by Jonathan Jackson, showed up at 5 p.m. August 5 and bought an inexpensive shotgun. She was recognized as Angela Davis and gave one of the men her autograph.

The next witness was Louis F. May, who had in August 1970 operated a motorized tram that took visitors from the main gate of the San Quentin prison to the prisoner visiting area. May said that on the day before the civic Center shootout he had seen Jonathan Jackson and Angela Davis at the prison, had seen them walking on a pathway, and had later seen them drive off in a yellow van.

The prosecution's case set forth the following thesis: Angela Davis had owned all the guns used in the escape attempt; she was in almost continuous company with Jonathan Jackson for days before the kidnapping; she had cashed several checks in the Bay Area and Jackson had disbursed large sums for an unemployed man; she was in the vicinity of the Marin Civic Center the day before the shootout; she had a romantic interest in freeing George Jackson as well as a revolutionary's interest in freeing the Soledad Brothers; the slain Jonathan's wallet contained the number of a public telephone at San Francisco airport; the escaping convicts said they were going to the airport; Angela was at the airport that day and departed in panic.

The defense did not present its list of witnesses to the prosecution until the day before their testimony. The first witness, Susan Castro, testified that on August 5, two days before the shootout, when guards West and Ayers said Angela was with Jonathan Jackson at the prison, that she was with her. She said she had lunch with Angela that day from noon until 2:30 or 2:45 at the home of Juanita Wheeler. Then she drove her to the Potero District of the City.

Susan Castro, it turns out, was active in the Committee To Free Angela Davis and had given a speech at a committee rally. Her luncheon companion, Juanita Wheeler, works for the *People's World,* the Communist newspaper in San Francisco. Thus, the entire luncheon alibi could only be supported by Mrs. Castro and Mrs. Wheeler, two witnesses whose bias was clear.

Carl Bloice, executive editor of *People's World,* also added an account of Angela during the days before the shootout. Bloice, a well known Negro Communist, testified that he had received a letter from Angela in July saying she would be in San Francisco the week of August 2, and he had made arrangements for her to stay with Juanita Wheeler. Bloice said that Angela had come to his office the mornings of August 4, 6, and 7, each day arriving about 8:30 in the morning. He recalled that on the 4th she stayed two and a half hours, on the 6th he was not sure how long she stayed, and on the 7th—the day of the shootout—she was there until 1 p.m. At that time he borrowed Mrs. Wheeler's car and drove her to San Francisco airport, and he carried her luggage inside and watched as she went to the PSA counter at 1:45 p.m. and bought a ticket to Los Angeles.

Bloice's testimony directly contradicted that of the eye-witnesses who placed Angela in Marin County on the 4th and 6th. Discussing the Bloice testimony, Lawrence V. Cott, former editor of *Combat*, noted that "It . . . revealed something about Bloice—for 19 months the Communists had bleated that Angela Davis was innocent of any involvement in the shootout, and journalist Bloice claimed to have intimate details of her whereabouts that would undeniably prove her presence elsewhere, and he had sat on the information and sat on the story, possibly the biggest one he will ever get in his lifetime. Not once in the *People's World* had he written about his personal knowledge of Angela's activities while federal and local law enforcement officers ransacked the nation looking for her—only to discover later that she had been spirited out of Los Angeles to Chicago and beyond with the help of the Communist Party."

The jury found Angela Davis innocent. Mr. Cott, after carefully studying the trial transcript, pointed out that "It chose to disbelieve the testimony of the witnesses who placed Angela Davis in Marin County during the critical days preceding the shootout, and depended instead on the alibis provided by her closest and most intimate friends, many of them members of the same secret organization, all of whom asserted that they had been alone with her, with no other outside witnesses, during the critical hours. . . . In believing the collection of alibi witnesses who had never lifted a finger or a telephone to cooperate with a police investigation, the jury also had to disbelieve the prosecution's witnesses, almost every one of whom admitted a failing, as opposed to the defense's witnesses, who had almost total recall."

After the trial, the jury reacted in an unusual manner. Ralph De Lange, a member of the jury, was so swept up in the enthusiasm for Miss Davis that he responded to cheers outside the courtroom by giving the revolutionary's clenched-fist salute, then explained to reporters: "I did it because I wanted to show I felt an identity with the oppressed people in the crowd. All through the trial, they thought we were just a white, middle-class jury. I wanted to express my sympathy with their struggle."

After the trial, more than 500 boisterous supporters—including five of the jurors who acquitted her—filled a club in San Jose to celebrate Angela's victory. The Soviet Union hailed Angela's acquittal as a "victory for the progressive American and world community." The official Soviet press agency, Tass, in a dispatch from New York said: "The charges were so unfounded that they were refuted even by the carefully selected jury, which did not include a single black or a single poor person."

The *London Daily Mail* hailed the verdict as "a milestone in America's tormented racial history." It said that the verdict "sensationally disproves that in the United States today a controversial black cannot get a fair trial from all-white jurors in a burgeois middle-class area where anti-Negro emotions have so long been potent."

The independent *Messaggero*, Rome's largest newspaper, said the trial had "elements of political and racial discrimination such as to threaten the fairness of American justice . . . All Americans breathed with relief at this reconfirmation of the democratic validity of the most sacred institution in the history of the nation."

Sweden's liberal *Expressen* concluded that those who argued that a black Communist could not get justice before an American court had been proved wrong. It said the verdict was not unexpected in view of the presectuion case.

Most radicals, however, did not consider the trial in any sense a vindication of the American legal system. Discussing this fact, Bernard Levin, columnist for the *London Times,* wrote: "Had she been found guilty, the verdict would have been proclaimed a perversion of justice on the part of racist America, and the judge and jury denounced as the willing tools of a conspiracy to destroy those brave freedom fighters who are struggling to liberate the United States from such abominable indignities as elections, free speech, open justice, etc., and to substitute for these shackles of imperialism an immeasurably more democratic system like that enjoyed at present by the citizens of, say, Czechoslovakia."

Mr. Levin continued: "Her acquittal on all charges against her might be thought to have made such an argument difficult to deploy, but those who think so must have forgotten the scene in Arthur Koestler's *Age Of Longing* in which the Russian delegate to the Western protest-meeting, when halfway through his speech, gets a message whispered to him by a Soviet official, and without pause or noticeable discomfiture puts his typescript back in his left-hand breast pocket, draws a similar-looking packet from his right-hand one, and proceeds to deliver the second half of a speech containing sentiments of an exactly opposite persuasion to those expressed in the first half of the speech he has just been making."

"So," declares Mr. Levin, "will it now be with Miss Davis. The argument was that she could not possibly expect a fair trial or an acquittal; . . . The argument will now simply be turned on its head, and the acquittal hailed as a victory, achieved by those who demanded it, over the forces of imperialist reaction which were compelled to retreat in the face of international working class solidarity. Exit Angela the Blessed Martyr, shamefully done to death by fascism; enter Angela the Living Soul Sister, liberated by her comrades from an otherwise certain death on the scaffold."

Henry Winston, national chairman of the Communist Party, U.S.A., declared that the freeing of Angela Davis was "a blow struck for liberty and peace throughout the world." Black Panther Party leader, Blaine Brown, took a totally hostile posture: "We do not give credit to the American judicial system for declaring her innocent. She has had to endure one year of prison unnecessarily because of that system." The Rev. Jesse L. Jackson, head of the Southern Christian Leadership Conference, said: "I think the verdict indicates that the trial should not have taken place."

The unfortunate fact may be that Kingman Brewster of Yale

[260]

University was right when he declared that a black radical could not receive a fair trial in America. Perhaps it is impossible to convict such an individual, even when the preponderance of the evidence indicates guilt. This is what we have seen in many cases, and the case of Angela Davis is no different. Columnist Holmes Alexander stated that, "The acquittal of Angela Davis proves a lot more than the justice and efficiency of our courts. It reminds us that we have built, not merely a merciful society, but a helpless one. We have not achieved the discipline to deal with the rebellion and anarchy which, quite aside from her trial, produced the kind of citizen that Miss Davis is."

Angela Davis will continue to be a symbol and a heroine to the radical left. The question which remains to be answered is what she and her supporters will become in the eyes of the American society as a whole. The fate of our society may rest in the balance.

Index

Boudin, Kathy, 82, 83
Braly, Malcolm, 239, 240
Brandeis University, 78, 83–87, 91, 92
Bras, Juan Maris, 45
Brewer, Marcia, 184
Brewster, Kingman, 196, 228, 260, 261
Brezhnev, Leonid Ilyich, 48
Brick, Steven A., 226, 227
Brotherhood of Sleeping Car Porters, 24
Brotsky, Allen, 220, 223
Browder, Earl, 125
Brown, Blaine, 260
Brown, H. Rap, 56, 57, 61, 62, 68, 70, 72, 204, 206, 223, 246
Brown v. *Board of Education,* 243
Buckley, William F., Jr., 113, 117
Bunche, Ralph, 29
Burnham, James, 72
Burnham, Margaret, 180, 211, 212
Burns, Haywood, 176, 218

California Law Review, 226
California Rural Legal Assistance, 157
California, University of, Los Angeles (UCLA), 79, 94, 103–105, 108–115, 117–119, 121–133, 168, 169, 180
California, University of, regents, 109–114, 117–119, 121–123
California, University of, San Diego, 78, 92, 97–99, 102, 103, 105, 127, 128
Calvert, Gregory, 64
Cambridge, Md., racial unrest, 69
Campbell, Dr. Angus, 253
Camus, Albert, 74, 75
Canaday, John, 121, 122
Cannella, John M., 184
Carmichael, Stokely, 11, 44, 45, 47, 50, 51, 60–62, 65, 68, 70, 206, 223, 246

Castro, Fidel, 45, 61
Castro, Susan, 257
Celona, Charles, 174
Challenge, 40
Chapman, Ervin N., 199
Che Lumumba Club, 79, 104
Chicago Daily News, 184
Christianity and Liberalism, 247
Christmas, William A., 169, 183, 214
Civil Rights Bill (1963), 38
Civilization and Its Discontents, 88
Clark, Dr. Kenneth, 36, 46, 47, 74, 101
Cleaver, Eldridge, 56, 59, 60, 68, 95, 154, 163, 204, 205, 211, 238
Clemenz, Manfred, 84, 85
Cleveland riots (1968), 63
Cluchette, John, 130, 133, 134
Columbia Journalism Review, 71
Combat, 258
Commager, Henry Steele, 100, 101
Committee to Free Angela Davis, 257
Common Sense, 158
Communists, communism, and the Negro, 23–27, 29, 30, 37, 39, 55–57, 59, 61, 63, 77, 79, 81, 93, 94, 96, 97, 104–106, 109–115, 117, 119, 121–129, 131, 132, 134, 135, 157, 172, 175, 178, 179, 181, 187, 189–191, 200, 207–220, 230–238, 253, 254, 257–260; see also New Left
Conant, James Bryant, 114
Congress of Racial Equality (CORE), 32, 33, 39, 41, 45–47, 49, 71, 221
Conrad, Nancy, 183
Conyers, Rep. John, 225
Cosby, Bill, 148
Cott, Lawrence V., 258
Council on African Affairs, 29
Cox, Donald, 190, 191
Crisis, The, 19, 20, 23

Fiedler, Leslie, 102, 103
Fleming, Alden, 256
Fleming, Peter D., 183
Forman, James, 40
Fortune Society, 217
Foster, William Z., 126
Fox, Jack, 82, 98
Franklin, Aretha, 212
Freedom House, 49, 50
French Revolution, 75
Freud, Sigmund, 88
Future Shock, 150

Galamison, Rev. Milton A., 37
Gardner, John, 73, 74
Garlington, Tyra, 97
Garrison, William Lloyd, 18
Garry, Charles, 220, 222, 223, 229
Garvey, Marcus, 12, 20–23, 27, 42
Garvey Movement, 20
Gavras, Costa, 212
Genêt, Jean, 139
Gide, André, 25
Gilbert, Dave, 65
Ginzburg, Eli, 100
Glaser, Daniel, 163
God That Failed, The, 25
Goethe University (Frankfurt), 78, 91, 92
Gomez, Joseph, 245
Graham, Jere, 159
Granma, 61
Graves, Ernest L., 185
Gray, Jesse, 37
Gray, William P., 197
Grier, Henry, 229
Guevara, Ernesto "Che," 65

Haddad, Ed, 71
Haley, Harold J., 169, 183, 185
Hall, Clarence W., 204, 205
Hall, Gus, 208
Hampton Normal and Agricultural Institute, 14

Handlin, Oscar, 37
Harlem, 29, 36–38, 53, 70, 244
Harlem Defense Council, 36
Harlem Rent Strike, 37
Harris, Patricia Roberts, 245, 246
Hawkins, Rev. Edler G., 202
Hayden, Tom, 64
Healy, Dorothy, 115
Hecksher, Mrs. August, 190
Heresy, Yes, Conspiracy, No, 113
Hershey, Lewis B., 52
Hetfield, George F., 72
Hicks, Rev. Dr. John J., 38
Higgs, Dewitt, 118
Hillenbrand, Martin, 178
Hilliard, David, 191, 192, 196, 197
Hitch, President, 118
Hoffer, Eric, 229
Hoffman, Abbie, 237
Holmes, Rev. John Haynes, 126
Hook, Sidney, 113–115
Hoover, Jerry, 255
House Committee on Un-American Activities, U.S., 210, 220
Howard, Charles, 29
Howard University, 52
Howell, Clark, 15
Huggins, Mrs. Ericka, 196, 215, 230, 231, 234, 239
Hughes, Governor, 64
Hughes, Langston, 80
Hunsinger, Mrs. June, 172, 173
Hutchings, Phil, 63

If They Come in the Morning, 177, 223
Innis, Roy, 221
International Labor Defense, 209
Irwin, Elisabeth, High School (New York City), 78, 80–84

Jackson, George L., 130–157, 159–168, 171, 182, 183, 193, 205, 214,

Roosevelt, Franklin D., 125
Rosenberg, Ethel and Julius, 216
Ross, Ronald O., 52, 53
Rothbard, Murray, 161, 164
Rousseau, 75
Rowan, Carl, 245
Rubin, Jerry, 237
Rubinstein, Rabbi Richard, 40
Ruby, Jack, 176
Rueben, Irving, 66
Rustin, Bayard, 40, 246

Saint-Just, 74, 75
Saltz, Amy, 82
San Diego, University of California at, 78, 92, 97–99, 102, 103, 105, 127, 128
San Francisco Examiner, 109
Santa Monica Evening Outlook, 128
Scheer, Robert, 49
Schmidt, Mary Jane, 228
Schuyler, George, 248
Scott King's Modern Europe, 101
Scottsboro Defense Fund, 209
Seale, Bobby, 11, 95, 187, 196, 205, 211, 215, 226, 228, 230, 231, 234, 239, 246
Sellers, Cleveland L., Jr., 50
Selma, March on, 72
Semple, Robert B., Jr., 244
Senate Internal Security Subcommittee, U.S., 124, 210
Shapiro, Barry, 92, 93, 103, 104
Shostakovich, Dmitri, 209
Shriver, Sargent, 64
Signoret, Simone, 212
Silone, Ignazio, 25
Singleton, Robert, 111
Sjollema, Baldwin, 204
Skolnick, Jerome H., 226, 227
Slevin, William, 175
Smith, Howard K., 206

SNCC: The New Abolitionists, 39
Snowden, Frank, 52
Soledad Brother, 139
"Soledad Brothers" case, 123, 130–168, 181, 215, 223, 231, 257
Solzhenitsyn, Aleksandr, 238
Sorbonne (Paris), 78, 84, 85
Souls of Black Folk, The, 19
Southern Christian Leadership Conference, 49, 58, 211, 221, 260
Southern Conference Educational Fund, 83
Sparks, Mrs. S., 39, 40
Spelman College, 31
Spina, Dominick A., 64
Spock, Dr. Benjamin, 49, 239
Stender, Fay, 158
Stern, Sol, 211, 212
Stockholm Peace Pledge, 29
Stokes, Carl B., 63
Stowe, Harriet Beecher, 13
Stringfellow, William, 36, 37
Stroll, Dr. Avrum, 98
Student Nonviolent Coordinating Committee (SNCC), 39, 40, 44–47, 50, 60, 61, 63, 70, 73
Student Violence, 128, 238
Students for a Democratic Society (SDS), 45, 63–65, 98, 99
Sullivan, Rev. Leon, 106
Suppression of the Black African Trade, 19
Susskind, Charles, 87
Swarthmore College, 105, 122
Swisher, Owen, 183

Tabor, Michael, 195
Taylor, Dr. Gardner C., 34
Television and riots, 69–73
Theodorakis, Mikis, 212
Thomas, Gary W., 169, 184
Thorne, John, 158, 220, 223
Tigar, Michael, 180, 181, 224
Time, 95, 221, 236, 238, 239